扎滚鲁克纺织品珍宝

新疆维吾尔自治区博物馆　编著

王博　王明芳　木娜瓦尔·哈帕尔　鲁礼鹏　著

文物出版社

阿贝格基金会

英文翻译　艾美霞（美）
摄　　影　刘玉生

文物出版社
责任编辑　李缙云　王　戈
责任校对　安艳娇
责任印制　张道奇

阿贝格基金会
责任编辑　瑞谷拉·肖特　王东宁

Textile Treasures of Zaghunluq

Xinjiang Uygur Autonomous Region Museum

Contributions by Wang Bo, Wang Mingfang, Minawar Happar and Lu Lipeng

Cultural Relics Press

Abegg-Stiftung

English Translation by Martha Avery

Photograps by Liu Yusheng

Cultural Relics Press

Editors   Li Jinyun, Wang Ge

Copy Editing   An Yanjiao

Printing   Zhang Daoqi

Abegg-Stiftung

Editors   Regula Schorta, Wang Dong-Ning

目 录

TABLE OF CONTENTS

序 一

中国西北部干燥的沙漠地带为当地出土的古代纺织品的保存提供了有利的气候条件。众所周知，纺织纤维的有机成分对环境影响非常敏感，包括水分、光照和温度等多种因素。正因如此，在历经几个世纪之后，很多出土的纺织品已经遭到自然条件的破坏。但在中国西北地区的考古学家们却发掘出了——而且目前还正在发掘中——很多因为干燥环境而能保留的古代纺织物品。这些存留不多的纺织品为了解几个世纪之前丰富多样的西北文化提供了珍贵的证据。通过对这些宝贵出土文物特别是纺织品的深入研究，有助于重新深化已成为沙漠地带西北古文化的认知。为了对这些极有价值的出土纺织品修复保护和研究资料进行整理，十五年来阿贝格基金会与当地考古研究所及各地博物馆之间展开了广泛的合作，包括联系互访、科研交流，并聘请阿贝格基金会纺织品保护修复专家到多个考古研究机构指导，协助当地工作研究人员对出土纺织品进行维护修复工作。

在合作过程中，萌发了出版以这些地区考古发掘纺织品珍宝为主题系列丛书的构想。与新疆维吾尔自治区博物馆合作的《扎滚鲁克纺织品珍宝》就是这套系列丛书的第一本。有意义的是阿贝格基金会 2000 年最早开始与中国联系合作的伙伴就是乌鲁木齐的同事们。

回首往事，出版《扎滚鲁克纺织品珍宝》是一段漫长的旅程，涉及了多种多样的挑战。我们的初衷就是想通过出版中英双语图录系列，介绍东西方各种不同处理古织品修复保护的技术方法，并更全面地展示这些纺织珍品，以便进一步研究古代纺织技术的发展特色。我们深信，这样的合作有着重要深远的影响力。这套丛书系列的出版不仅有助于了解当地纺织品的特点，更有助于理解评价东西方纺织技术之间的影响和发展。

在此，我们特别感谢北京科技大学冶金与材料史研究院的韩汝玢教授。如果没有韩教授的经验、知识、权威以及她不懈的督促推动，阿贝格基金会是不可能有这样的一段旅程。韩汝玢教授从一开始就是我们敬重的合作伙伴。由于她对东西方不同工作过程和方式的了解，使她能够在这样的东西合作中无数次地架起相互理解的桥梁。由于她的努力，这段漫长的旅程终于有了令各方满意的结果。美国宾夕法尼亚州的王东宁博士也满腔热忱地对韩汝玢教授的工作给予了全力的支持和协助。

在出版发行的过程中，我们深感幸运的是能与文物出版社的李缙云先生和王戈女士一起合作。同时，我们对一起合作的新疆维吾尔自治区博物馆表示衷心的感谢，尤其是原馆长田先洪先生。从合作起始，他就对本项目给予了高度关注和全力支持。我们在此还要特别感谢此书的主要作者王博先生。在他专业考古发掘研究的生涯中，王博先生始终非常重视纺织品在考古学中的贡献和意义。他的研究成果为更好地了解丝绸之路纺织品的历史和纺织技术的发展作出了重要贡献。

多米尼克·凯勒

阿贝格基金会董事长

FOREWORD

The dry and arid desert sands in north–west China have provided a favourable climate for the preservation of textiles. The organic material that textile fibres are is very susceptible to environmental impacts such as water, light or heat. Over centuries much is lost, but what has survived and has been – and still is – excavated by Chinese archaeologists gives evidence of rich and varied cultures of centuries ago. The traces these cultures have left are scarce, but the in-depth preoccupation with the wealth and quality of especially the textile finds will advance the knowledge of these cultures from the times when the land in which they lived was more welcoming than today's desert lands. Since fifteen years the Abegg-Stiftung has the privilege to cooperate with a number of regional Archaeological Institutes and Museums on issues of conservation and preservation as well as subsequent publication of these extraordinary and highly significant textiles. In past years there were extensive contacts with mutual visits, scientific exchanges and study stays by an expert on behalf of the Abegg-Stiftung at various institutions to assist in the conservation and preservation of archaeological textiles.

In the course of these cooperative efforts the idea nascent to publish a series of books dealing with the textile treasures from certain regions and find spots. It is meaningful that the first of these volumes is a cooperation between the Museum of the Xinjiang Uygur Autonomous Region and the Abegg-Stiftung, as it was in Urumqi where we from Switzerland initiated in the year 2000 our contacts with Chinese colleagues.

The journey to complete "Textile Treasures from Zaghunluq" was long and challenging for all concerned. The aim was also to interweave Chinese and Western methods of dealing with ancient textiles and to present them in an extensive documentation and number, also in the aim to supply to further research. We believe that the result will benefit multiple purposes and further the understanding and estimation of the importance of theses textiles in China as well as in the West.

This journey would have simply been impossible for the Abegg-Stiftung without the experience, knowledge, authority and above all unfailing dedication of Professor Han Rubin of the University of Science and Technology Beijing, Institute of Historical Metallurgy and Materials, who from the beginning was our esteemed partner. Her singular understanding of not only the Chinese way of working but also the Western proceedings has enabled her to innumerable times build bridges between the different cultures and understandings. Thanks to her this now already long journey has been of benefit to all concerned. As of lately she has been assisted by Dr Wang Dong-Ning, Allentown PA, who has been as enthusiastic as Professor Han about the common cause.

It was fortunate, that with Mr Li Jinyun and Ms Wang Ge of Cultural Relics Press (Wenwu Chubanshe) a third formidable and dedicated partner could be found to achieve the goal of an exemplary publication.

Our thanks go also to the authorities of the Museum of the Xinjiang Uygur Autonomous Region and especially to its (former) director Mr. Tian Xianhong, who has taken an a special interest in this project and has given it his full support. But most of course we want to thank the main author Mr. Wang Bo who throughout his career has thought of textiles as important in his profound archaeological considerations. With such an approach, he has greatly contributed to better understanding of historic textiles along the Silk Roads.

Dominik Keller
Abegg-Stiftung
President of the Board of Trustees

序　二

　　《扎滚鲁克纺织品珍宝》一书即将问世，这是继《中国新疆山普拉——古代于阗文明的揭示与研究》一书出版后，新疆维吾尔自治区博物馆与瑞士 Abegg 研究所合作出版的第二本与新疆考古出土纺织品研究相关的专著，是一件值得庆贺的事情。

　　扎滚鲁克，是新疆南疆偏远的一个小村名。"扎滚"，维吾尔语是指一种油料作物，与"鲁克"相联，意谓"生长扎滚的地方"。扎滚鲁克村位于塔克拉玛干大沙漠的南缘，且末县托格拉克勒克乡附近。这里分布着五处古墓地，1985年、1996年和1998年间，我馆考古工作人员曾三次在这里发掘（一号墓地发掘165座墓，二号墓地发掘2座墓），共发掘167座墓。出土纺织品500余件，资料丰富、精彩。

　　本书选取了扎滚鲁克一、二号墓地出土的 86 件纺织品珍宝，以毛织品为主，还有丝织品和棉织品等。纺织品色彩艳丽，蓝、红、黄、绿等色明快、光洁。精细的毛布，如绞缬、晕繝、毛绣和挖花织物；保存完整的服饰，如长袍、直筒裤、毛布裙、毛布开襟上衣、百衲毛布套头裙衣；多种多样纺织品，除平、斜纹组合毛布外，还有毛纱、毛罗、毛绉、缂毛、栽绒毯和编织帽、绦、带等。出土的织物，同时还有丝织品绢、绮、缣、缦、纨、锦和刺绣，棉织品仅平纹棉布一种。

　　扎滚鲁克墓地发掘的墓葬，经研究分为三期考古文化。出土纺织品较多的第二期文化年代为公元前 8 世纪～公元 3 世纪中期，第三期文化墓葬年代为公元 3 世纪中期～6世纪，其间延续了 14 个世纪。这些毛纺织品无疑反映了这一时期古代新疆毛纺织业发展的一些情况，或许也能反映丝绸之路毛纺织业发展的水平。

　　今天的且末县，古称且末国，是古代丝绸之路、两汉西域三十六国塔里木盆地南缘的一个绿洲城邦小国。班固撰《汉书·西域传》记载："且末国，王治且末城，去长安六千八百二十里。户二百三十，口千六百一十，胜兵三百二十人。"扎滚鲁克古墓出土的遗物，反映出古且末国在社会经济文化发展中，形成了独特的丝绸之路文化现象。它们具有兼容并蓄的多元文化的态势，与中原、北方草原以及西方都有着密切的文化联系，构成了文化因素的多样性。本书的出版将有助于学者们的研究，随着学者们的比较分析，推想将可能会有精彩的发现，从而揭示出古代且末国及早期新疆毛纺织业发展的脉络。

在这里，我们要感谢 Abegg 研究所的董事长 Dominik Keller 对这项工作的支持，要感谢参加指导工作的 Dr. Regula Schorta。同时，还要感谢北京科技大学的韩汝玢教授为促成这次合作付出的努力，感谢 Angelika Sliwka 在我馆的短期指导。

最后，衷心祝愿，我们与世界著名的古代纺织品收藏、保护、研究中心——瑞士阿贝格基金会 ABEGG-STIFTUNG 建立的合作，能够长久地进行下去。

田先洪

新疆维吾尔自治区博物馆原馆长

FOREWORD

"Textile treasures of Zaghunluq" is the second book to be published as a cooperative effort by the Museum of the Xinjiang Uygur Autonomous Region of China and the Abegg-Stiftung, a research institute and museum in Switzerland. It follows the publication of "Sampula in Xinjiang of China— Revelation and study of Ancient Khotan Civilization" back in 2001, and is devoted to research of textiles excavated in Xinjiang. We celebrate its publication.

Zaghunluq is the name of a small village in a remote part of southern Xinjiang. *Zaghun* is a Uygur word that refers to a kind of crop used to extract oil. When tied to *luq*, the term means a place where *zaghun* is growing. The village of Zaghunluq is located on the southern rim of the Taklamakan desert near the Toghraqliq township of Qiemo (Cherchen) County. Five ancient cemeteries are distributed around this place. During three campaigns in 1985, 1996, and 1998, archaeologists from our museum excavated 167 graves here, 165 of which were from Cemetery #1, and two of which were from Cemetery #2 (in 1989, the Cultural Relics Administration Office of Bayin'gholin Mongol Autonomous Prefecture excavated two tombs). More than 500 textiles were recovered from these two sites, which produced a wealth of beautiful material.

We have chosen 85 textiles for display in this book, from among all the excavated items of Cemeteries #1 and #2. The textiles are predominantly made of wool, although there are also some of silk and cotton. They include lustrous shades of blue, red, yellow, and green, and the finely woven fabrics include a number of techniques such as tie-dying (*jiaoxie*), shading (*yunjian*), wool embroidery (*mao xiu*), and brocading (*wa hua*). Relatively well-preserved garments include long gowns, straight tubular trousers, woolen skirts, woolen jackets that are open in the front, and a woolen patchwork pullover dress. In addition to tabby and twill, weaving types include different kinds of woolen gauze (*mao sha, mao luo*), woolen crêpe (*mao zhou*), woolen tapestry (*ke mao*), carpets. Furthermore there are braided hats, ribbons, and belts. Among the excavated textiles are various kinds of silk tabby such as *juan, jian, man,* and *wan,* monochrome (*qi*) and multicolored figured silks (*jin*), and embroideries. The cotton weavings are only done in tabby weave.

After extensive research, we have ascertained that the dating of graves at the Zaghunluq cemeteries can be divided into three periods or archaeological cultures. Many of the excavated textiles were found in Second-period culture graves and are believed to date from the 8th century BC to the 3rd century AD. Third-period culture graves date from the 3rd to the 6th centuries AD. The entire period of the five cemeteries spans sixteen centuries. Zaghunluq textiles reflect the circumstances of evolving weaving technologies in ancient Xinjiang, as well as the level of weaving industries along the Silk Road.

Today's Qiemo County was called the State of Qiemo in ancient times. During the Eastern and Western Han dynasties, it was part of an alliance of small oasis states among the 36 states strung along the southern border of the Taklamakan desert. In Book of Han (*Hanshu*), Chronicle of the western regions (*Xiyu Zhuan*), Ban Gu records, "A King ruled over the Qiemo walled city, which was 6,820 li from Chang'an. It held 230 households and contained 1,610 inhabitants. Its valiant soldiers numbered 320."

Objects excavated from the Zaghunluq graves reflect the fact that the ancient State of Qiemo formed a unique culture along the Silk Road. During the course of socio-economic development, Qiemo accommodated a diversity of cultures that showed close cultural ties to the Central Plains, but also to the northern steppe regions and to the west. This allowed for a diversity of cultural factors. This book's publication will greatly benefit scholars who are researching the subject. Comparative analysis may aid in new discoveries that reveal the pulse of development of early woolen textile industries in ancient Qiemo.

At this point, we would like to extend our great appreciation to Dominik Keller, Chairman of the Board of the Abegg-Stiftung, for his support of this endeavor. We extend our thanks to Dr. Regula Schorta, who directed the work. We want to thank Professor Han Rubin of the Beijing Science and Technology University, for the tremendous effort she put into facilitating our cooperation, and we thank Angelika Sliwka for her valuable help in training staff at our Museum.

Finally, we extend heartfelt thanks to the Abegg-Stiftung in Riggisberg, Switzerland, a renowned institution dedicated to the collecting, conserving, and researching of ancient textiles. We thank them for establishing cooperative relations with us, and we hope that these will continue to grow for a long time to come.

Tian Xianhong

Former Dicector of the Xinjiang Uygur Autonomous Region Museum

第一章　扎滚鲁克墓地概述

王　博　鲁礼鹏

　　扎滚鲁克墓地位于塔克拉玛干沙漠南缘、且末县托格拉克勒克乡扎滚鲁克村附近。这里有五处古墓地，相距不是很远，大体呈东西向排列，分布在 5 平方公里的范围内。其中一号墓地最大，其余的墓地都比较小，面积多在 1000~7000 平方米。1985 年、1989 年、1996 年和 1998 年，四次对一号墓地进行了考古发掘，1996 年发掘了二号墓地。两个墓地共发掘墓葬 169 座：一号墓地 167 座，二号墓地 2 座。[1] 经过长时间的资料整理、分析研究，目前对扎滚鲁克一、二号墓地的分布、墓葬形制及年代、考古文化现象有了一些认识。

一　墓葬的分布和形制

　　扎滚鲁克一号墓地位于扎滚鲁克村西 2 公里绿洲边缘的戈壁地带，东经 85°28′29″，北纬 38°07′16″，海拔高度 1270 米。二号墓地处于兰干村与扎滚鲁克村交界地带的"黑沙梁"上（图 1）。

---

1 巴音郭楞蒙古自治州文管所：《且末扎滚鲁克墓葬 1989 年清理简报》，《新疆文物》1992 年第 2 期，第 1~14 页；新疆博物馆文物队：《且末县扎滚鲁克五座墓葬发掘简报》，《新疆文物》1998 年第 3 期，第 2~18 页；新疆维吾尔自治区博物馆考古部、巴音郭楞蒙古自治州文物管理所、且末县文物管理所：《且末扎滚鲁克二号墓地发掘简报》，《新疆文物》2002 年第 1、2 期，第 1~21 页；新疆维吾尔自治区博物馆、巴音郭楞蒙古自治州文物管理所、且末县文物管理所：《1998 年扎滚鲁克第三期文化墓葬发掘简报》，《新疆文物》2003 年第 1 期，第 1~19 页；新疆博物馆、巴州文管所、且末县文管所：《新疆且末扎滚鲁克一号墓地》，《考古学报》2003 年第 1 期，第 89~130 页。

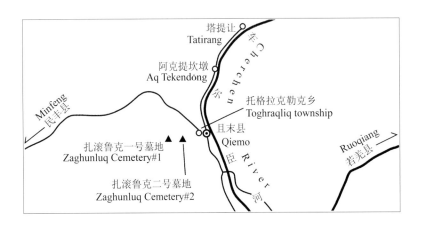

1　扎滚鲁克一、二号墓地位置示意图
　Location of Zaghunluq Cemeteries #1 and #2

By Wang Bo, Lu Lipeng

OVERVIEW OF THE ZAGHUNLUQ CEMETERIES

Five ancient cemeteries are located along the southern rim of the Taklamakan Desert near the village of Zaghunluq in Toghraqliq township of Qiemo (Cherchen) County. They are arrayed in roughly an east-west direction, and are not far from one another—they all lie within an area of five square kilometers. Among the five, Cemetery #1 is the largest. All the rest are relatively small with areas covering between 1000 and 7000 square meters.

In 1985, 1989, 1996, and 1998, we carried out excavations in Cemetery #1, working over the course of four seasons. In 1996, we also worked in Cemetery #2. Altogether, we excavated 169 individual graves, 167 of which were from #1 and two of which were from #2.[1] After extensive analysis of the resulting material, we have a better understanding of the archaeological phenomena underlying these graves, of their distribution, their structure, and their dating.

DISTRIBUTION AND STRUCTURE OF THE GRAVES

The Zaghunluq Cemetery #1 is located at East longitude 85° 28′ 29″, and North latitude 38° 07′ 16″. It is two kilometers to the west of the town of Zaghunluq in the *gobi* belt bordering the oasis. It stands at 1,270 meters in elevation above sea level. Cemetery #2 is on the 'black sand ridge' in the zone between the villages of Langan and Zaghunluq (fig. 1).

---

1 Balinguoleng Menggu Zizhizhou wenwu guanlisuo: «Qiemo Zhagunluke muzang 1989 qingli jianbao [Brief report on the 1989 excavation of Zaghunluq Cemetery, Qiemo]», *Xinjiang Wenwu* 2, 1992, pp. 1–14. – Xinjiang Bowuguan wenwu dui: «Qiemo xian Zhagunluke wu zuo muzang fajue jianbao [Brief report on the excavation of the five ancient cemeteries at Zaghunluq in Qiemo county]», *Xinjiang Wenwu* 3, 1998, pp. 2–18. – Xinjiang Bowuguan kaogusuo, Balinguoleng Menggu Zizhizhou wenwu guanlisuo, Qiemo xian wenwu guanlisuo: «Qiemo Zhagunluke er hao mudi fajue jianbao [Brief report on the excavation of graveyard no. 2 at Zaghunluq, Qiemo]», *Xinjiang wenwu* 1-2, 2002, pp. 1–21. – Xinjiang Weiwuer Zizhiqu Bowuguan, Balinguoleng Menggu Zizhizhou wenwu guanlisuo, Qiemo xian wenwu guanlisuo: «1998 nian Zhagunluke di san qi wenhua muzang fajue jianbao [Brief report on the 1998 excavation of the Third-period culture graveyard of Zaghunluq]», *Xinjiang wenwu* 1, 2003, pp. 1–19. – Xinjiang Weiwuer Zizhiqu Bowuguan, Balinguoleng Menggu Zizhizhou wenwu guanlisuo, Qiemo xian wenwu guanlisuo: «Xinjiang Qiemo Zhagunluke yi hao mudi fajue baogao [Graveyard no. 1 of Zaghunluq, Qiemo, Xinjiang]», *Kaogu Xuebao* 1, 2003, pp. 89–136.

（一）墓葬的分布及保存状况

扎滚鲁克二号墓地，分布面积不大，南北长 280 米，东西宽 150 米。1996 年发掘的两座墓葬位于墓地的北偏东处，东西向分布，相距 20 米。编号分别为：96QZIIM1、96QZIIM2。[2]

扎滚鲁克一号墓地，分布面积很大，有 3.5 万平方米。对该墓地首次较大规模发掘应该是 1996 年 10~11 月间的清理工作。当时重点放在墓地的南部区域，选择了五个发掘点。其中有一个发掘点选在南东区，四个发掘点选在南西区，共发掘墓葬 102 座。1998 年 10~11 月间进行了第二次较大规模的发掘，发掘墓葬 58 座，选择了六个发掘点。其中有一个发掘点选择在 1996 年南西区的第一发掘点附近，1985 年和 1989 年的发掘点也选择在这一带。其他的五个发掘点中，第一、二两个发掘点发掘的墓葬比较多一些，其他发掘点发掘的墓葬相对少一些。

在扎滚鲁克一号墓地进行的四次发掘，共有十个发掘点（图 2）。

2 1985 年、1989 年发掘时，并没对墓地进行划分，所以墓葬编号为 85QZM1~5，89QZM1、89QZM2。1996 年发掘了二号墓地，故出现了一、二号墓地之分， 编号分别为：96QZIM1~M102，96QZIIM1、96QZIIM2，1998 年发掘的编号为：98QZIM103~98QZIM160。

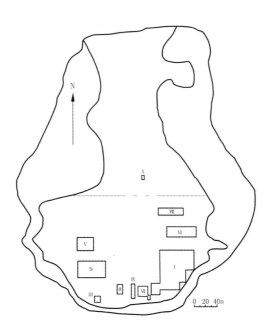

2 一号墓地墓葬发掘点分布示意图
Location of the ten excavation sites of Cemetery #1

DISTRIBUTION AND STATE OF PRESERVATION OF THE GRAVES

Zaghunluq Cemetery #2 covers a relatively small area, 280 meters in length from north to south and 150 meters from east to west. The two graves excavated in 1996 were situated on the eastern side of the northern part of the cemetery and stood to east and west of each other, separated by around 20 meters. Our numbering system designates these two graves as 96QZIIM1 and 96QZIIM2.[2]

Zaghunluq Cemetery #1 covers quite a large area that includes 35,000 square meters. The first extensive excavation work at this site was carried out in October and November of 1996. The emphasis at that time was placed on the southern part of the cemetery where five sites were selected for excavation. Among these, one excavation site was selected in the southeast region and four in the southwest region. Altogether 102 graves were excavated. A second extensive excavation was undertaken in the months of October and November, 1998, during which 58 graves were excavated from six excavation sites that had been selected. Among these excavation sites, one was near the site in the southwest chosen during the 1996 excavations, at the same time the excavation sites for 1985 and 1989 were selected from this region. Among the other five locations, the first and second excavation sites produced quite a few graves whereas the others produced relatively fewer.

Zaghunluq Cemetery #1 has therefore seen four separate excavations and altogether we have worked at ten excavation sites (fig. 2):

2 The numbers are to be read as follows: 96 – year of excavation; QZ – Qiemo township, Zaghunluq village; II – cemetery #2; M1 – grave (Chinese mu) number 1. During excavations in 1985 and 1989, a distinction between the two cemeteries was not made and therefore the original numbers were 85QZM1 to 85QZM5, 89QZM1, and 89QZM2. During excavation of Cemetery #2 in 1996, the distinction between cemeteries #1 and #2 became clear and cataloguing numbers were therefore given as follows: 96QZIM1 to 96QZIM102, 96QZIIM1, and 96QZIIM2. The 1998 excavations were given the numbers 98QZIM103 to 98QZIM160.

Ⅰ.1996 年南东区发掘点，清理墓葬 88 座（96QZIM1~M3、96QZIM5~M13、96QZIM15~M23、96QZIM25~M33、96QZIM35~M43、96QZIM45~M53、96QZIM56~M59、96QZIM61~M63、96QZIM66~M69、96QZIM71~M73、96QZIM75~M78、96QZIM81~M102）；

Ⅱ.1996 年南西区第三发掘点，清理墓葬 2 座（96QZIM55、96QZIM60）；

Ⅲ.1996 年南西区第四发掘点，清理墓葬 1 座（96QZIM65）；

Ⅳ.1996 年南西区第一发掘点（是 1998 年第五发掘点，也是 1985 年和 1989 年发掘点），共清理墓葬 10 座（85QZM1~M5、89QZM1、89QZM2、96QZIM4、96QZIM14、96QZIM154）；

Ⅴ.1996 年南西区第二发掘点，清理墓葬 9 座（96QZIM24、96QZIM34、96QZIM44、96QZIM54、96QZIM64、96QZIM70、96QZIM74、96QZIM79、96QZIM80）；

Ⅵ.1998 年南区第一发掘点，清理墓葬 27 座（98QZIM103、98QZIM104、98QZIM107~M109、98QZIM112~M114、98QZIM118~M120、98QZIM123、98QZIM125~M127、98QZIM130、98QZIM132、98QZIM136、98QZIM140、98QZIM143、98QZIM148、98QZIM150~M153、98QZIM158、98QZIM159、98QZIM160）；

Ⅶ.1998 年南区第二发掘点，清理墓葬 20 座（98QZIM105、98QZIM106、98QZIM109、98QZIM110、98QZIM115、98QZIM117、98QZIM122、98QZIM128、98QZIM131、98QZIM133、98QZIM135、98QZIM137、98QZIM138、98QZIM141、98QZIM142、98QZIM145、98QZIM149、98QZIM155~M157）；

Ⅷ.1998 年南区第三发掘点，清理墓葬 4 座（98QZIM111、98QZIM121、98QZIM139、98QZIM147）；

Ⅸ.1998 年南区第四发掘点，清理墓葬 1 座（98QZIM144）；

Ⅹ.1998 年北区第一发掘点，清理墓葬 4 座（98QZIM116、98QZIM124、98QZIM129、98QZIM146）；

Ⅺ.1998 年北区第二发掘点，清理墓葬 1 座（98QZIM134）。

Ⅰ.1996: 88 graves were excavated from the southeast region's excavation site (96QZIM1–M3, 96QZIM5–M13, 96QZIM15–M23, 96QZIM25–M33, 96QZIM35–M43, 96QZIM45–M53, 96QZIM56–M59, 96QZIM61–M63, 96QZIM66–M69, 96QZIM71–M73, 96QZIM75–M78, 96QZIM81–M102);

Ⅱ.1996: 2 graves were excavated from the southwest region's third excavation site (96QZIM55, 96QZIM60);

Ⅲ.1996: 1 grave was excavated from the southwest region's fourth excavation site (96QZIM65);

Ⅳ.1996: 10 graves were excavated from the southwest region's first excavation site (which was the fifth excavation site in 1998 and also an excavation site in 1985 and 1989) (85QZM1–M5, 89QZM1, 89QZM2, 96QZIM4, 96QZIM14, 96QZIM154);

Ⅴ.1996: 9 graves were excavated from the southwest region's second excavation site (96QZIM24, 96QZIM34, 96QZIM44, 96QZIM54, 96QZIM64, 96QZIM70, 96QZIM74, 96QZIM79, 96QZIM80);

Ⅵ.1998: 27 graves were excavated from the southern region's first excavation site (98QZIM103, 98QZIM104, 98QZIM107–M109, 98QZIM112–M114, 98QZIM118–M120, 98QZIM123, 98QZIM125–M127, 98QZIM130, 98QZIM132, 98QZIM136, 98QZIM140, 98QZIM143, 98QZIM148, 98QZIM150–M153, 98QZIM158–M160);

Ⅶ.1998: 20 graves were excavated from the southern region's second excavation site (98QZIM105, 98QZIM106, 98QZIM109, 98QZIM110, 98QZIM115, 98QZIM117, 98QZIM122, 98QZIM128, 98QZIM131, 98QZIM133, 98QZIM135, 98QZIM137, 98QZXIM138, 98QZIM141, 98QZIM142, 98QZIM145, 98QZIM149, 98QZXIM155–M157);

Ⅷ.1998: 4 graves were excavated from the southern region's third excavation site (98QZIM111, 98QZIM121, 98QZIM139, 98QZIM147);

Ⅸ.1998: 1 grave was excavated from the southern region's fourth excavation site (98QZIM144);

Ⅹ.1998: 4 graves were excavated from the northern region's first excavation site (98QZIM116, 98QZIM124, 98QZIM129, 98QZIM146);

Ⅺ.1998: 1 grave was excavated from the northern region's second excavation site (98QZIM134).

扎滚鲁克一号墓地98%以上的墓葬都遭到不同程度的破坏。根据发掘的情况，盗掘程度分为以下几种：

第一，是比较彻底的盗掘，墓室的葬具、尸体及随葬品，盗掘一空，几乎没有残留东西。此类墓葬有的可能经过正式的发掘。

第二，只是为了挖取墓口的盖木及芦苇秆、蒲草等。此类墓葬多缺失棚盖，或严重破坏了棚盖的结构，葬式及随葬品保存基本完好。

第三，只是为了盗掘墓主人的头饰。此类墓葬显然是盗宝者所为。他们找到墓葬后，先从墓室的中部向下挖掘，发掘至死者的屈腿关节时，通过腿关节推测到人的头部位置，而后再寻找死者的头部，盗取金饰件。所以，墓葬死者的头部皆被移动，且放置在了其颈部附近。死者的膝关节因长期暴露于外，日晒风蚀，变白变朽。墓内金饰缺失。

这样以来，无论盗掘的程度如何，皆保存了墓葬的基本形制，只是第二种被盗墓葬，棚架结构破坏严重；第三种被盗墓葬，不仅破坏了棚架，而且缺失了死者头饰。不过，部分墓葬保存了较完整的死者个体，对研究埋葬人数、葬式及其随葬品，提供了较科学的资料。

More than 98% of the graves at Zaghunluq Cemetery #1 had been damaged to a certain extent by grave robbers. The damage included the following types, as ascertained by excavation data:

First, relatively complete robbing with the grave chamber, the corpse, and accompanying grave goods all being removed. Graves were left essentially without anything inside. It is possible that this type of grave had been subjected to official excavation in the past.

Second, robbery undertaken merely to take the wood that was covering the grave opening, and the reed. This type of grave normally had lost any covering structure or the cover had been severely damaged but the form of the grave itself and the accompanying grave objects were basically well preserved.

Third, robbery undertaken to remove the head ornaments of the occupant of the grave. This kind was normally done by grave robbers seeking treasure. After locating a grave, they would go directly downward from the center of the grave into the chamber. Digging down to the leg joints of the corpse, they would estimate the head position by the position of the leg joints and then look for the skull and take its gold face covering. The occupant's skull in such instances had therefore generally been moved and was often found near the neck bones. The knee bones of the corpse in such instances were exposed for a long time and were whitened or rotted away by exposure to the elements. Any gold ornaments in these graves were gone.

Regardless of damage from grave robbers, all of the graves maintained their basic structure or form (other than the canopy which was sometimes destroyed by the second type of robbery). The third type of robbery not only destroyed the canopy but also led to the loss of the head ornaments. Nonetheless, the complete remains of some corpses in other graves provided adequate scientific data to evaluate the numbers of buried corpses, the types of corpses, and the types of their accompanying grave goods.

（二） 墓葬形制

扎滚鲁克一号墓地和二号墓地发掘的 169 座墓葬，在考古文化分期上可以分为三期，墓葬形制上有一些变化。[3]

第一期文化墓葬，仅在一号墓地发现了 1 座（96QZIM61）。为长方形竖穴土坑墓，墓向呈东北—西南向。墓葬已被盗墓者扰乱，骨架不全。从残留的骨骼看为单人葬，死者是成年女性。另外，人骨架中的盆骨、部分胸腰椎骨、左肩胛和肱骨处于解剖位置，由此看应该是仰身葬，头向东北。出土了红衣陶壶、木纺轮、木杵（带有重石）和锥形小木件等。

第二期文化墓葬，发掘了 138 座（包括二号墓地的 2 座）。根据墓葬墓口和墓室的演变，其形制大体可以分为五种类型。

A 型，为长方形竖穴土坑墓；B 型，为长方形二层台墓；C 型，为单墓道长方形竖穴棚架墓；D 型，为洞室墓；E 型，为多室墓。[4]

---

3 本文对墓葬形制的分类作了新的调整。
4 85QZM1 和 85QZM2 是 1985 年发掘墓葬，从平面图上看，这两座墓葬可以看作是一座墓的两个墓室。这样一来，在墓葬形制分类的统计上，会少一座墓葬。

STRUCTURE OF THE GRAVES

The 169 graves excavated in the course of archaeological work at Cemeteries #1 and #2 have been divided into three archaeological periods. The structure of graves changed over the course of these three periods.[3]

Only one grave was found in Zaghunluq Cemetery #1 that belonged to **First-Period Culture** graves, namely 96QZIM61. This was a rectangular, vertical-shaft type earthen grave. It was oriented in a northeast-southwest direction. The grave had been robbed, was in disarray, and contained an incomplete skeleton. From remaining bones, this appeared to be a grave for one person, with the occupant being an adult woman. Placement of various body parts, including a part of the chest and ribs and the left shoulder, showed that the corpse appeared to have been dismembered. The head appeared to have been placed towards the northeast, and the body appeared to have been lying on the back, facing upwards. This was deduced from the position of some of the bones. In addition, a wooden spindle , a wooden pestle (*chu*) with heavy stone weight, and a small awl-shaped wooden implement were found in the grave, as well as a ceramic pot with red coating.

A total of 138 **Second-period culture** grave numbers were given during excavation, including the two in Cemetery #2.[4] Five grave types can be distinguished, as determined by the structure of grave openings and the grave chambers. These are listed as types A, B, C, D, and E. Type A was a rectangular, vertical earth pit (shaft grave). Type B was a rectangular grave with two platform levels. Type C was a rectangular, vertical pit with a single grave entry and pillar-supported canopy. Type D was a chamber grave with niche and E a multi-chambered grave.

---

3 This book provides a new approach to the way grave types are categorized.

4 The two graves 85QZM1 and 85QZM2 have been excavated in 1985 and were given their classification numbers at that time, cf. note 2 above. From their ground plan can be seen that they should be considered as being two chambers of one grave. Because of this, the total number of graves now is reduced by one.

A 型，长方形竖穴土坑墓，88 座。主要分布在一号墓地 1996 年南东区发掘点。墓口大都呈椭圆形，墓室底部多是圆角长方形，室壁略外斜，呈敞口状。也有的墓口缘边上面保存着棚架的痕迹，即残棚木、蒲草、芦苇秆和柽柳编席等，甚至墓室填土中夹杂着芦苇秆、蒲草，说明墓葬口缘上曾架设过棚架。不过，有的墓葬没有保存任何的棚架痕迹。所以，长方形竖穴土坑墓中又可以细分出棚架墓和非棚架墓。

　　这一类型墓葬保存完整的有 1 座（96QZIM27），位于 1996 年南东区发掘点（图 2，Ⅰ），墓向呈东北—西南向。墓口呈不规则的椭圆形，长径 1.8 米，短径 1 米。墓壁外斜，墓底也呈椭圆形，敞口状，墓深 0.86 米。墓室里葬两个小孩，同包裹在一张毛毡里面，用细毛绳扎捆。小孩头向，一东北，一西南，两脚相对，仰身。毛毡上盖一胡杨半圆木木棺。墓室西角有 1 件角杯，东面有 1 件带流小陶罐，皆在棺外。棺内北角随葬 1 件角杯。

A total of 88 graves were of the Type A grave structure. These were excavated mainly from the southeast region of Zaghunluq Cemetery #1 in 1996. The grave openings were mostly elliptical, the grave chambers were mostly rectangular at the bottom but with rounded corners, and the walls of the chambers leaned slightly outwards. Some of the graves had traces of canopies near the vicinity of their openings, also remaining bits of reeds or willow mats and so on. These indicated that canopies had been laid down near or around the opening of the graves. Other graves did not reveal any trace of a canopy, however. Therefore, this type of rectangular, vertical-pit earthen shaft grave can be further subdivided into those with canopies and those without.

One of the Type A graves was preserved in complete form, namely 96QZIM27, which was located in the 1996 southeast region's excavation site (fig. 2, field I). The orientation of the grave was northeast–southwest. The opening was an irregular elliptical form, with a diameter at the widest part of 1.8 meters and at the narrowest of 1 meter. The walls of the grave tilted outwards, and the base of the grave was also elliptical. The grave was 0.86 meters deep and contained the corpses of two children. They were wrapped together in a piece of woolen felt that had been tied up with rope made of fine wool. The two children were placed foot to foot, one with the head to the northeast and the other with the head to the southwest; both were lying on their backs. A wooden coffin made of half a log of poplar was placed over the felt. A cup made of horn was recovered from the western corner of the chamber and a small ceramic container was found on the eastern side of the chamber, both of these being outside the coffin. Another horn cup was inside the coffin, at its northern corner.

B 型，长方形二层台墓，26 座。主要分布在一号墓地 1998 年南区第一发掘点。这一类型的墓葬非常规整，二层台也比较明显，可以看出墓口和墓室的界线。虽然大多数墓葬的二层台上未发现棚架，但根据墓葬设置二层台这一现象，可以认为初建时应该有棚架。

这一类型的墓葬有 1 座（96QZIM30）保存完整，位于 1996 年南东区发掘点（图 2，Ⅰ），墓向呈东南—西北向。墓室保存完好，墓口呈圆角长方形，长 2.4 米，宽 1.74 米。墓口二层台上纵向铺设了 3 根细圆木，圆木长 2.2 米，径 0.06 米。圆木上置有芦苇草秆。墓底呈圆角长方形，墓深 0.77 米。墓室里仅发现 3 只、分属于 3 个小孩个体的半干尸脚，用平纹毛布包裹，属解肢葬。随葬的 1 件角杯立放在东南壁的裂缝处（可见下葬时，墓室壁上已出现了裂缝）。

98QZIM113 是保存较好的一座墓，位于 1998 年南区第一发掘点（图 2，Ⅵ）。墓向呈东—西向，棚架缺失，在填土中发现一些毛织物残片。墓口长 4.36 米，宽 2.9 米，二层台宽 0.5~0.82 米，深 0.5 米。墓深 1.34 米。4 人葬，皆为仰身屈肢，双手交叉于腹部，头下有枕头。A、B 两个体头向东，C、D 两个体头朝西。C 个体为女性，A、B、D 个体为男性（图 3）。

这座墓葬保存有较好的服饰、编织帽、皮靴等。随葬品有陶钵、木桶、木纺杆、钻木取火器、角勺、角梳、芦苇束捆和彩色羽毛、骨串珠等，还有鞭杆、皮荷包、皮箭袋和木箭。

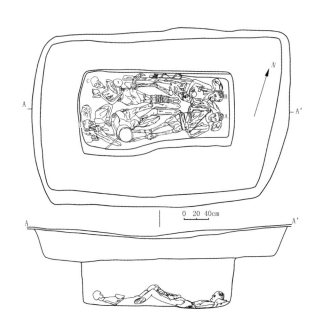

3 98QZIM113 墓平、剖面图
Plan and cross section of grave 98QZIM113

A total of 26 graves of Type B were excavated, that is, rectangular graves with two levels, an upper platform and a lower pit. They were mainly located in the 1998 southern region of Cemetery #1, at the first excavation site. This type of grave was extremely regular and the two levels or platforms were quite distinct. One could clearly see the dividing line between the opening to the grave and the chamber of the grave. Although mostly no canopy was found in this type of grave, one can surmise that in the early period there had been canopies, because of the two-leveled nature of the graves.

One example of this Type B grave was well preserved and complete (96QZIM30). It was located in the 1996 southeast region's excavation site (fig. 2, field I),with a southeast-northwest orientation. The chamber had been well preserved, the opening was rectangular with rounded corners, 2.4 meters long and 1.74 meters wide. Three narrow logs of wood had been placed lengthwise on the opening of the second level: these were 2.2 meters in length and 0.06 in diameter. Reed had been placed on top of the logs. The base of the grave was rectangular with rounded corners. It was 0.77 meters deep. Only three half-desiccated feet belonging to three children were found in the chamber. They were wrapped in a tabby-weave woolen cloth. This burial was of the type that buried dismembered corpses. Inside the grave, one horn cup was found that had been placed in a crack at the southeast wall. Clearly there was already a crack in the chamber at the time of burial.

Grave 98QZIM113 was relatively well preserved, located in the 1998 southern region's first excavation site (fig. 2, field VI). Oriented in an east-west direction, its canopy was already gone. Fragments of woolen textiles were found in the disturbed earth. The opening to the grave was 4.36 meters long and its width was 2.9 meters. The second-level platform was between 0.5 and 0.82 meters wide and was 0.5 meters below the surface. The grave itself was 1.34 meters deep. Four people were buried in this grave, all face upwards, with flexed limbs, both hands crossed over the chest, and with pillows under the heads. The heads of Persons A and B faced east; the heads of Persons C and D faced west. Person C was female; A, B, and D were male (fig. 3).

Well-preserved objects were found in this grave, including braided hats and leather boots. Grave objects included an earthen bowl, a wooden pail, a wooden spindle, a wooden drill for making fire, a ladle made of horn, a comb made of horn, bundles of reed, colored feathers, a necklace made of stringed pieces of bones, also a horse whip, a leather pouch, a leather quiver for holding arrows, and the wooden arrows themselves.

C 型，单墓道长方形竖穴棚架墓，20 座。分布在一号墓地 1996 年南西区的第一、三、四发掘点；1998 年北区第一、二发掘点，南区第四发掘点（图 2，Ⅱ～Ⅳ，Ⅹ～Ⅺ，Ⅸ），比较分散。二号墓地发掘的 2 座墓葬皆属于这一类型。此类墓葬虽然皆被盗掘，但有的葬式比较清楚，一号墓地的 96QZIM14、96QZIM24 墓和二号墓地的 96QZIIM1 墓都出土了不少的遗物。

96QZIM14 墓是保存比较好的一座，位于 1996 年发掘南西区第一发掘点（图 2，Ⅳ）。墓向东西向。墓道处于墓室的西北角，墓道和墓口都有二层台，台面宽和深皆为 0.8 米。墓道平面呈梯形，长 3 米，深 0.8 米。墓口长 7 米，宽 5.6 米。墓室底为圆角长方形，东西长 5 米，南北宽 3.6 米。墓室壁较直，深 1.4 米。墓室中间有一根粗立柱，立柱顶部呈"Y"字形，高 2 米，直径 0.2 米。在墓室有一根直径 0.2 米的残檩木，残长 2.3 米，原应搭放在立柱上。二层台上放置着草绳捆扎的麻秆及树枝，其上横搭着棚木。在棚木上面残留着分层的苇草和柽柳编席。

19 人葬。大体上是沿墓室四壁方向摆放，皆仰身屈肢、双手置于身体两侧，成年人 15 人，其中男性 4 人，女性 11 人。另有小孩 2 人，还有 2 人年龄、性别不清。

这座墓葬保存了较好的服饰，包括上衣、帽饰等，还有铺盖的毛布毯、毛布单。随葬器物大都放置在死者附近，有单耳罐、砺石、木弓、打纬木刀、木竖箜篌、弓囊附件、木梳、木腰牌、长齿木梳、木纺轮、木拐杖、木碗、长方形木盒、绊马索等，还有石珠、玻璃珠、铜环以及加工木件、漆木棒、苇秆束捆、帽、毛布袋等（图 4）。

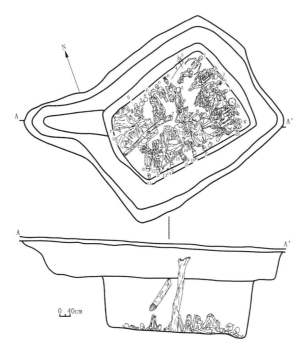

4 96QZIM14 墓平、剖面图
Plan and cross section of grave 96QZIM14

Type C graves had a single grave passage or entryway and were rectangular vertical shaft type earthen graves with canopy. Twenty of these were excavated. They were distributed in the 1996 southwest region of Cemetery #1, in the first, third, and fourth excavation sites, also in the first and second excavation sites of the 1998 northern region as well as the fourth excavation site of the 1998 southern region (fig. 2, fields Ⅱ – Ⅳ , X – Ⅺ , Ⅸ). These Type C graves were quite dispersed. The two graves excavated from Cemetery #2 both had this type of grave structure. Although all of the graves of this type had been robbed, some of the burial structures were still clear and quite a few cultural objects were recovered from Graves 96QZIM14 and 96QZIM24 of Cemetery #1 and from Grave 96QZXIIM1 of Cemetery #2.

Grave 96QZIM14 of Cemetery #1 was well preserved and was situated in the 1996 southwest region's first excavation site (fig. 2, field IV). Its orientation was east-west. The entryway was in the northwest corner of the chamber and both entryway and grave opening had a double-platform structure with both width and depth of the platform being 0.8 meters. The entryway was stair-stepped, 3 meters in length and 0.8 meters deep. The opening to the grave was 7 meters long and 5.6 meters wide. The chamber's base was rectangular with rounded corners, and measured 5 meters from east to west and 3.6 meters from north to south. Its walls were relatively vertical and were 1.4 meters deep. A thick pillar with a forked top had stood in the middle of the room, which measured 2 meters tall and had a diameter of 0.2 meters. Another fragment of a log was also found in the chamber. It was 20 cm in diameter and 2.3 meters long and had originally been placed in the fork of the upright pillar. Hemp stalks and branches tied together with hemp rope had been placed on the second platform, on top of which the wood of the covering was placed crosswise. Remaining traces of reeds and of Chinese tamarisk were on top or originally on the surface of the cover.

Nineteen people were buried in this grave. They were mostly placed with their heads facing outwards against the four walls of the grave. All were laid face upwards with flexed limbs and with hands placed on either side of the body. Of fifteen adults, four were men and eleven were women. There were also two children, and two more whose age and gender were unclear.

The relatively well-preserved clothing from occupants of this grave included upper garments, hats, also woolen carpets and blankets made of woolen cloth. Grave goods accompanying the burial were generally placed near the dead persons, and such goods included a single-handled jar, whetstones, a wooden bow, a wooden sword for beating the weft, two wooden harp-like instruments called an upright *konghou*, a bow case, wooden combs, wooden waist plaques, a long-toothed wooden comb, wooden spindles, wooden walking sticks, a wooden bowl, a rectangular wooden box, horse hobbles, and so on. There were also stone beads, glass beads, a copper ring, and processed wooden articles, a lacquered wooden stick, bundles of reed, hats, a woolen-fabric bag, etc. (fig. 4).

D 型，偏洞室墓。1 座（98QZIM128）。位于一号墓地1998年发掘的南区第二发掘点（图2，Ⅶ），为方形墓道偏洞室墓。墓道处于墓室的东北，方形，西南—东北长5米，西北—东南宽4.2米，深1.3米。墓道壁斜直，底部有一方坑。偏洞室处于墓道的西南壁上，呈龛状。洞室呈东南—西北向，长1.58米，宽1.06米，高0.5米。单人葬，成年女性。仰身屈肢，头向西南。保存有服饰，腰部右侧随葬木腰牌。

E 型，多室墓。2 座。98QZIM111 墓有一个很大的墓圹，建有二层台。沿二层台的四面建了9个小墓室，有竖穴室或偏洞室。

1985 年发掘的 85QZM1 和 85QZM2[5] 两座墓也是在一个大的墓圹里，或可以称作两室墓，位于 1996 年南西区第一发掘点（图2，Ⅳ）。85QZM1 墓室处于墓圹的南部，竖穴，长 1.75 米，宽 0.8 米，深 0.3 米。死者为婴儿，上面盖椭圆形木盆状的胡杨木盖板，盖板长 1.3 米，宽 0.55 米，厚 0.08 米。其上再覆盖芦苇和沙土。婴儿被包裹在内为白色、外为绛红色的两层毛织物里面，外面捆扎着红、蓝色羊毛线绳。膝盖以下有两道，膝部一道，肩部一道，胸部也斜捆了一道。头戴内为红色、外为蓝色的绒帽。仰身，置于一片长 40 厘米、宽 15 厘米的白毡上，头部枕有以毡片制作的枕头。面部裸露，双眼覆盖长 3 厘米、宽 2 厘米、厚 0.3 厘米的黑色石片。鼻孔塞有红色毛线绳。婴儿呈沉睡状，保存得相当完好，全长 51.5 厘米。在婴儿头旁，放置着用羊乳房皮缝制的喂奶器和 1 牛角杯。另外，在 85QZM1 墓室西北 0.8 米处，还发现了殉葬的羊头。

5　85QZM1和85QZM2是1985年发掘墓葬的编号，从平面图上看，这2个编号可以看作是一座两室墓。

The Type D grave can be called a 'chamber grave with niche or recess' and only one of these was excavated, namely 98QZIM128. It was located in the 1998 southern region's second excavation site of Cemetery #1 (fig. 2, field Ⅶ). It had a square-shaped entryway on one side. This was on the northeastern side of the chamber, and was 5 meters from southwest to northeast and 4.2 meters from northwest to southeast. It was 1.3 meters deep. The walls of the entryway were slanted and there was a square pit in the floor. The recess was on the southwest side of the entryway, and was in the shape of a niche. This niche was oriented in a southeast-northwest direction, with a length of 1.58 meters and a width of 1.06 meters. It was 0.5 meters high. This grave was occupied by one person, a female adult. She was lying on her back with legs flexed and head towards the southwest. Articles of clothing were preserved in the grave, and on the right side of the grave-occupant's waist was a wooden plaque or belt buckle.

The Type E grave was multi-chambered and two of these were excavated. In 98QZIM111 there was a very large grave hall, built in two layers or with a double platform. Along the platform were 9 small chambers on all four sides, among which some were vertical-shaft chambers and some were 'side-shaft' chambers.

The two graves excavated in 1985, 85QZM1 and 85QZM2, were also located in a large grave area, and one could say they were one two-chambered grave. They were located in the 1996 southwest region's first excavation site (fig. 2, field Ⅳ). The chamber of 85QZM1 was located in the southern part of the tomb. It was a vertical pit, was 1.75 meters long, 0.8 meters wide, and 0.3 meters deep. The occupant was a child who had been covered with a piece of poplar wood that was in the shape of an oblong basin. This piece of wood was 1.3 meters long, 0.55 meters wide, and 0.08 meters thick. It was covered with reeds and sandy earth. The child was wrapped in woolen cloth, white on the inside and red on the outside – i.e., in two layers of woolen fabric. A soft rope made of red and blue sheep's wool was wound around this bundle. There were two turns of rope under the knees, another on the knees, one on the shoulder area and another, diagonal one across the chest. The head covering or bonnet was made of unspun wool, red on the inside and blue on the outside. The body was on its back, on a white felt mat that was 40 cm long and 15 cm wide. The head was resting on a pillow made of fragments of fabric and unspun wool. The face was exposed and the eyes were covered with flat, black stones that measured $3 \times 2 \times 0.3$ cm. The nostrils were stuffed up with red-colored wool. The child appeared to be in a deep slumber and was extremely well preserved. The whole bundle was 51.5 cm long. Beside the child's head were placed a milk feeder made of a sheep's teat and a drinking horn. In addition, the head of a sheep was found 80 cm to the northwest from grave 85QZM1.

85QZM2在85QZM1的西北2米处。墓室口长5.35米，宽3米；墓室底长3.1米，宽1.55米；墓深2.4米。为长方形二层台墓。

　　墓口有两级二层台，在第一级台面上的棚盖分为四层。第一层是30厘米厚的芦苇层，其中部有一长60厘米、宽30厘米的开口，上面盖着厚毛布长衣、毡毯和马鞍垫等，毡毯上还放着1件陶碗。芦苇层上面还有带角羊头殉牲、牛角杯，并发现了殉马头和一条马腿（膝部以下作了除去骨头的处理，并将干草塞进了马腿皮内）。第二层是苇编席，长3.8米，宽2.4米。第三层是马皮、鹿皮和牛皮。第四层是柽柳编席。第二级台面上有长短不一的25根胡杨木，长2.6米，直径0.15～0.25米（图5）。

　　5人葬。里面的1男、3女四具为干尸，其中1男、1女干尸保存得相当完好，两具女干尸则有不同程度的腐烂。

　　墓室近底部铺柽柳编席，长1.3米，宽2.75米。席下是30厘米深的腰坑，上面放置着长短不齐的14根胡杨木。

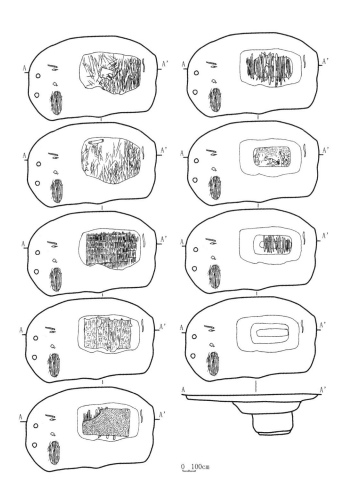

5　85QZM1和85QZM2 墓平、剖面图

Plan, cutaway views and cross section of graves 85QZM1 and 85QZM2

Grave 85QZM2 was 2 meters from 85QZM1, to its northwest. This grave's opening was 5.35 meters long and 3 meters wide; the length and width of the bottom of the grave measured 3.1 and 1.55 meters. The depth of the grave was 2.4 meters. This was a rectangular two-tiered platform type of grave with two levels in the chamber opening. Four layers could be discerned as composing the covering. The first layer was a 30-cm-thick layer of reeds, in the middle of which was an opening measuring 60 by 30 cm. On top of the reeds was a thick woolen gown or robe, a felt carpet, and, on top of this, a saddle cushion and one ceramic bowl.

At the level of the layer of reeds, but placed at some distance from the grave itself, was also a sacrificed sheep's head with horns, a cup made of cow horn, and a sacrificed horse's head and one horse leg. (Below the knee, the bone of this leg had been removed and grasses had been stuffed under the skin.) The second layer of the grave covering was a mat made from reed, 3.8 meters long and 2.4 meters wide. The third layer was horsehide, deer hide, and cowhide. The fourth layer was composed of mats made of Chinese tamarisk. Finally, twenty-five pieces of poplar (*huyang*) of varying lengths had been placed on top of the second tier, these were approximately 2.6 meters long, with diameters between 15 and 25 cm (fig. 5).

Five people were buried in this grave. Four, among them one man and three women, were naturally desiccated mummies, and among these the man and one of the women had been well preserved. Two more female corpses were in varying degrees of decay.

Close to the bottom of the grave chamber were tamarisk woven mats that were 1.3 meters long and 2.75 meters wide. Under these was a thirty-centimeter-deep waisted pit, on top of which had been placed fourteen pieces of poplar of varying lengths.

第三期文化墓葬，发掘了 30 座，分布于一号墓地（1998 年发掘 19 座，1996 年发掘 11 座）。

形制变化比较明显，有三种类型：A 型，长方形竖穴土坑墓；B 型，方形竖穴土坑棚架墓；C 型，偏洞室墓。

A 型，长方形竖穴土坑墓。10 座。这类墓葬与第二期文化的同名墓葬差别明显，主要表现在第三期文化的墓坑相对要规整一些，较深，没有发现棚架遗迹。有的墓室残留木棺，或有木尸架葬具。

B 型，方形竖穴土坑棚架墓。3 座。这一形制仅发现于第三期文化墓葬，木棚架皆已破坏。墓室里皆发现残箱式木棺。

C 型，偏洞室墓。17 座。这一形制的墓葬与第二期文化的同名墓葬差别也比较明显，墓道为比较窄的长方形竖穴，多是单偏洞室，面积比较大。偏洞室残留木架式葬具。同时还发掘 1 座墓葬（96QZIM40），是双偏洞室墓。

98QZIM133 墓位于一号墓地 1998 年南区第二发掘点（图 2，Ⅶ）。墓道口呈长椭圆形，长 3 米，宽 2.3 米。墓道深 1.3 米。偏洞室在墓道的东南一侧，底与墓道底平齐，室口由木栅栏封堵。墓室呈长方形，长 2.16 米，宽 0.64~0.72 米。室顶较平，高 0.64 米。单人葬，仰身直肢。头向东北，面向东南。保存着残损服饰和随葬器物，器物放置在头的东侧，有陶罐、漆木奁、铜镜、木纺轮和马鞍等。同时，在漆木奁里盛着 2 颗饰珠（玛瑙珠、玻璃珠）和白色棉布扎包。另外，填土中发现 1 件铁针，插在白色绢带上（图 6）。

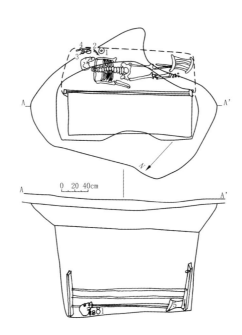

6 98QZIM133 平、剖面图
Plan and cross section of grave 98QZIM133

Thirty graves were excavated that belonged to **Third-Period Culture** graves. these were located in cemetery #1 (19 were excavated in 1998, 11 were excavated in 1996). There was a clear difference in grave structure from Second-period culture graves, with three types of graves being distinguished, called here A, B, and C. Type A was a rectangular, vertical-shaft earthen grave. B was a rectangular vertical-shaft earthen grave with canopy, and C was a 'niche or recess-chamber grave.'

Type A. Ten graves belonged to this type. Notable differences distinguished these graves from Second-period culture graves. Third-period culture graves were comparatively more standardized, they were deeper, and no traces of canopies were found. Some of the grave chambers had traces of wooden coffins, or of wooden platforms on which the body had been laid.

Type B. Three graves were excavated. This type was found only in Third-period graves. Wooden canopies had already been destroyed. In all Type B graves, the remains of box-style coffins were found.

Type C. Seventeen graves were excavated. Again, differences from Second-period graves were apparent. The entryway was relatively narrow, they were rectangular, vertical shaft graves, most of them with one recess-chamber only, and their size was relatively large. Traces or remains of wooden burial platforms remained. One grave was excavated (96QZIM40) that had two side chambers.

Grave 98QZIM133 was situated in Cemetery #1, at the 1998 southern region's second excavation site (fig. 2, field Ⅶ). The opening had an elliptical shape, 3 meters long and 2.3 meters wide. The grave was 1.3 meters deep. The recess chamber was on the southeast side of the shaft, and its floor was level with the bottom of the shaft itself. The entry to the chamber had been blocked with a wooden railing. The chamber was rectangular, 2.16 meters long and 0.64 to 0.72 meters wide. The ceiling of the room was quite level and was 0.64 meters high. This was a grave for one person, who was lying on her back with limbs extended. The head was in the northeast; the face was facing southeast. Fragments of clothing and accompanying grave goods were present. To the east side of the head were placed an earthen jar, a lacquered wooden toilet box (*lian*), a copper mirror, and a wooden spindle, a wooden saddle was placed at the feet. The lacquered box contained two beads, one made of agate and one of glass, and was itself wrapped in white cotton fabric. In addition, an iron needle was discovered stuck into a strip of white silk fabric in the disturbed earth around the chamber (fig. 6).

（三）葬具

在第一期文化墓葬中没有发现葬具。第二期文化墓葬的葬具主要有裹、铺的毛毡，或铺柽柳编席、苇草、羊皮等。第二期文化墓葬发现的木葬具不多，96QZIM27 墓发现一具半圆胡杨木木棺，木棺长 0.92 米，径 0.26 米，盖在小孩身上。在 96QZIM154 和 96QZIIM2 墓葬发现了尸床，不高，较大。同时，在有的墓室里发现残木架，可能是放随葬品的，不排除放置尸体的可能。在 96QZIM83 墓出土一具木架，木架两侧立有木棍，系扎着两根长而细的原木，原木上横向放置小原木棍，木架上铺着羊皮和柽柳编席。

第三期文化墓葬里出现了箱式木棺，不过，没有一具完整的。木板都经过细致地加工，表面也比较平整，方柱形四腿制作得很规整，榫卯结构。另外，还发现木架葬具。98QZIM110 墓的木架保存完整，由细原木制作，呈梯架形式。木架上面残留着毡片。

GRAVE GOODS

No grave goods were found in graves belonging to the First-period culture.

Objects found in Second-period culture graves were primarily felts for both wrapping things and placing under things, or mats made out of Chinese tamarisk, reeds, sheepskins and so on. Not many wooden grave goods were found in Second-period graves. A wooden coffin made of half a section of a poplar tree was found in 96QZIM27. It was 0.92 meters long, had a diameter of 0.26 meters and was placed over the body of a child. In 96QZIM154 and 96QZIIM2 large 'beds' or platforms for the corpse were found that were fairly large but not tall. At the same time, the remains of wooden racks were found in some of the grave chambers, which may have been used for placing burial goods to accompany the deceased although we do not exclude the possibility that they were used as a deathbed for the corpse. A wooden rack or frame was retrieved from 96QZIM83 that had erect wooden poles on either side tied to two long narrow logs. Small logs were placed crosswise on these larger logs; and sheepskins and mats that were made of Chinese tamarisk were spread on this structure.

Box-type coffins appeared in Third-period culture graves, although no complete example was found. The wood of these coffins had been carefully worked, with surfaces that were relatively smooth. Square pillar-like legs were quite well executed and the structures used tenon and mortise construction. There were also wooden platforms or deathbeds. The one in 98QZIM110 was well preserved and complete, had been made from fine logs and was in trapezoid form. Remnants of felt were found on the top of the rack.

（四） 第二、三期文化墓葬的葬式和葬俗

扎滚鲁克一、二号墓地发掘的169座墓葬中，98％的墓葬因盗掘遭到破坏，影响了对埋葬人数的判断。

比如单墓道竖穴棚架墓，墓室都比较大，根据保存较好的一些墓葬看，应该属于丛葬墓。[6]但96QZIM54只保存了两具个体，98QZIM116和98QZIM144也只保存了四具个体，而98QZIM121、98QZIM124、98QZIM129、98QZIM134和98QZIM139则破坏得连一具完整个体都没有发现。

在这里对墓葬埋葬人数多少的判断，主要依据墓室底部保存个体的多少。这样的计算，也考虑到盗墓者的破坏及盗掘原因等因素。统计起来，肯定会有一些偏差，所以埋葬人数只是一个参考数据。不过，多数墓葬的埋葬人数是可信的。

在第二期文化的138座墓葬中，经过仔细研究，发现114座墓葬大体上能看出埋葬的人数，占到了墓葬数的83％，基本上可以反映扎滚鲁克墓葬的葬式和葬俗。情况如下：

单人葬墓31座，两人合葬墓36座，三人合葬墓17座，四人合葬墓10座，五人合葬墓5座，六人合葬墓1座，七人合葬墓3座，九人葬墓1座，丛葬墓10座（10人葬、11人葬、13人葬、14人葬、17人葬和34人葬墓各有1座，19人葬墓2座，24人葬墓2座）。

这里面有成人和小孩的单人葬、成人合葬和小孩合葬、成人与小孩的合葬、小孩解肢葬等，以成人合葬和小孩合葬为主。有的个体生前在手背饰刺青。

6　丛葬，我们将埋葬10人以上的墓称作丛葬墓，说明埋葬的人很多。

GRAVE TYPES AND FUNERARY CUSTOMS OF SECOND- AND THIRD-PERIOD CULTURE GRAVES

Among the 169 graves excavated in Cemetery #1 and Cemetery #2 at Zaghunluq, 98% had been robbed and damaged. This affected any determination of how many people had been buried in them.

Some of the graves probably had more than ten people. For example, graves with a single entryway and vertical shaft with canopy had fairly large chambers. Relying on graves that were well preserved, the ones that were less preserved, but large, probably belonged to what we call 'mass graves'.[5] In 96QZIM54, however, only two individuals were found, and in 98QZIM116 and 98QZIM144 only four were found, while 98QZIM121, 98QZIM124, 98QZIM129, 98QZIM134 and 98QZIM139 were so destroyed that not a single complete individual was discovered.

Determination of how many people were buried in each grave mainly depended on how many skeletons remained on the floor of the chamber. This took into consideration such factors as damage by grave robbers and the underlying reason for the robbery. Due to disturbance by robbers we certainly missed out on some people, so the numbers that are given here are estimates only. Nonetheless, the figure given for most of the graves is reliable.

Among 138 Second-period culture graves, it was possible, through careful analysis, to figure out how many people had been buried in 114 of them. The graves for which we were confident of the number of people thus constituted 83% of the total. The following therefore can generally reflect the burial customs and practices of Zaghunluq, which are as follows.

Thirty-one graves had a single occupant. Thirty-six had two people buried together, seventeen had three people, ten had four people, five had five people, one had six people, three had seven people, one had nine people, and there were ten 'mass graves' of over ten people (one each of 10, 11, 13, 14, 17, and 34 people, two of 19 people, and two of 24 people).

Among the graves were burials of a single child or a single adult, graves of adults buried together with children, of adults buried with adults and children with children, of dismembered children, and so on, but the primary type of grave was that of adults buried together and children buried together. Some of the individuals had been tattooed on the back of their hands while still alive.

5 By 'mass graves,' we mean graves in which more than ten people were buried together.

在葬式上以仰身屈肢葬、双手交叉置于胸腹为主，约占了95％；少数是仰身右侧和左侧屈肢、仰身直肢、俯身直肢葬。同时，大多数个体腿下都放置了支腿棍，以支持死者的屈肢葬式。支腿棍，一般不作细致的加工，将柽柳树枝折成40~50厘米的长度即可，有的一端缠红毛线或红羊毛。死者头向没有规律，夫妻合葬者有同向的，也有反向的。丛葬墓死者大都头向沿墓室四壁方向排列。

第二期文化墓葬有随葬牲畜和动物骨骼的习惯，有绵羊头、山羊头和羊角、羊肩胛骨、羊排骨、羊排骨串，马头骨和马下颌、马肩胛骨、马肋骨，牛头骨和牛角以及狐狸腿、狗皮等。羊骨相对比较多，其次是牛和马，其余的都是在个别墓葬中有所发现。另外，还发现马、鹿、牛和羊的皮革。

从埋葬情况看，有人死后以彩绘面的习俗，许多墓葬随葬的角勺勺体内壁残留有红彩颜料，在一些干尸上也能看到彩绘的花纹。葬俗上还存在用片石盖眼，布、皮蒙面，以及用金片和面糊封口的习俗。个别死者的颈颌部放置有垫颌木块，托着下颌，以防止死者的嘴张开，有一垫颌木块上刻有涡纹。不论男女，多饰长辫，戴帽，包脚蹬皮或着毡靴，穿袍裙或皮衣、裤，并且习惯于束腰、戴项链、发上饰串珠等。串珠有料珠、铜珠、石珠和骨珠。服饰以毛、布为主，也发现很少的原可能也是服饰的残丝织物。随葬器物以木器、陶器为多，还有石、骨、铜铁器和毛制品等，一般都是实用品，包括生活用品和生产工具等。

第三期文化墓葬，多为单人葬，仰身直肢，头向大体是东北向，可以看作是葬式上的一个规律。仍然保留了殉牲现象，只是比较单一，主要是羊。

The primary form of burial was to have the body facing upwards with flexed legs and with the two hands placed crosswise over the chest or abdomen. This accounted for around 95% of burials. A minority were resting on either the right or left side, with flexed legs; some had straight legs, and some were lying prostrate with legs outstretched. The majority of corpses had supports placed under their legs in order to support the flexed-leg-style burial. Mostly, these supports were not well finished or finely made. They were made of Chinese tamarisk branches that had been broken into sections of 40 to 50 cm in length. Some of them were wrapped around with red woolen thread or with red sheep's wool. There was no standardized way of head placement. Some couples that were buried together had their heads placed in the same direction but others had their heads placed in opposite directions. In mass graves, most of the bodies were placed with their heads facing the four walls of the chamber, i.e., lined up around it.

Second-period culture graves exhibited the custom of accompanying the deceased with sacrificed domesticated animals and the bones of animals. These included the heads of sheep and the heads of goats, also goat horns, the shoulder bones of sheep, the ribs of sheep, the spines of sheep, horse's heads and horse's lower jaws, horse's shoulder blades, horse's ribs, cow skulls and cow horns, foxes legs, dog hides, and so on. Sheep bones predominated, after which came cow and horse bones. The others were found only in certain graves. In addition, the hides of horses, deer, cows and sheep were found.

Another custom found in many graves was that of painting the face after the person had died. Traces of red material could be found inside many of the horn ladles found in graves, and also on many of the corpses. Another burial custom was to place stone pieces over the eyes, and to use cloth or leather to cover the face. Yet another was the custom of using a piece of gold foil together with flour paste to stop up the mouth. Some of the necks of some corpses were supported with pieces of wood in order to prop up the lower jaw and prevent the mouth of the deceased from falling open. One of these supporting pieces of wood had been carved with circular whorl patterns. Whether male or female, all corpses were adorned with braided hair, wore hats, and had their feet wrapped and placed in leather or felt boots. They wore either cloth or fur garments and if they wore a jacket or a gown it was customary to tie it in at the waist. They wore necklaces and their hair was adorned with strings of different kinds of beads, made of seeds, copper, stone, or bone. Clothing was mainly made from woolen cloth, but a small number of fragments of silk textiles were also found that originally may have been clothing. Items accompanying the burials were made primarily of wood or ceramics, but there were also items made of stone, bone, copper and iron, and also items made of wool. Mostly the items were for practical use, including items of daily use and tools for production.

Third-period culture graves were mainly single-occupancy burials, with the body facing upwards and limbs outstretched. The head orientation was mainly toward the northeast, which could be regarded as a general practice. The custom of sacrificing animals was still maintained in this period, but it was focused on only one kind of animal, namely sheep.

二　第二期文化墓葬出土器物的文化特点

第二期文化墓葬出土了不少的随葬品，分三类：生活用品、生产工具和纺织品等。[7]

（一）生活用品

生活用品中的陶器、铁器、铜器、骨角器和漆器都是实用品，木器也多为实用品，发现少量的冥器。生活用品中还有石器、皮制品、装饰品等。

陶器，许多陶器上都有烟炱，说明曾用作炊器。典型器物有带流陶罐、陶钵、圜底陶罐、钵形陶罐、单耳陶罐和双系小陶罐，其次是单耳陶杯、无耳陶杯、单耳陶碗、陶壶和陶饼等。陶器特点是手制，以细砂泥质褐灰或褐红色陶胎、黑色陶衣为主。其次是夹砂红陶，个别的器物腹部有刻划的样纹。

带流陶罐，都是开口流，束颈，溜肩，深鼓腹，带状耳处于颈肩部位。多数是素面，有1件腹部饰有刻划纹。器物有圜底和平底之分。陶钵，口比较大，圜底。器物大小、腹壁、底部都有些变化，有深弧腹陶钵、直弧壁弧底陶钵、折腹（肩）陶钵三种类型。深弧腹陶钵少，直弧壁弧底陶钵相对多一些，最多的是折腹（肩）陶钵。双系陶罐，直口，短颈，深弧腹，颈肩部饰双系。器物大小、器底都有变化，分圜底和平底两种。单耳陶杯，器形变化明显，有的是束颈、折肩明显，圜底；有的是束颈，弧、鼓腹圜底；有的则是束颈，平底；有的则是弧腹平底。耳分颈肩耳和口肩耳两种，底变化较大，有圜底单耳陶杯和平底单耳陶杯。圜底陶罐，多数有些束颈，个别的颈部呈弧壁状。领部或高、或低有些变化，鼓腹，尖底或圜底。单耳陶罐，敞口，溜肩，鼓腹。大小差异较大，均为细砂泥质褐灰陶，素面，手制，上黑色陶衣。耳都是带状耳，分口肩耳和颈肩耳两种。器底变化较大，有圜底陶罐和平底陶罐。陶壶，领比较高，鼓腹。多为素面，有1件颈部刻划正、反两排三角纹，三角纹内饰以平行线。器底有些变化，有圜底陶壶和平底陶壶。钵形罐，敛口，弧腹，颈肩没有分界，圜底。单耳碗，口较大，有敛口或口微敞的差别，圜底。无耳陶杯，或敞口，或微敞，深弧腹，圜底。

7　在这里不介绍纺织品。

CULTURAL ATTRIBUTES OF ITEMS EXCAVATED FROM SECOND-PERIOD CULTURE GRAVES

Second-period culture graves produced quite a few accompanying grave goods, which can be divided into three categories: items of daily use, tools for production, and woven items[6].

ITEMS OF DAILY USE

The ceramics, iron objects, copper vessels, lacquered items and articles made from bone and horn found in graves were all for practical use. Most of the wood items were also for practical use; few burial objects, called *mingqi* in Chinese, were discovered. In addition, other daily use items discovered were made of stone, and leather, and there were some ornamental items.

Ceramics: Many of the ceramic items had traces of soot on them, indicating that they had been used in cooking. Representative objects included ceramic jars with spouts, ceramic pots, round-bottomed ceramic jars, ceramic bowls, single-handle jars, double-handle jars and so on. Second in number were cups, single-handle cups, no-handle cups, one-handle bowls, kettles, plates, and so on. The ceramics were notable for being formed by hand, with a base of fine sandy clay that was either grayish or brownish-reddish with a black slip. Next to these came sandy-clay red ceramics, with a few of the items having incised patterns around the middle.

The ceramic jars with spouts had constricted necks, curved shoulders, rounded bodies, and a handle placed between neck and shoulder. Mostly these were plain, i.e. without ornamentation, but one had an incised pattern on the middle part. The vessels could be divided into those with round bottoms and those with flat bottoms. In the case of the bowls, the mouth or opening was relatively large, and bottoms were rounded. There was great variation in the size of the vessels, as well as in the shape of bodies and bottoms, which fell into three main types. Ceramic bowls with a deeply curved belly were rare; straight-walled bowls were more common, but most common were bowls with a curved shoulder. There was great variation in size of vessel and in their bases, some of which were rounded, some flat. The variation was notable among single-handle cups, depending on the curve of the body, the shape of the bottom, the size of the top opening and so on. Some had handles attached to the neck and some to the shoulder. There was considerable variation in the length of the neck of vessels, and the roundedness or pointedness of the bottoms.

Articles made of iron: Damage to these was considerable with many items of unknown original shape. There seem, however, to have been iron swords, iron knives, iron nails, and iron pieces of various kinds. The cross-section of the iron sword was diamond-shaped, there were iron rivets with elliptical heads on them, and there was one small fragment of an iron knife from which it could be seen that the blade was one-sided, not double-sided.

6 Textiles are not discussed in this section, but cf. the catalogue part of this book.

铁器，残缺严重，器形不明，似有铁剑、铁刀、铁钉和铁块等。铁剑截面呈菱形，铁铆钉有椭圆钉帽，残铁刀有一小块，为单面刃。

　　铜器，有铜刀、铜镞、铜镜和铜饰等。铜刀有方首铜刀和弧首铜刀。方首铜刀，直柄，两面刃；弧首铜刀，柄有些弯曲，两面刃，尖锋。铜镞三翼形，刃薄，锋尖，铤由圆渐变为长方形。铜饰呈近半圆或椭圆柱形，有一件上面有 4 个穿孔。

　　骨角器，角勺、角杯、角筒、角罐和骨角梳都很具代表性。有一些特殊器物，如骨套、小方形角扣饰、小角器、骨带扣、刻纹骨板和骨把手，有的残缺严重或用途不明。角勺，系牛角切割为一半，刮削打磨制成。许多角勺内壁或多或少粘附着橘黄或橙红色颜料，应该是给死者绘面后剩余的颜料。角勺器形有些差异，分作三种类型：一种是勺体狭长，壁高，前端呈铲状；一种是勺体椭圆形，较宽，有长柄和短柄之分；还有一种加工精细，勺体也呈圆形或椭圆形。角杯，多是小孩的随葬品，保持着牛角的原形。杯底形状有些变化，一种是锥尖底，底部没做任何加工；一种是小平底，两头切平。有的小平底角杯的小头塞有小圆木板，有的则是弧底。角罐，用三块角料拼接，以牛筋线缝合制成，敞口，束腰，鼓腹，凹底。角罐分单耳角罐和无耳角罐。单耳角罐，腹耳，用牛角制作，以牛筋线缝于罐壁上。骨角梳，器形差别不大。骨梳用大动物的肢骨制作。角梳大多用牛角，有的是刀削磨制而成，有的则用锯加工出梳齿，制作得比较精细。梳背有些变化，一种是平头梳，呈方形或长方形，个别的柄部呈束腰形式；一种是脊头梳型，梳柄背部起一个三角形或近三角形的脊，两侧雕刻着纹饰，有的齿也比较长。另外，还有一种是圆头梳，梳柄背部呈圆弧形，有的在两侧也雕刻了装饰。

Articles made of copper: There were copper knives, arrowheads, mirrors, and items for ornamentation. There was both a knife with a handle with square cross-section and a knife with a handle with curved cross-section. The knife with square cross-section had a straight handle and both sides of the blade had a cutting edge, the knife with curved cross-section had a slightly bent handle, the blade had a cutting edge on both sides, and a sharp point. The arrowheads had three flanges or 'wings,' with thin blades and sharp tips, the tang gradually progressing from round to rectangular. Copper ornaments were semi-circular or elliptical and one had four holes in it.

Bone and horn items included horn ladles, horn cups, horn tubes, and horn jars. Bone and horn combs were very representative. There were some special items such as a bone cover, small square horn buttons, a small horn item, a bone buckle, a bone tablet with engraved linear decoration, and a bone handle, as well as objects which had been severely damaged or the use of which was unclear. Horn ladles, cow horns cut in half, had been cut and polished. Many had traces of orange-yellow or reddish pigments still adhering to them which may have been what remained after painting the faces of the deceased. Horn ladles came in three kinds: in one, the ladle body was long and thin with high sides, with the front end like a shovel. In another, the ladle body was oblong, relatively wide, with either long or short handles. The last was a kind that had been finely made, with the ladle body either round or elliptical. Horn cups were mainly found accompanying the graves of children, and they were left in the basic shape of a cow horn. There was variation in the base of these cups, some being pointed without any modification at all, and others flat-bottomed with the two sides cut level. Some small flat-bottomed horn cups had round wooden boards tucked into the top, while some had curved bottoms. Horn jars: three pieces of horn material were tied together with cow sinews or tendons to form a composite item with wide rim, girded waist, rounded belly and concave bottom. The horn jars can be divided in such with one ear and such without. The ear, attached to the belly, was made from cow horn and stitched to the jar with sinew. Bone and horn combs: there was not much variation among these. Bone combs were made from the bones of large animals; horn combs generally used cow horns. Some were cut and polished with a knife, some were made with a saw, and relatively finely finished. The back of the combs had some variation: one kind had a flat head, either square or rectangular; some handles were waisted. One kind had a spine-formed head, with the back of the handle being triangular or nearly triangular, with decorative elements protruding on both sides. Some combs had relatively long teeth. Another kind had a round top, with a curved back to the handle forming an arch, and also protruding decorative elements on both sides.

装饰品，有铜耳环、铜环、铁戒指、金口饰和串珠等。串珠形式多样，有的是串珠饰品，如项链、发饰串珠等。大多数是零星的饰珠，有骨珠（包括海贝、珊瑚珠、蚌壳）、石珠（包括石坠、云母饰片、玛瑙珠和绿松石）、玻璃珠和铜珠等。耳环是由铜丝拧成椭圆形的环。铜环是宽体椭圆形环，环里存一残铁块。铁戒指由宽而薄的铁片弯曲而成。金口饰盖在死者的口部，薄，有系眼。项链由各种饰珠组合，或为骨珠，或为石珠和玻璃珠。骨珠由动物骨制作，有管状、菱角形和圆形等。蚌壳呈椭圆形，壁薄。海贝大小有别，珊瑚珠近圆柱状，中间穿孔。石珠主要是绿松石，还有玛瑙珠和浅蓝色石珠，形状有柱状、管状、梯形、扁圆形。云母饰片刻成了花瓣状。玻璃珠，分圆鼓形和球形两种，中间穿孔。铜珠呈环节状，截面椭圆。

皮制品，有船形皮囊、皮荷包、皮袋和皮刀鞘、皮带等。船形皮囊很特别，分内外两层，内层是一个封闭性的船形盒，上面刻有图案和两个系孔，系孔上残留有毛线；外层是套，上部开口呈船形，后侧壁呈方形。内外两层用皮条缝扎在一起，由短线、弧线勾勒出一些图案化纹饰。皮荷包呈半圆形，由皮扣、皮盖、皮身和皮缀饰组成。皮盖周边加工出弧形的花边，非常精致。皮袋不大，有口小底大的梯形袋和方形袋等。

皮刀鞘，一种是木胎刀鞘，外面包裹牛皮，呈长三角形，鞘口边缘上有一系眼，尾部曲折。刀鞘上绑缚有细皮条，出土时和砺石粘附在一起。一种是皮刀鞘，鞘口一侧有穿孔的耳。鞘尾呈尖状，镶铁环。皮带，皆残，牛皮缝制，有的残皮带上保存着骨带扣。

漆器，大都残缺严重，不能复原。器形有漆盒、残漆碗、漆桶、漆盖、漆木盘和漆木棒等，还发现 1 件残漆木片。漆器都是木胎，漆面光洁，或亮或暗，有些变化。有的漆器为黑漆底，绘红彩云纹。漆桶较为完整，用原木制成，口部平齐，壁上加工有二层台。桶的底壁四周有固定桶底的穿孔，表面涂黑漆。漆木棒上缠缚着很薄的麻和树皮，表面涂黑漆。

Ornamental articles included copper earrings, a copper hoop, an iron ring, a gold mouthpiece, and strings of beads. The many different kinds of beads included bone beads (including shells, coral, clamshells), stone (including stone pendants, a piece of mica, amber and turquoise), glass, and copper. Earrings were made of copper wire curved into an oval ring. The broad copper hoop had an elliptical shape, inside there was a fragmentary piece of iron. The iron ring was made of a broad, thin sheet of iron bent into a ring. The thin gold mouthpiece was placed over the dead person's mouth and had a series of holes in it. Necklaces were made of all kinds of beads, bone, stone, or glass. Bone beads were from animals, including tube shaped, lozenge shaped and round. Clamshells were elliptical, with thin walls. There were all sizes of shells. The coral was nearly round and tubular, with holes pierced through the middle. The main stone used for beads was turquoise, but there were also amber and a light-blue-colored stone, with shapes including tubular, trapezoid, and oblate. The mica ornamental piece was square and cut to a petal-like shape. Glass beads were both round and drum-shaped and had holes pierced through the middle. The copper beads were clustered to form a tube, their cross-section was elliptical.

Leather items: these included a boat-shaped leather sack, a leather pouch, leather bags, a leather scabbard or sheath and a leather belt. The boat-shaped leather sack was quite special, with an inside- and outside-layer. The inside layer was boat-shaped with carved patterns and two finely worked holes. Traces of wool threads remained in the holes. The outer layer was a cover, the upper part having a boat-shaped opening, the back side being square, with leather strips to tie the inside and outside layers together. Patterns included short curved and interlocking lines. The leather pouch was half-moon shaped and included leather buttons, leather cover, leather body and leather stitching. The rim of the cover had a very finely worked decorative border of arches. The leather bags were small, either trapezoidal with a narrow opening and larger bottom, or square. The leather knife scabbards: one kind was a long triangular shape, with a hole for tying at the opening. It had a wooden core, was wrapped in cow leather and was bound at the end with fine leather strips. During excavation, this was found close to a whetstone. Another kind of knife sheath made of leather had a handle or 'ear' with a hole in it at one side of the opening. The end of this was pointed and was inset with an iron hoop. A leather belt was found in fragments, it was made of cow leather. Some of the leather pieces retained fragments of a bone buckle.

Lacquer objects: most of these were severely damaged and could not be reconstructed. The shapes included lacquer boxes, fragments of lacquer bowls, a lacquer bucket, lacquer covers, lacquer wooden basins, a lacquered wooden stick and so on. A fragment of a thin lacquered wooden piece was also discovered. All of the lacquer pieces had a wooden core. There was considerable variation in how lustrous or dark the lacquer was. Some of the lacquer objects were black and painted with red cloud patterns. The lacquer bucket was relatively complete. It was made out of a log, the mouth was regular and even, the walls had been worked and constituted two different levels. Holes were found at fixed intervals in the bottom part of the tube; the surface was painted with black lacquer. The top of the lacquer stick had been wrapped with a thin layer of bark and hemp, its surface was painted with black lacquer.

木器，多用原木雕刻制作，分制组合的比较少，其中木竖箜篌、木盒、木筒、木桶、刻纹双连小木杯、木盘、木梳和木腰牌很有特点。另外，还有木手杖、木花押、木带扣、钻木取火器、双范式木器、木管、木板和彩绘木板、木叉、加工木件、木别子、带流木罐、单耳木杯、单系木碗、单耳木碗、单柄木钵、单系木罐、木盆、木勺等，多是实用器，有的用途不明。

木竖箜篌是扎滚鲁克第二期文化具有代表性的木器之一，也是目前新疆乃至以东地区发现的年代最早的箜篌实物之一。发现3件，虽缺失弦和蒙皮，但音箱、颈、弦杆保存完好，木料为当地的胡杨和柽柳枝，说明属本地制造品。同时外表打磨光滑，器形规整且很美观。木盒为长方形，子母口，用削、刮、凿等方法雕刻打磨而成，多刻涡旋纹，最精彩的是狼羊纹木盒、鸟纹木盒。木筒和木桶皆为圆柱形，结构上略有些变化，有的上面刻画了纹样，如鹿羊纹木筒、涡旋纹木筒、鹿纹木桶、驼鹿纹木桶等都很精彩。刻纹双连小木杯，残，原木刮挖雕刻而成，近圆形，切平的圆口。器表锥刺连点、曲线组合的纹饰。木盘形状差异较大，分为无足盘和四足盘两种。无足盘，形状有不少的变化，如凹边木盘、椭圆形木盘和长方形木盘等。长方形木盘器形大都比较规整，多为平底。凹边木盘不大，大体呈长方形，有一个边内凹，弧底。椭圆形木盘变化较大，有的盘口一端窄，一端宽，呈船形或菱形。四足木盘，盘多呈长方形和近方形，也有圆形或者长椭圆形的，有的四足与盘为整体雕刻制作，有的四足是组装而成。盘内有盛放食物的痕迹。木梳形式变化较大，一种是组合型木梳，用几块小木板粘合，或刻出齿槽的长方形梳柄，齿是单独削制，且附有边齿；一种是沟槽嵌齿型，梳柄为小圆木棒，在镶齿一面凿刻出长方形的沟槽，梳齿并排镶嵌其中，齿根截面为方形；一种是卯孔嵌齿形，梳柄为小圆木棒；也有长方形和多边形，皆在梳柄上钻出一个个卯眼（齿孔），再将齿根镶嵌于卯眼之中制成。

Wooden objects: these were mostly made of logs. Composite pieces, fewer in number, included harp-like, upright stringed instruments called a *konghou*. Other pieces included a wooden box, wooden tubes, wooden buckets, two wooden conjoined cups with incised pattern, wooden basins, wooden combs, and wooden waist plaques. There were also wooden staffs, a wooden seal stamp, wooden belt buckles, wooden implements for making fire, wooden objects with double mold, wooden tubes, wooden boards, painted wooden boards, wooden forks, pieces of worked wood, wooden brooches, wooden jars with spout, one-handled wooden cups, wooden bowls, one-handled wooden bowls, one-handled wooden bowls of *bo* type, one-handled wooden jars, wooden basins, wooden ladles and so on. All of these items were for practical use, although the use of some was unclear.

The three *konghou* instruments that were found in the graves dated from the Zaghunluq Second-period culture and were some of the key wooden objects to be discovered. They represent the earliest such instruments found to date in Xinjiang and indeed in the eastern region. They lacked strings and skin covering over the sound box but included the sound box, neckpiece and pegs for holding the strings, which were all preserved in complete form. The wood used in their construction was local poplar *huyang* and Chinese tamarisk, showing that the instruments had been made locally. The outer surfaces were polished to a luster, and the shape of the instruments was very beautiful.

The wooden boxes were rectangular, with lipped lid and with various techniques used in construction, including paring, scraping and chiseling, followed by carving and polishing. Designs included mostly carved whorl patterns. The most exquisite boxes were those which had wolf-and-sheep patterns and bird patterns. The wooden tubes and buckets were made of logs and were all rounded pillar shapes, with variation in structure. Some were carved with patterns, such as a tube with deer and sheep, a tube with whorl patterns, a bucket with deer, or a bucket with camel and deer. These were quite beautiful. The two small wooden conjoined cups with carved decoration had been carved from a log, scraped, scooped out, carved and polished. They had a near to round shape, and the round opening was cut even. The surface of the cups was carved with rows of aligned dots, in curved lines forming patterns. The wooden basins came in many fairly large forms, including those without legs and those with four legs. There was not much variation in the shape of those without legs. Examples include wooden basins with one inward-bent side, elliptically shaped wooden basins and rectangular wooden basins. All of the rectangular basins had a fairly regular shape, most with flat bottoms. There were not many wooden basins with an inward-bent side and they were generally rectangular in shape, with curved bottoms. There was greater variation among the elliptically shaped wooden basins. Some had mouths that were narrow on one end and wide on the other, like a boat or lozenge shape. The four-legged wooden basins were mostly rectangular or nearly square, although there were also round or long elliptical shapes. Some of the basins with four legs were carved in one piece, the legs together with the body of the basin, others had their legs inset. Traces of food remained inside the basins.

许多梳柄上刺刻着花纹，有"S"形纹、波浪纹、"几"字纹、锯齿纹、菱格纹、"V"形纹、"M"形纹、曲折纹、三角纹、三角网纹和鹿纹等。木腰牌，佩于腰部，有系孔。腰牌分圆形和长方形两种，圆形木腰牌，有的饰方形柄，刻纹有圆点、涡纹、半月纹、弧线纹、放射状弧线纹、"S"形纹等；长方形木腰牌皆有长方形柄，柄上钻系孔，也有倒梯形柄的。刻纹有正、倒三角纹和涡纹等。

石器，比较少，有砺石、石眉笔和石眉墨。砺石呈长条形，为灰黑色或红褐色细砂岩砾石磨制，有圆形的系，带钻孔和明显的使用痕迹。首部有些变化，分为平首型和弧首型。石眉笔纵面锥体，截面近圆形。石眉墨残缺严重，形状不规则，有一道磨槽。

墓葬里出土了一些颜料、面食、麦子和粟。颜料呈粉末状，有红色、白色、赭红色和橘红色。麦子和粟发现得少，面食有圆形、椭圆形和半球形的小饼。羊排骨串和羊排骨很有特点，是相连的三四条羊肋骨，羊排骨串上有木棍，类似现代的烤排骨串形式。

Wooden combs varied considerably, with one kind being a composite comb, using either small wooden boards bound together or having a handle with a carved-out groove for the teeth. These were cut individually, and there were also two side teeth. One kind with inlaid teeth had a comb handle that was a small, raw wooden stick. In inlaying the teeth a long rectangular channel had been carved into one side, into which the teeth were inset in a row. The cross-section of each individual tooth was square. One kind had teeth inlaid into mortise holes, with the comb handle being a small round wooden stick. There were also rectangular and multi-sided types of comb handles. All of the teeth were set into holes in the handle of the combs.

Many of the comb handles had been incised with patterns, including S-patterns, wave patterns, *ji*-character patterns, zigzag patterns, diamond patterns, V-type patterns, M-shape patterns, twisted patterns, triangular patterns, triangular networks and also deer patterns. The wooden waist plaques, girdle ornaments found near the waist area, had lines of holes for tying. The waist plaques could be divided into two types, round and rectangular. Some of the round-shaped wooden waist plaques had square handles, they were decorated with carved dots, whorls, half-moon patterns, also curving lines, radiating arches or S-patterns. All of the rectangular wooden waist plaques had rectangular handles and holes for tying were drilled into the handles. There were also inverted trapezoid handles. The incised patterns included upright and upside-down triangles and whorls.

Stone implements were relatively rare. They included whetstones, stone eyebrow pencils, and mineral pigments. The whetstones were long and made from either grey-black or orange-brownish colored sandstone; they had round holes for tying to the belt and there was clear evidence of their being used. The tops of these items varied: some were flat and some were curved. The eyebrow pencils were close to circular in cross-section, in length they were like a drill. The eyebrow pigments were somewhat deteriorated and irregular in shape, and came with a grinder.

Pigments were excavated that were in powdered form and included red, white, reddish brown or burnt ochre, and orange-red. Food made of flour was found in the graves, also wheat and millet. Not much wheat and millet were found, but round, oval and conical-shaped little cakes made of flour. Strips of sheep ribs that were found were quite special—three or four sheep's ribs would be linked to wooden sticks, similar to the sticks used in cooking spareribs today.

（二）生产工具

分为一般生产工具和马具两种。

1. 一般生产工具有石器、木器、铁器、骨器和皮制品等。

石器，有石球、石磨盘和石臼。石球，磨制，圆形。石磨盘呈马鞍形，大小变化不大。石臼都比较小，器形有变化，有的呈船形，斜弧壁，平底；有的是錾耳圆体形状。

木器，有木弓、木矢、捕鸭木器、木耜、木臼、木纺轮、打纬木刀、鞣皮木刮刀、长齿木梳和木针等。木针，是缝缀用具。木纺轮、打纬木刀是纺织用具。不少木纺轮保存完整，有的保存了纺杆或纺轮。长齿木梳可能是加工毛毡的辅助性工具，梳体大，将7根柽柳枝分别削刮成长梳齿（梳齿锥尖，尾部削得比较扁），而后粘成三角形。

打纬木刀，分为刀柄和刀体，由木板削刮而成。刀柄有变化：一种，刀柄和刀体分界明显，两面刃；一种，刀柄和刀体分界不明显，柄长方形，单面刃。刀背上有线的勒痕。鞣皮木刮刀是加工兽皮的工具，形似弯刀，柄截面圆形，刀体弯，钝刃（有人认为是类似于飞去来器一类的打猎工具）。木弓、木矢和捕鸭木器都是狩猎器具。木弓，弦缺失，弓的质地有些变化，一种是木质；一种是木、骨角质。一般来说木质的力量要小，而木、骨角质的力量大，射程远。木矢，由木棍刳削打磨制成，杆尾有涂彩和粘贴翎羽的痕迹。箭头有些变化，有方体形、方体倒刺形、菱体倒刺形、三棱体倒刺形、圆头形等。捕鸭木器，为一弯形的木棍，上面残留了缠缚网线的痕迹。木耜、木镰刀和木臼都是农业生产工具。木耜残损严重，不见木柄，仅保留了小部分木耜头，为近长方形的铲头。木臼有柄，为整木刳挖雕刻而成，器形较小，呈椭圆形。另外，还出土了木镰刀，比较小，是冥器，由木刀和木柄组成。

TOOLS USED IN PRODUCTION

Tools used in production could be divided into general tools and horse implements.

General tools included wooden articles, stone, iron, bone, and leather articles.

Stone: Objects included stone balls, stone grinding basins, and stone mortars. The stone balls were polished and round in shape. The stone grinding basins resembled a horse's saddle and there was not much variation in size. The stone mortars were all quite small and there was great variation in their shape. Some were boat shaped, with curved walls and flat bottoms, some had handles or ears and round bodies.

The wooden articles included bows, arrows, implements for catching ducks, wooden shovel-shaped implements, wooden mortars, wooden spindles and whorls, wooden sword beaters for beating weft threads, wooden knives for softening hides, long-tooth wooden combs and wooden needles. The wooden needles were for sewing and stitching. The wooden spindles, and the sword beaters were for making textiles. Quite many of the spindles were preserved in complete condition, but some of them retained only the spindle and some the whorl. The long-toothed wooden comb was perhaps an accessory for processing woolen felt. It was large and had seven teeth made of sticks of peeled Chinese tamarisk (the teeth were pointed at the end, the rear part was peeled to relatively flat), prepared individually and then stuck together in triangular form. The wooden sword-shaped beaters were composed of handle and body, which had been cut or pared from wooden boards. The beater and handles varied, some having clear distinctions between handle and body, with both blade sides sharpened, others having no evident distinction between handle and body, but rectangular handles and only one sharpened side of the knife. Traces and grooves due to the warp threads were visible on the back of the beaters. The knife for softening hides was a tool for processing animal skins. It was curved, with a handle that had a round cross-section. Since the knife blade was curved and blunt, some people thought it was a hunting tool similar in function to a boomerang. The wooden bow and arrows and the device for catching ducks were hunting items. The wooden bows lacked their string, the material of the bows themselves varied. Some were made of wood, some of wood with bone and horn. Generally speaking, the wooden bows were less powerful, while the ones made of wood, bone and horn had the ability to shoot further. The wooden arrows were made of polished wooden sticks. Their tail ends were painted and they had traces of feather fletching stuck on them. There were various kinds of arrowheads, some square, some square-bodied and barbed, some diamond-shaped and barbed, some triangular and barbed, and some round. The piece for catching ducks was like a curved wooden stick, with traces of a net still on it. The wooden shovel, wooden sickle, and wooden mortar were all agricultural implements. The wooden shovel had suffered severe damage and lacked a handle. The only part left was a small piece of the wooden blade, which had a nearly rectangular head. The mortar had a handle and was formed as one piece out of a hollowed piece of wood. It was quite small, with an elliptical body. One small wooden sickle that was excavated was clearly a burial object (*mingqi*). It was composed of a wooden blade and a wooden handle.

铁器，只有木柄铁刀一种。铁刀的镶嵌方式有变化，分作横向镶嵌铁刀和纵向镶嵌铁刀。横向镶嵌铁刀，圆木棍柄，柄前端横穿一长方形孔，内残存部分锈蚀铁刀。这类铁刀可能是镰刀。纵向镶嵌铁刀，长圆柄，前端中空，内保留有锈蚀铁刀，有缠绑丝麻的痕迹。

皮制品，主要是箭箙，外包兽皮，内由木筋定形，大都呈长方形。箭箙上有皮条及木挂钩，以备悬挂之用。箙里面除保存有木矢外，还有钻木取火母器。

骨器，有骨针和箭簇。骨针磨制，很精致，柄端有一圆形穿孔。箭簇，三棱形，铤稍残，有倒刺。

2. 马具，有木马镳、木杆皮鞭及木鞭杆、绊马索及木结具和弓形木绳扣。

木马镳，圆柱形，上面钻两孔。有的保留树皮，用柽柳木棍制作。绊马索及木结具，绊马索由粗毛绳和两个木结具及细绳组成。木结具在结构上有些变化，分为"凹"字型和"凸"字型两种。绊马索上多用"凹"字型结具，绊马时将细绳绕过马腿，绳环套在木结具上即可。木杆皮鞭及木鞭杆，只有1件保存了皮鞭鞘，鞭杆两端各套有一装饰骨管。木鞭杆，分作圆木棍鞭杆和长方形鞭杆。长方形鞭杆，杆头钻有两个固定鞭鞘的穿孔，遗留有捆绑的痕迹。圆木棍鞭杆，有一些变化，分直杆、钻孔杆、刻槽钻孔杆和螺旋纹杆。

直杆，杆头和杆尾既无穿孔也无系绳槽；钻孔杆，杆头钻孔，以加固鞭鞘，杆尾钻提带孔或刻系绳槽，有的木杆上刻花纹、涂黑色；刻槽钻孔杆，杆头刻系绳槽以捆绑鞭梢，杆尾穿孔或刻系绳槽，有的杆头系绳槽缠着白色毛线绳，杆尾也缠有原白色和棕色毛线绳；螺旋纹杆，两头削刮成螺旋纹形式，一边有拴鞭鞘的痕迹。弓形木绳扣，是捆绑用具，呈"V"形，两端削有系绳环槽，扣体经刮削、烧烤弯曲加工制作。

Iron items: Only one kind was found, iron knives with wooden handles. These included variations in how the blade was attached to the handle. Some were attached crosswise, and some lengthwise. Those attached crosswise had a rounded handle with a rectangular hole at its front end retaining traces of the rusted iron knife. This kind of iron knives may well have been sickles.

Those attached lengthwise had long rounded handles, hollowed at the front, with traces of rust remaining inside. Some sickles had traces of silk and hemp on them.

Leather-made objects included mainly a quiver for arrows which had animal skin wrapped around it. It had a wooden bracing on the inside and was generally rectangular in shape. At the upper end, the quiver had leather thongs with wooden hooks, for hanging purposes. Inside the quiver, in addition to wooden arrows, was a fireboard for making fire by friction.

Bone items included wooden needles and arrowheads. The needles were polished and finely made, with a round hole in the handle end. The arrowheads were triangular in shape and barbed, the tang somewhat damaged.

Horse Implements

Horse implements included wooden horse bits, wooden whips with leather lash and wooden whip handles, hobbles, and bow-shaped toggles or fasteners for ropes. The wooden horse bit cheeks were round, with two holes. Some of these objects still had bark on them, and had been made of sticks of Chinese tamarisk. The hobbles were made of thick woolen rope and two wooden pieces joined to thinner ropes. The wooden pieces showed variation in construction, and could be divided into those that were indented and those that protruded. The hobbles mostly were of the indented type. When hobbling a horse, the thin rope would be tied around the horse's legs, the rope loops would go around the wooden knobs in order to be tightened. Of all the whips, only one was found with its leather lash preserved, its whip stick was decorated with a bone tube on either end. The wooden whip-sticks came in round and rectangular shapes. The rectangular ones had two holes drilled in the top end, in order to fasten the whip lash, and there were remains of fibers that had been tied on them. The round whip sticks were varied in form, some straight, some with holes, some with grooves and holes, and some had spiral patterns. The straight ones did not have holes in either top or bottom and also showed no grooves to tie a lash. Of those with holes, one type had a hole at the top of the stick for fastening a solid whip tip, a hole or a groove at the bottom served for fastening a rope to attach the whip to the wrist; some of the wooden sticks had patterns carved in them, painted with black pigment. The whip sticks with holes and grooves had a hole or a groove at the top of the stick for attaching the whip lash, and a hole or a groove at the bottom, some had a rope made of white wool bound to the groove at the top of the stick and natural white and brown colored wool rope wrapped around the bottom end of the stick. The stick with spiral patterns was carved at both ends with a spiraling line, the remains of a whip lash were bound to one end. The bow-shaped wooden toggles were used to for binding, they had a V-shape and a circular groove at both ends to attach ropes. The body of the toggles was pared and scraped to give it a bent form.

三　第三期文化墓葬出土器物的文化特点

扎滚鲁克墓地盗掘最严重的是第三期文化墓葬，随葬物品大体上分为三大类：生活用品、生产工具和纺织品等。[8]

（一）生活用品

生活用品包括陶器、生土器、漆木器、铜器、铁器、骨角器、玻璃器、装饰品、皮制品、食品和纸文书等。

陶器，有单耳罐、陶罐、残陶壶颈等，都是泥质，以灰陶为主。陶器多是手制，出现了轮制，素面，无任何的纹饰。陶器中，除陶壶的残颈外，陶罐和单耳陶罐器形风格相似、统一，特别是平底陶罐、单耳陶罐，应该是三期文化的代表性器物。

生土灯，直接用生土块雕刻，呈不规则的方梯形，椭圆形口，弧壁，内底呈圆形。口沿有黑灰，内底残存灯芯和似油渣的东西，应该是灯。

---

8 在这里不介绍纺织品。

CULTURAL ATTRIBUTES OF ITEMS EXCAVATED FROM THIRD-PERIOD CULTURE GRAVES

Third-period culture graves were the most severely robbed of all graves at Zaghunluq. Articles found in these graves could be divided into three main categories: items for daily life, tools for production, and implements for weaving.[7]

ITEMS FOR DAILY LIFE

Items for daily life items included ceramic vessels, unfired ceramic wares, lacquered objects, copper, iron, and bone and horn objects, glass objects, decorative objects, objects made of leather, food, and paper documents.

Ceramics: there were single-handle jars, pottery jars, fragments of kettle spouts and so on, all of which were made of clay with grey-pottery predominating. Most of the ceramics were formed by hand, but wheel-formed pieces did appear. They were all unadorned, without any patterns. With the exception of the kettle spout fragments, the jars and single-handle jars had a similar style, that is, a unified approach. The flat-bottomed ceramic jar with one handle can be taken as a defining object of Third-period culture.

Lamps made from unfired clay were fashioned directly into irregular square or trapezoid shapes, with elliptical mouths, curved walls and round inside bottoms. There were ashes on the mouth and wick remains were found on the inside, together with dregs of oil, so these were probably lamps.

---

7 Weaving implements are not discussed here.

漆木器，比较多，有木盘、木碗、单柄木罐、木篦、木梳、木匕、漆匕、木耳杯、漆耳杯、漆案、筷子和袋口夹棍等。木器多是手工加工，同时也出现了旋切技术，器形规整。圆木盘，有的是旋切加工，有的是手工雕刻。制作得都比较精致。器物有大小的差别。单柄木罐，颈和腹部有明显的旋切纹痕迹，有假圈足。木梳和木篦，皆呈马蹄形，纵截面为楔形。边齿稍宽，中齿细密。筷子，柽柳枝两头截断制成，保留有树皮。袋口夹棍，是皮袋口上的夹棍，皆为半圆的细木棍，两头削有系绳槽。木匕和漆匕，造型相似，皆长柄，匕体面平，呈梨形。漆匕涂有红、黑色漆。木耳杯、漆耳杯，木耳杯都是仿漆耳杯，削刮制作，粗糙，大小差异很大。

　　漆耳杯制作相对精致一些，器形也很典型，木胎，胎上有一层丝绢，杯内涂红漆，外表是黑漆。漆案，木胎，案体为弧角长方形，窄边，长方形耳。木漆案以红漆作底，深红、黑、黄色绘三角、枝花和鸟纹等。漆木奁，木胎，旋切加工，施红漆，奁盖上有黄、黑彩绘植物图案。

Lacquer wares were common in Third-period culture graves. There were lacquered wooden basins, wooden bowls, single-handle wooden jars, wooden combs, wooden fine-toothed combs, wooden *bi* ladles, lacquer ladles, wooden ear-cups, lacquer ear-cups, lacquer tables, chopsticks, clamp sticks for pouches and so on. Most of the wooden implements were made by hand and then processed, but at the same time turning technology seems to have appeared, for the shape of the objects was quite regular. Some round wooden basins were made by turning; others were carved by hand. All were relatively finely made. Objects came in large and small sizes. Single-handle wooden jars: the neck and body of these clearly showed traces of turning, with a false foot ring. Wooden combs and fine-toothed combs: all were in the shape of horse's hooves, with cross-sections that were wedge-shaped. The side teeth were wider, the middle ones more fine. Chopsticks: these were made from Chinese tamarisk branches that still showed traces of bark. Clamp sticks for pouches: these were pairs of slender wooden sticks with half-circle cross section and a carved groove at both ends; they were placed at both sides of the opening of a leather pouch and tied together with a rope. Wooden ladles and lacquer ladles: these were similar in shape, all long-handled, with flat ladle tops and bodies in the shape of a pear. The lacquer ladles were painted with both red and black lacquer. Wooden ear-cups, lacquer ear-cups: the wooden cups were made to copy the lacquer cups. They were scraped out, rather rough and came in great variation in size.

Lacquer ear-cups were made more finely, and came in a standard shape. They had a wooden core on which a layer of tabby silk (*juan*) was placed; red lacquer was painted inside the cup, black lacquer on the outside. The lacquer tables had a wooden core; they were rectangular with rounded corners, narrow sides and rectangular handles. One wooden lacquered table had red lacquer as the base, with dark red, black, and yellow painting of triangle, flower and bird patterns. The lacquered wooden *lian*-type toilet box had a turned wooden core, was painted with red lacquer, and was decorated on the lid with plant patterns drawn in yellow and black.

铜器，比较少，有勺、镜、带扣和扣饰等。铜勺，残缺严重。长柄勺，柄为螺纹形式。铜镜，圆形，镜面纹样浅而模糊，为卷草一类的纹样。铜带扣及铜饰扣，皆发现于死者腰部。

铁器，数量少，发现一些器形不明的铁块和铁刀。铁刀保存在残骨鞘内，是骨鞘铜首铁刀。

骨器，在墓葬填土中收集到一件骨带扣，长方形，为双孔式带扣。

玻璃杯，残，可以复原。淡绿白色，吹制。口大底小，斜直口。杯腹部冷加工磨琢三排椭圆纹，上、中排 13 个，下排 7 个。底部为一磨制的单圆纹。

装饰品，有玛瑙珠、玻璃珠、骨珠和贝饰等。玛瑙珠截面呈不规则六棱形，玻璃珠有棕黄色柱形珠和蜻蜓眼珠。蜻蜓眼玻璃珠为蓝色，呈菱形，上面有长椭圆形的眼纹。贝饰，大小有些差别。鹰爪饰系鹰的趾骨，尖部缠有很小的一块金箔。

皮制品，有一件圆形皮奁，稍残，圆形，羊皮包面。奁内有文书、铁针、木篦、玻璃珠、残丝毛织品和线。有一件皮袋，由麻线缝制，呈长方形，袋口用夹棍、麻绳绑缚。

食品、谷物，发现了一些面食，有油炸的菊花饼、麻花、桃皮形小油饼、薄饼等，还有葡萄干串和连骨肉。发现一些谷粒，保存较好，出土时和杂草、棉布混在一起。

纸文书，原用于包裹粉末状物品，染有红色。文书分成了两条，残存四行文字：

　　□□
　　望叹□
　　煮热伏相
　　□万福□□□

其中"望"、"煮"两字上部残缺。可能是一封家书。

Copper items were relatively scarce and included a spoon, a mirror, belt buckles and button-like ornaments. The spoon was badly damaged; it had a long handle with a thread-like patterns on it. The mirror was round and had indistinct patterns on its surface, somewhat like scrolls. The copper belt buckles and button-like ornaments were all found near the deceased's waist.

Iron objects were rare. Fragmented iron pieces and an iron knife were found. The knife was found inside a damaged scabbard made of bone. The handle was made of copper, the blade of iron.

Bone items: one bone belt buckle was collected from the backfill of a grave, it was rectangular, with two holes in it.

Glass cup: this was broken but could be reconstructed. It was a light green / whitish color, and was blown glass. The mouth was large, the base small and it had slanting vertical walls. The middle part of the cup had wheel-cut polished faceting, three rows of oblong-to-round facets, 13 in the top and middle rows and 7 in the bottom row. The bottom part was polished in a single round facet.

Ornaments: These included agate beads, glass beads, bone beads and shell ornaments. The agate beads' cross-section was an irregular six-sided diamond, the glass beads included brownish-yellow tubular-shaped beads and dragonfly-eye beads. The dragonfly-eye glass beads were blue, and in the shape of a diamond; eye patterns on them were elliptical. Shells came in a great variation in size. The eagle-talon ornament consisted of an eagle's toe bone with its talon covered with a small piece of thin gold foil.

Leather items included a round leather toilet case (*lian*), slightly damaged, round in shape, with a sheepskin wrapping. Inside it was writing, an iron needle, a wooden fine-toothed comb, glass beads, fragments of silk and wool textiles and yarn. There was one leather bag, sewn together with hemp, that was rectangular in shape, its opening closed with clamp sticks, and hemp rope to bind them together.

Food: grains and some food made from wheat were found, including some chrysanthemum-flower cakes fried in oil, dough twists, peach-skin type small oil-fried cakes, thin cakes and so on. There were also strings of raisins and strings of ribs. Some of the millet was relatively well preserved. At the time of the excavation, the grain was found mixed with weeds and cotton cloth.

Written script on paper: this was originally wrapped around powdered material that seemed to be red dye pigment. The writing was preserved in two fragments and had four remaining columns of characters. Among these characters, the uppermost ones of the two middle columns were fragmentary and hard to decipher. This piece of writing may have been a family letter.

（二）生产工具

分一般生产工具和马具两种。

1. 一般生产工具，包括石球、木耜、木纺轮、木弓、木箭和铁针等。

石球，残。呈椭圆形，深黄色砂岩，表面粗糙，剥蚀严重。

木耜，是木柄木耜。木耜呈长方形，尾部有一短柄用毛绳将它绑缚在木柄上。

木纺轮和石膏纺轮，木纺轮分椭圆形和圆形两种，石膏纺轮皆为扁圆形。

铁针，1件保存完好，基本没有锈蚀。制作得比较精致，呈银白色，磨制。针眼部，扁，钻圆形的孔眼。

木弓和木箭，保存了一些木和骨角质的残件，中腰、弓弭等。木箭的箭头缺失，保存有衔口。

TOOLS USED IN PRODUCTION

These were divided into general tools and horse implements.

General tools included a stone ball, a wooden shovel, wooden whorls, wooden bows, wooden arrows, iron needles, and so on.

The fragment of a stone ball was elliptical in shape and made of dark yellow sandstone, the surface was rough, and badly deteriorated.

The wooden shovel (*si*) had a long wooden handle; the shovel part was rectangular and had a short handle which was used to tie it to the long handle with a woolen rope.

Wooden whorls and clay whorls, the wooden whorls were of elliptical and round types, the clay whorls were all a flattened round in shape.

Iron needles: one was preserved in complete and good form, basically without any rusting. It was well made, was silvery white in color and was polished. The eye part of the needle was flattened and bored with a round eye.

Wooden bow and arrows: also preserved were some wood and bone or horn fragments, grip, bow tips and so on. The arrowheads on the wooden arrows were missing, but the tang hole was preserved.

2.马具，有马鞍和鞍桥、木鞭杆、马络和马镳、马肚带及骨带扣、木扣等。

马鞍和鞍桥，有的保存较完整。马鞍的前后桥都是木制的，而鞍体质地有些变化，或为木质，或为皮、毡包裹杂草制成。有的马鞍的前后桥由细木棍制成，即将细木棍一剖为二，弯曲成半圆形的鞍桥，鞍体的两侧皆呈"凸"字形，由动物皮作面，内包苇秆制成。鞍体由麻绳缝制，边缘针脚细而密，中部针脚比较粗。另外，在马鞍上拴系有粗毛线绳、皮袋、条带纹毛布袋、山羊的小腿（保存皮毛）、编织带等。

马络和马镳，马络由皮马络体、毛缰绳、铁衔和木镳组成。铁衔锈蚀，中间由套环相连，两端也是环圈，杆截面呈方体。木镳削制，上面钻两个穿绳孔。马镳分木马镳和角质马镳，镳体截面形状变化很大，分圆柱形、长方形和弧角形。角质马镳呈细羚羊角形，钻孔里还残留着锈蚀严重的铁铆钉。

木鞭杆，皆缺失鞭鞘，只留下了鞭杆。鞭杆形式有些变化，分两种形式，一种是在杆头钻孔以固定鞭鞘，杆尾钻提带孔；一种是在杆头刻系绳槽以拴系鞭鞘。

马肚带及带扣，马肚带与马鞍一起出土，由毛编织带和带扣组合。

带扣呈方形，骨扣、骨舌。有1件骨带扣，由骨体和铁舌组合，骨体呈束腰的"弹头"形式，铁舌显得大而粗糙。

木扣，有两种形式，一种是近长方体，在一侧刻槽，呈"凹"字形；一种是圆柱体，呈哑铃形。最初在绊马索上发现了此类木扣，后来在马饰物品上也发现了类似的扣饰。

Horse implements

These included saddles and saddle-arches , wooden whip-sticks, horse bridles, horse bits, girths and bone girth-buckles, wooden buckles, and so on.

Some of the horse saddles and saddle arches were well preserved, the front and rear arches were made of wood, but there were variations in the saddle itself, some were wood, some were leather or felt, wrapped around various grasses. Some of the front and back arches of the saddles were made of thin wooden sticks. These were split lengthwise and bent to form the half-round shape of the arch. The two side bars of the saddle were ⊔-shaped and covered with animal skins, with reeds on the inside. The saddles were stitched with coarse hemp yarn, with stitching around the bottom outline that was very finely done, while the middle part of the saddles was more crudely made. Thick ropes made of wool, leather bags, woolen strips, bags from wool cloth with striped patterns, goat's legs (with the hair still on them), braided belts and so on were tied to the saddles.

The horse bridle and horse bits: the bridle was made of different materials including leather bands, woolen reins, an iron mouthpiece and wooden bit side pieces. The iron mouthpiece was rusted, single-jointed with two small rings in the middle, ended in two rings on the sides and was square in cross-section. The wooden bit cheeks were tapered and had two holes drilled into them for the leather bands. The horse bit cheeks (side pieces) were divided into wooden bits and horn bits. There was great variation in the cross-section of the horse bits, including round, rectangular, and curved. Horse bit cheeks made of horn were crafted from fine antelope horns, pierced with iron rivets that had been severely rusted.

The wooden whips lacked any lashes, and only had the staff part left. These came in various shapes and were of two kinds. One kind had a hole drilled into it at the top end of the staff, for fastening the lash, and another hole at the tail end, for fastening a hand strap; another kind had a groove carved at the upper end for tying the lash.

The girths and buckles: girths and saddles were excavated together. Girths were made of woolen braided belts with buckles. The buckles were square with both buckles and prongs made of bone. One buckle was made of bone, in a shape reminiscent of a warhead, and had an iron prong which was large and quite crude.

There were two kinds of wooden toggles. One was nearly rectangular, and had a notch carved on one side; another kind was cylindrical, and looked like a dumbbell. This kind of wooden toggles was first found on horse hobbles, and later similar toggle adornments were also found on horse adornments.

四 墓葬的分期和年代

扎滚鲁克一号和二号墓地发掘的墓葬，延续时间比较长（公元前 10 世纪～公元 6 世纪），有 1600 年。墓葬所显现的文化内涵也有大的差异，分出了三期文化。第一期文化代表了扎滚鲁克墓地早期墓葬的文化现象，可惜只发现了 1 座（96QZIM61）；第二期文化发掘墓葬 138 座，数量最多，因而成为扎滚鲁克墓地的主体文化；第三期文化代表了扎滚鲁克墓地晚期墓葬的文化特征，发掘 30 座，虽然数量不多、破坏严重，但非常重要。

从墓葬出土器物、服饰、葬具及墓葬形制等因素，分析这三期文化的年代，感觉情况有些复杂。

首先，第一期和第二期文化墓葬，仅依靠墓葬形制及出土器物进行年代的推测，有比较大的困难，所以采集 ^{14}C 标本进行了年代测定。第一期文化的 96QZIM61 采红柳样本，测年为公元前 1508±76 年，感觉略为偏早。

在第二期文化墓葬中选取了 6 座墓葬的碳标本，采样进行 ^{14}C 测年：1. 85QZM2 取 ^{14}C 样标本，测年为公元前 1010±115 年；2. 85QZM4 取 ^{14}C 样标本，代年为公元前 740±120 年；3. 96QZIM1 取红柳枝 ^{14}C 样标本，测年为公元前 792±60 年；4. 96QZIM4 取红柳枝 ^{14}C 样标本，测年为公元前 388±59 年；5. 96QZIM14 取红柳枝 ^{14}C 样标本，测年为公元前 761±61 年；6. 96QZIM24 取红柳枝 ^{14}C 样标本，测年为公元前 986±61 年。这里面 85QZM2、96QZIM24 的测年，略显早一些。除 96QZIM4 外，其余 3 座墓葬标本测年比较接近，可以作为第二期文化的上限年代来考虑。96QZIM4 取红柳枝 ^{14}C 样标本，测年为公元前 388±59 年，也是一个非常可信的年代。

DATING AND DESIGNATION OF GRAVES INTO DIFFERENT PERIODS

The graves of the Zaghunluq Cemeteries #1 and #2 extended over some 1,600 years, from the 10th century BCE to the 6th century CE. The culture or cultures that they embody experienced great changes and can be divided into three periods.

The First-period culture represented the cultural phenomena of the early period of the Zaghunluq graves, but unfortunately only one grave from this period has been discovered to date, namely 96QZIM61. A total of 138 graves were excavated that belong to the Second-period culture. This constituted the largest number of graves, and therefore represents the main culture of Zaghunluq. The Third-period culture displays the cultural attributes of the late period of graves, of which 30 were excavated. Although the number was smaller, and the graves had been severely damaged, these graves were extremely important.

Analysis of these three cultural periods from excavated objects, garments, grave goods and grave structures turned out to be extremely complex. We encountered difficulties in relying only on excavated objects and grave types in the First-period and Second-period culture, and therefore we gathered carbon-14 samples to aid in dating determination.

Our sample from the First-period culture grave, 96QZIM61, was red tamarisk and the dating came out to be 1,508 BCE plus or minus 76 years. We feel that this date may be on the early side. We selected samples from six graves among the Second-period culture graves for carbon-14 analysis. The results were as follows.

1. Grave 85QZM2 – 1,010 BCE ± 115 years.
2. Grave 85QZM4 – 740 BCE ± 120 years.
3. Grave 96QZIM1 – 792 BCE ± 60 years.
4. Grave 96QZIM4, samples of red tamarisk branches – 388 BCE ± 59 years.
5. Grave 96QZIM14, samples of red tamarisk branches – 761 BCE ± 61 years.
6. Grave 96QZIM24, samples of red tamarisk branches – 986 BCE ± 61 years.

Of these samples, the results from 85QZM2 and 96QZIM24 were rather early. Except for 96QZIM4, the other three dates were relatively close to each other and can be thought of as representing the upper limit of the dating of the Second-period culture. The sample from grave 96QZIM4 resulted in a carbon-14 dating of 388 BCE ± 59 years, which we believe is a very credible dating.

同时，在分析扎滚鲁克二号墓地及附近同文化类型的加瓦艾日克墓地年代时，[9] 发现第二期文化墓葬可能延续的时间会更长一些，可以到公元 3 世纪。

第三期文化的墓葬形制、葬具及出土器物、织物等，风格相对比较统一，又有汉文文书及一些年代比较明确的器物，所以年代推测为公元 3 ~ 6 世纪，学术界都比较认可。

初步推测：第一期文化，墓葬年代在公元前 10 世纪前后；第二期文化，墓葬年代在公元前 8 世纪 ~ 公元 3 世纪中期；第三期文化，墓葬年代在公元 3 世纪中期 ~6 世纪晚期。

这一次在纺织品的研究中，选取织物的墓葬是 33 座，其中：

第二期文化有 25 座墓葬（85QZM2~85QZM4、96QZIM4、96QZIM14、96QZIM34、96QZIM54、96QZIM55、96QZIM59、96QZIM64、96QZIM65、96QZIM68、96QZIM69、96QZIM71、96QZIM99、98QZIM100、98QZIM103、98QZIM113、98QZIM114、98QZIM124、98QZIM129、98QZIM136、98QZIM139、98QZIM147 和 96QZIIM2）。

第三期文化有 8 座墓葬（96QZIM49、96QZIM60、98QZIM105、98QZIM122、98QZIM131、98QZIM141、98QZIM149 和 98QZIM156）。

在三期文化的年代分析上，感觉第一期和第三期文化推测年代较为适宜，而第二期文化的时间则延续较长，有 1100 年。在分析出土纺织品时，发现可以作进一步的分期研究，至少可以再分出早、晚两个时间段，即早段和晚段。划分情况如下：

早段，有 85QZM2~85QZM4、96QZIM4、96QZIM14、96QZIM64、96QZIM68、96QZIM69、96QZIM71、96QZIM99、98QZIM100、98QZIM103、98QZIM113、98QZIM114 和 98QZIM136 等 15 座墓葬。其时间初步推测为公元前 8~ 前 3 世纪末。

晚段，有 96QZIM34、96QZIM54、96QZIM55、96QZIM59、96QZIM65、98QZIM124、98QZIM129、98QZIM139、98QZIM147 和 96QZIIM2 等 10 座墓葬。其时间初步推测为公元前 3 世纪末 ~ 公元 3 世纪中期。

9 龚国强：《新疆且末考古发掘有新收获》，《中国文物报》1997 年 5 月 25 日；中国社会科学院考古研究所考古科技实验研究中心：《放射性碳素测定年代报告》（二四），《考古》1997 年第 7 期；中国社会科学院考古研究所新疆队、新疆巴音郭楞蒙古自治州文管所：《新疆且末县加瓦艾日克墓地的发掘》，《考古》1997 年第 9 期。

In evaluating similar graveyards of the same culture to those in Cemetery #2 of Zaghunluq, specifically the Jiawa'airike gravesite, we feel that Second-period culture graves may well extend into the 3rd century CE.[8]

Excavated items from Third-period culture graves, including textiles, have a relatively uniform style. In addition, written items with Chinese characters and other items can be dated with relative accuracy. These factors allow us to date Third-period culture to the 3rd to 6th centuries CE. Authorities in the field generally accept this dating.

Therefore, we make an initial hypothesis as follows: First-period culture graves date from around the 10th century BCE. Second-period culture graves date from the 8th century BCE to the mid-3rd century CE. Third-period culture graves date from the 3rd to the 6th centuries CE.

We have selected textiles from 33 graves for further research, among which are the following.

Second-period culture: 25 graves: 85QZM2–85QZM4, 96QZIM4, 96QZIM14, 96QZIM34, 96QZIM54, 96QZIM55, 96QZIM59, 96QZIM64, 96QZIM65, 96QZIM68, 96QZIM69, 96QZIM71, 96QZIM99, 98QZIM100, 98QZIM103, 98QZIM113, 98QZIM114, 98QZIM124, 98QZIM129, 98QZIM136, 98QZIM139, 98QZIM147, and 96QZIIM2.

Third-period culture: 8 graves: 96QZIM49, 96QZIM60, 98QZIM105, 98QZIM122, 98QZIM131, 98QZIM141, 98QZIM149, and 98QZIM156.

We feel that our dating with regard to the First- and Third-period cultures are appropriate, whereas the Second-period culture extends for a very long time, some 1,100 years. In the process of analyzing excavated textiles, we have found that we can further subdivide this long time into shorter periods, at the very least divide it into early and late segments. The result of this division into two further categories is as follows:

The early phase of Second-period culture included 15 graves: 85QZM2–85QZM4, 96QZIM4, 96QZIM14, 96QZIM64, 96QZIM68, 96QZIM69, 96QZIM71, 96QZIM99, 98QZIM100, 98QZIM103, 98QZIM113, 98QZIM114, and 98QZIM136. We tentatively date this group of graves from 8th century BCE to late-3rd century BCE.

The late phase of Second-period culture included 10 graves: 96QZIM34, 96QZIM54, 96QZIM55, 96QZIM59, 96QZIM65, 98QZIM124, 98QZIM129, 98QZIM139, 98QZIM147, and 96QZIIM2. We tentatively date this group of graves from late-3rd century BCE to mid-3rd century CE.

8 Gong Guoqiang: «Xinjiang Qiemo kaogu fajue you xin shuohuo [New results from the archaeological excavations at Qiemo in Xinjiang]», *Zhongguo wenwu bao* 25. Mai 1997. – Zhongguo shehui kexueyuan kaogu yanjiusuo kaogu keji shiyan yanjiu zhongxin: «Fangshexing tansu ceding niandai baogao (24) [Radiocarbon Dating Report (24)]», *Kaogu* 7, 1997. – Zhongguo shehui kexueyuan kaogu yanjiusuo Xinjiang dui, Xinjiang Bayinguoleng Menggu Zizhizhou wenguansuo: «Xinjiang Qiemo xian Jiawa'airike mudi de fajue [Excavation of the Jiawa'airike cemetery in Qiemo county, Xinjiang]», *Kaogu* 9, 1997, pp. 21–32.

五　对扎滚鲁克第二、三期文化的认识

在上面叙述扎滚鲁克墓葬文化现象时，感觉第二期和第三期文化之间差异很大。它们反映了且末国历史发展过程中，不同时期的文化现象。

（一）　对扎滚鲁克第二期文化的认识

1. 对扎滚鲁克第二期文化的认识。

古且末国，地处古代且末水流域，即今天的车尔臣河水系一带。

它"西北至都护治所二千二百五十八里，北接尉犁，南至小宛可三日行"，"西通精绝"，东连若羌。由此看来，且末国辖境大体在车尔臣河山前地带，可延伸至今北部的沙漠深处。无论从地域还是从时间上，都能感觉到扎滚鲁克第二期文化与且末立国前后及早期发展的历史有着密切的关系，墓葬反映的情况再现了古且末国的文明。

第二期文化墓葬出土了不少的保存树皮的木头，可以看出一些树种，如柳树、白杨、胡杨、柽柳、沙枣树等。同时，用于覆盖墓口的有芦苇、蒲草、驴草等。这些树种和草类植物和现在扎滚鲁克村附近的植被没有什么区别，属于干旱性沙漠气候生态环境。第二期文化墓葬中出土了数件铁刀，其中的横向安置刀体的推测是镰刀，同时还出土了马鞍形石磨盘、残木耜，并发现一定数量的陶器，说明这里出现了农业经济。这与《汉书·西域传》"自且末以往皆种五谷"的记载相符。从若羌仰且末谷的情形来看，应该有一定规模的灌溉农业生产，而且存在园艺种植。正与史书记载：土地无雨，决水种麦，耒耜而田作，不知用牛的情况相符。

墓葬出土的服装用料主要是毛布，也有皮衣，随葬器物中有马鞭、绊马索，这些都说明养畜业比较发达。从出土的动物骨和皮可以认定，饲养的牲畜有绵羊、山羊、马、牛等。墓葬中出土了弓箭、捕鸭器、狐狸腿、鹿皮、鱼骨、鸟禽羽毛等，反映了居民的狩猎生产。

CURRENT UNDERSTANDING OF ZAGHUNLUQ SECOND- AND THIRD-PERIOD CULTURES

Analyzing the circumstances of Zaghunluq cultures, as dated above, we have a sense of great disparity between Second-period and Third-period cultures. This reflects the history of the State of Qiemo and reflects the various cultural phenomena associated with different periods.

ZAGHUNLUQ SECOND-PERIOD CULTURE

The ancient state of Qiemo was located in the drainage area of Qiemo, which today is known as the Cherchen river system.

In ancient chronicles this was located as follows: «distant from the seat of the Governor-General 2,258 *li* to the northwest, connecting in the north with Weili, and a three-day's journey south to Xiaoyuan (Little Wan) ... To the west reaching Jingjue»,[9] to the east connecting with Shanshan (modern Ruoqiang). From this it can be seen that the jurisdiction of the State of Qiemo was in general the area 'in front of' the mountains and the Cherchen River, and that it extended to what today is deep into the northern part of the desert. Whether from a geographical or a chronological perspective, we feel that Second-period Zaghunluq culture was closely linked to the period when the Qiemo State was being established and its early historical development. The graves reflect circumstances that are seen in the ancient Qiemo civilization.

Second-period culture graves produced many types of wood that still retain their bark, from which we could discern the species of trees. They included willow, White poplar, Euphrates poplar (*huyang*), Chinese tamarisk, oleaster, and so on. The reeds and grasses covering the grave openings included Common reed, Calamus, and Kingcup. There is no great difference between these plants and trees and the vegetation currently growing in the vicinity of Zaghunluq. They belong to an arid ecology.

Many iron knives were excavated from Second-period culture graves, among which were some that we surmise were sickles. They were used to cut cross-wise. At the same time, we excavated saddle-shaped grindstones, pieces of wooden shovels (*si*), and a number of ceramic pieces that indicated that an agricultural economy had appeared at this place. This tallies with the recorded statement in the Book of Han (*Hanshu*), Chronicle of the Western Regions: «From Qiemo come the five grains.»[10] From this statement, i.e. that Shanshan relies on Qiemo grain, we can see that there must have been a certain degree of irrigated agricultural production. Horticulture was practiced

---

9 [Han] Ban Gu (comp.), [Tang] Yan Shigu (comm.): Hanshu [*History of the Former Han*]. 12 vols, Beijing: Zhonghua Shuju, 1964 (abbreviated as HS 1964), vol. 12, p. 3879 (chapter 96).

10 HS 1964 (see note 9 above), vol. 12, p. 3879 (chapter 96).

2.埋葬习俗及死者间关系，对推测居民社会的组织结构形式、社会性质有一定帮助。扎滚鲁克墓地第二期文化的墓葬反映大多是成人的丛葬、多人葬，小孩的单人葬和合葬，葬式以仰身屈肢葬为主，这些特点具有明显的普遍意义及规律性，同时显示出社会组织结构可能是以血缘家族为基础。

　　3.在且末县城附近与第二期文化内涵相似的墓地，除了扎滚鲁克村的五处墓地外，在车尔臣河流域还有兰干墓地和加瓦艾日克墓地。它们在墓葬形制、葬俗、随葬器物、服饰等都表现出考古文化上的一致，特征明显。墓葬出土的手制陶器，以黑衣陶为主，器物类型以陶钵居多，其次是各种陶罐、陶杯，包括带流罐、圆底罐、单耳杯等。黑衣陶器在塔克拉玛干沙漠南缘地区同时期的一些墓地也有发现，如洛浦县山普拉墓地的一期、于阗县圆沙古墓群的H墓地、民丰县尼雅遗址的1993年3号墓地等，但器物的组合及器物造型风格差异较大，陶器的用色趋向一致则说明地区间的文化渗透性还是比较强。同时，也反映出绿洲间的相对隔离及居民组群的相对独立，使得文化上保留了自身的一些特点。

in this place as well. It is just the way the historic writings also state: «This land lacked rain, water was dammed up to plant millet, shovels were used to work the land, they did not know how to use cows.»[11] This statement corresponds to the archaeological data.

Woolen fabrics were the primary material used in textiles that were excavated. Items of clothing were also made of leather, and horse whips and hobbles were among accompanying grave goods. All of these indicate that animal husbandry was well developed. From the animal bones and hides that were excavated, we can deduce that animals being raised included sheep, goats, horses, and cows. The bows and arrows, gear for catching ducks, the fox legs, deer skins, fish bones and feathers of certain birds all reflect a hunting practice among inhabitants as well.

The burial practices and all the things relating to the buried people at Zaghunluq allow us to make hypotheses about the social structure of inhabitants and are helpful in evaluating the nature of society at the time. Zaghunluq Second-period culture graves generally include mass graves of adults, graves of several people, single graves of children as well as multiple children in one grave. The burial style was to have the body facing upwards with limbs flexed. All of these attributes were fairly standard and significant, indicating perhaps that the organizational structure of society at the time was based on family lineage or clan.

Cemeteries in the vicinity of Qiemo County and other graves that are similar to Second-period culture graves include not only the five cemeteries in the neighborhood of Zaghunluq but also the Langan cemetery and the Jiawa'airike cemetery, both also in the Cherchen river valley. The archaeological culture of these sites is the same in terms of grave structure, burial practices, accompanying grave goods, clothing and so on. The attributes are clear. Hand-formed ceramics excavated from these sites generally have a black slip, and the objects are mainly ceramic bowls (bo), plus all kinds of jars and cups, including those with spouts, round-bottomed jars, single-handle cups and so on. Other black-slip ceramic wares have been discovered on the southern rim of the Taklamakan desert that date from the same period. These include ceramics from the First Period of the Shanpula (Sampul) cemetery in Luopu (Lop) county, the H cemetery in the Yutian (Keriya) county Yuansha (Yumbulak Kum) graves, the #3 cemetery excavated in 1993 in the Niya site in Minfeng county, and so on. Although the range and style of the ceramic items differs from place to place, the consistent use of the same colors demonstrates the importance of the substantial cultural interrelationship between these places.

The overarching trend shows that the absorptive capacity of cultures in these regions was quite strong, while at the same time the relative separation between oases, and the relative independence of their inhabitants, allowed their cultures to preserve unique features.

---

11 [Wei] Yang Xuanzhi (comp.), Zhou Zumo (collated and annotated): *Luoyang qielan ji jiaoshi* [*Record of the Monasteries of Luoyang. Critical Edition*], Beijing: Zhonghua Shuju, 1963, p. 185. – Din Cheuk Lau et al. (ed.), *ICS Concordances to Works of Wei-Jin and the Northern and Southern Dynasties Historical Works No.1: A Concordance to the Luoyang Qielan Ji*, Hongkong: Chinese University Press, 2003, p. 50.

4. 班固撰《汉书·西域传》记载："且末国，王治且末城，去长安六千八百二十里。户二百三十，口千六百一十，胜兵三百二十人。"它东连若羌，"西通精绝"，和塔里木盆地南缘的扜弥、于阗、莎车诸国一样，都是古代丝绸之路、西域三十六国塔里木盆地南缘的一个绿洲城邦小国。在社会经济文化发展中，自然形成了丝绸之路文化现象。它们具有兼容并蓄的多元文化的态势，与中原、北方草原以及西方都有着密切的文化联系，构成了文化因素的多样性。

墓葬出土的经锦、纨、缦、绢等一类丝织品和漆器都是中原的输入品，出土的海贝、珊瑚珠有可能产自东南沿海，或产于印度洋。

墓葬出土的木竖箜篌，保存有音箱、颈和弦杆等，木料是当地的胡杨和柽柳枝，说明属本地制造品。同时，箜篌是世界上最古老的弦乐器之一，名称多样，最早的实物出自公元前2500年前后的乌尔城王室墓地，应该是西方文化向东流传的见证。从敦煌壁画和陕西古代雕塑中的箜篌乐器来看，与扎滚鲁克古墓地出土的箜篌乐器有些相像，说明中原竖箜篌的原型来自西域，具体的东传时间可能是在两汉以前通过新疆塔里木盆地南缘传入内地。

动物纹是草原居民比较喜好的一种装饰纹样，广布于亚欧草原地带。墓葬中出土的一些雕刻动物纹的木器，动物有狼、羚羊、绵羊、鹿、骆驼等。动物的姿态有反转式、立式或半立式和卧式等。其中反转式动物纹在新疆山地草原的阿拉沟、库兰萨日克、博孜墩等墓地皆有发现，同时它也是鄂尔多斯式、斯基泰式、南西伯利亚式青铜器及中亚塞克文化中的传统纹样。鸟首纹在新疆境内尚未见资料报道，但在鄂尔多斯、斯基泰艺术中都占有重要的位置。

As recorded in the Book of Han (*Hanshu*), Chronicle of the Western Regions (*Xiyu Zhuan*), written by Ban Gu: «A King ruled over the Qiemo walled city, which was 6,820 li from Chang'an. It held 230 households and contained 1,610 inhabitants. Its valiant soldiers numbered 320.»[12] This state extended east to Shanshan, «to the west reaching Jingjue,»[13] and, like the states of Yumi, Yutian, and Shache on the southern rim of the Tarim Basin, it was situated along the ancient Silk Road, and was one of an alliance of 36 States or oases on the southern rim of the Tarim Basin.

In the course of socio-economic development, geographical considerations determined the phenomenon of the Silk Road culture. All of these States had a diversified culture that integrated cultures of different regions. They were connected with cultures of the central plains, the northern steppe, and the west, which meant they were a composite of diversified cultural factors.

In terms of excavated textiles, the warp-faced patterned silks, the fine silk fabric called *wan*, the fabric called *man*, the thin tough silk tabby *juan* as well as the lacquer articles were all imports from the central plains. The excavated shells and coral beads may have derived from coastal areas in the southeast or perhaps the Indian Ocean.

The upright *konghou* harp that was excavated with its preserved sound box, neck and pegs was most likely locally made. The wood used was Euphrates poplar and Chinese tamarisk. At the same time, the *konghou* is one of the most ancient stringed instruments known in the world. It goes by many names. The earliest actual example found to date was from the royal cemetery in the city of Ur, dating to around 2,500 BCE. This instrument is evidence of the transmittal of western culture toward the east. In *konghou*-like instruments depicted on the walls of Dunhuang and from the sculptures at Shaanxi we can see a resemblance to the *konghou* excavated from the Zaghunluq cemetery. This shows that the original form of the upright konghou harp came into the central plains from the western regions, and that the specific time of its transmittal was perhaps prior to the eastern and western Han dynasties, as it passed along the southern rim of the Tarim basin in Xinjiang.

Animal motifs are one of the key decorative patterns used by people of the steppe, and are widely distributed along the band of Eurasian steppe. Some of the wooden articles excavated from the tombs have such motifs carved into them, including antelope (or gazelle), wolves, sheep, deer, and camels. The animals are depicted with reversed hind-quarters and in standing, half-standing, or crouching posture. The reversed hind-quarters posture has also been found in the steppe and mountain regions of Xinjiang, from Alagou, Kulansarike, Baozidong and other cemeteries. At the same time, this style is a traditional motif in Ordos, Scythian, and South Siberian bronzes, as well as in the Saka culture in Central Asia. Bird-headed patterns have not yet been reported in Xinjiang, although they have a prominent position in Ordos and Scythian arts.

12   HS 1964 (see note 9 above), vol. 12, p. 3879 (chapter 96).
13   HS 1964 (see note 9 above), vol. 12, p. 3879 (chapter 96).

5.从第二期文化墓葬出土的大量毛织物，可以感受到古代扎滚鲁克居民的服装是以毛织物为主。塔里木盆地南缘出土毛织物比较多的墓地有小河、扎滚鲁克和山普拉，在时间上小河墓地年代要比扎滚鲁克墓地早，而山普拉墓地的年代相对要晚一些。

在汉文史料中记载的精细毛纺织品称作"罽"，如"金缕罽"、"绩罽"等。《汉书·高帝纪》，八年（公元前199年）三月诏："贾人毋得衣锦、绣、绮、縠、絺、紵、罽。"古代中原汉政府重农轻商，贬低商人，所以禁止他们穿着罽衣料。同时，史料中也记载了一些产罽的国家。《汉书·西域传》记载：罽宾（Kashmir）"其民巧，雕文刻镂，治宫室，织罽，刺文绣，好治食"；《后汉书·西域传》记载，大秦国（罗马帝国）"刺金缕绣，织成金缕罽、杂色绫"。同时，如乌弋山离（Kandahar，今阿富汗赫拉特〈Herat〉一带）"畜产、五谷……钱货……皆与罽宾同"；安息（Parthia，古波斯）物类，所有民俗与乌弋山离、罽宾同；大月氏（Indo-Scythia，阿姆河上游一带，大夏〈Bactria〉故地，强大时及至印度河上游）物类，所有民俗、钱货与安息同等，这些国家也都有可能产罽。以上列举的这些国家都在今天新疆的西面。

As seen from the large quantity of woolen textiles excavated from Second-period culture graves, we can deduce that most of the clothing worn by Zaghunluq inhabitants was made of wool. Areas from which woolen textiles have been excavated in some quantity along the southern rim of the Tarim Basin include Xiaohe, Zaghunluq, and Shanpula. In terms of dating, the Xiaohe graves are earlier than those at Zaghunluq, while those at Shanpula are somewhat later.

In Han-dynasty historical chronicles, the terms for fine woolen fabrics are described as *ji*, *jinlü ji*, *huiji*, and so on. The Records on Emperor Gaodi of the Book of Han (*Hanshu*) say, in an edict of the third month of the eighth year (199 BCE): «Merchants are not allowed to wear garments of multicolored patterned silk (*jin*), embroidery, damask on tabby (*qi*), *hu* silk, *chi* linen, *zhu* silk, and woolen *ji*.»[14]

The Chinese government of the ancient central plains officially despised merchants and venerated farmers, so it forbad merchants to wear clothing made of *ji* woolens. During this same time period, historical records document that certain countries were producing just these fabrics. The Chronicle of the Western Regions of the Book of Han (*Hanshu*) records the following, regarding a place called Jibin (today's Kashmir), «The people are talented, literate, build buildings, rule from palaces, weave *ji* fabrics, embroider patterns, enjoy cooking.»[15]

The Chronicle of the Western Regions of the History of the Later Han (*Hou Hanshu*) records, for the country of Da Qin, the Roman Empire: «embroideries with drawn gold thread, woolen *ji* weaves with twisted gold thread, multicolored *ling* damasks».[16] At the same time, for Wuyishanli, in the region of Herat in today's Afghanistan, it is said: «Regarding stock-animals, the five field crops, coinage,　it is identical to Jibin.»[17] Also Parthia (Anxi, ancient Persia) was said to have the same folk customs as Wuyishanli and Jibin. And similarly, Kushan (Da Yuezhi or Da Rouzhi, a region on the upper reaches of the Amu Darya, the former Bactria, that in its height had extended to the upper reaches of the Indus) had the same folk customs and coinage as Parthia, and so on. It is possible that all these countries also produced *ji* fabrics. All of the above mentioned countries are to the west of today's Xinjiang.

---

14 HS 1964 (see note 9 above), vol. 1, p. 65 (chapter 1).

15 HS 1964 (see note 9 above), vol. 12, p. 3885 (chapter 96).

16 [Song] Fan Ye (comp.), [Tang] Li Xiandeng (comm.): Hou Hanshu [*History of the Later Han*], 12 vols, Beijing: Zhonghua Shuju, 1973 (abbreviated as HHS 1973), vol. 10, p. 2919 (chapter 88).

17 HS 1964 (see note 9 above), vol. 12, p. 3889 (chapter 96).

扎滚鲁克第二期文化墓葬出土的精细毛纺织品，有毛绣、缋罽、缂毛、毛绉、毛罗、挖花、晕繝、绞缬染和夹缬毛布等。它们或许反映了这一时期古代新疆毛纺织业发展的一些情况，同时也代表着此期丝绸之路毛纺织业发展的水平。随着学者们对扎滚鲁克纺织品的比较分析研究，推想经过一段时间可能会有更加精彩的发现，揭示古代且末国及早期新疆毛纺织业发展的脉络，逐渐发现古且末国的毛纺织业非常发达。

　　新疆是中国最早种植草棉的地区，发现了不少东汉时期的棉布，一般认为至高昌国时期（公元 460~640 年）有了较为发达的棉花种植业及纺织业。扎滚鲁克第二期文化墓葬出土西汉时期的棉布衣，是目前所知新疆境内出土棉布中年代比较早的一件。这将有助于我们对棉布输入时间、棉花种植时间的推测。

　　墓葬中出土的丝织品除了经锦，还有纬锦。纬锦是丝线加捻、纬线显花的丝织物。纬锦在古代新疆出现的时间，一般认为古代吐鲁番地区始于公元 4 世纪，同时在《吐鲁番出土文书》中也有高昌织锦"绵经绵纬"的记载。

　　营盘墓地 99BYYM66 墓纬锦与佉卢文书同出，也当在公元 4 世纪。扎滚鲁克墓地出土了属第二期文化晚段（早于公元 3 世纪中期）的纬锦，这是一个需要注意的问题。

The fine woolen textiles excavated from Second-period culture graves at Zaghunluq included wool embroidery (*mao xiu*), multicoloured wool weaves (*huiji*), tapestry (*kemao*), crêpe (*mao zhou*), gauze (*mao luo*), brocading (*wa hua*), shading of hues (*yunjian*), tie-dyeing (*jiaoxie ran*), and clamp-resist dyed woolen cloth (*jiaxie*). They reflected the state of wool weaving technology at this period in ancient Xinjiang, and at the same time they represented the level of wool weaving technologies along the Silk Road.

After more thinking and theorizing, scholars doing comparative analysis of Zaghunluq textiles may be able to offer even more extraordinary evidence that shows the pulse of development of the ancient State of Qiemo and early Xinjiang woolen industries. They may gradually discover that the woolen textile industry of Qiemo was extremely sophisticated.

Xinjiang was the earliest region in China to grow cotton. Quite a few Eastern Han-period cotton textiles have been found and it is generally thought that by the time of the State of Gaochang (460 to 640 CE), the region had a relatively well-developed cotton-growing industry as well as weaving industry. The Western-Han period clothing made of cotton fabric excavated from Second-period culture graves at Zaghunluq represent some of the earliest pieces found within Xinjiang and known to date. This may be helpful to our thinking about the dates from which cotton fabric was imported into China and when cotton was planted.

In addition to warp-faced silk *jin*, weft-faced compound silk weaves were also excavated from graves at Zaghunluq. In weft-faced compound silk, the silk threads are given a twist and it is the weft threads that show the pattern. It had generally been thought that weft-faced *jin* began to appear in Xinjiang at Turfan, starting in the fourth century. At the same time, in one of the documents found in excavations at Turfan, *jin* weaves from Gaochang with «warp and weft of spun silk» are mentioned.[18] From the Yingpan cemetery Grave 99BYYM66 a weft-faced *jin* was excavated together with a Kharosthi record that was dated to the fourth century.

The fact that weft-faced *jin* was excavated from late Second-period culture graves at Zaghunluq (which date to before the mid-3rd century CE) deserves attention.

18 Guojia wenwuju wenxian yanjiushi (ed.): *Tulufan chutu wenshu [Excavated documents from Turfan]*, 10 vols, Beijing: *Wenwu* chubanshe, 1981, vol. 1, p. 181. See also *Wenwu* 6, 1978, p. 6.

（二） 对扎滚鲁克第三期文化的认识

《魏书·西戎传》记载，"南道西行，且志国（且末国）、小宛国、精绝国、楼兰国皆并属鄯善也"。又《后汉书·西域传》载，"小宛、精绝、戎卢、且末，为鄯善所并"，事情发生在东汉末年。"后其国并复立"，复立的时间不很清楚，至隋炀帝大业五年（公元 609 年），隋朝在且末设郡。第三期文化的年代，似与史书记载的"为鄯善所并"至且末设郡前这一时期的历史关系更为紧密。

1. 公元 3~6 世纪是且末国历史上一个重要时期。第三期文化墓葬发现的汉文纸文书和"（延）年益寿大宜子孙"文句锦上的墨书汉字（96QZIM60:2，第四章图 73）都能说明且末国已进入使用汉文字的文明时代。

2. 墓葬形制、葬具、葬俗和陶、木器的组合关系，以及陶、木器的造型风格，与尉犁县营盘墓地出土的器物非常相似，其次是察吾呼沟三号墓地、阿斯塔那古墓群一期墓葬等。并且和尼雅遗址、洛浦山普拉晚期文化，以及罗布泊东汉墓所反映的情况，也有相似之处。扎滚鲁克第三期文化现象，明显地是与"为鄯善所并"这一历史相关，是鄯善国文化侵入的结果。同时，从陶器形制上看，应该受到了甘肃省河西及中原文化的影响。

3. 墓葬出土的农业生产工具与第二期没有大的变化，也有木耜和谷粒。不过，第三期文化墓葬出土的食品为更加精细的面食，同时还出上了葡萄串，可能还有油料，反映出扎滚鲁克居民更为稳定的定居农业经济现象。从第三期文化时期出现的纺织品可以看出，居民服饰的用料有了明显的变化，应该是以丝、棉织物为主，毛织物很少。从丝织物出土的数量，还很难判断是纬锦多，还是经锦多。不过纬锦比较单一，而经锦的品种明显要多。棉布的质量有所提高。

ZAGHUNLUQ THIRD-PERIOD CULTURE

The Chronicle of the People of the West (*Xi Rong zhuan*) of the Book of Wei records: «The Southern Route heads west to: the kingdom of Qiemo, the kingdom of Xiaoyuan, the kingdom of Jingjue, the kingdom of Loulan, which are all dependencies of Shanshan.»[19] Also the Book of the Later Han, Chronicle of the Western Regions, states: «Xiaoyuan, Jingjue, Ronglu, and Qiemo were annexed by Shanshan.»[20] This occurred in the latter years of the Eastern Han dynasty.

«Later, these small States were re-established,»[21] although the dates of this are unclear. By the year 609, or the fifth year of the Sui emperor known as Sui Yangdi, the Sui dynasty established a *jun* or prefecture in the place known as Qiemo. Zaghunluq Third-period culture seems to bear a close relationship to the time span spreading between the re-establishment of the kingdoms and the establishment of Qiemo as prefecture.

The third to sixth centuries were an extremely important period in the history of the State of Qiemo. Paper with Han Chinese characters on it, and the ink-written Han Chinese characters on a *jin* silk (96QZIM60:2, cat. no. 73), both found in Third-period culture graves, indicate that the State of Qiemo had entered a literate age by this time with the use of written Han-characters.

The composite relationship of the form of graves, grave utensils, funerary practices, and ceramic and wooden objects, as well as the stylistic shape of ceramic and wooden objects, are very similar to excavated objects from the Yingpan cemetery in Yuli county. They are also similar to Cemetery #3 at Chawuhugou, and the First-period graves at the Astana site. Moreover, the circumstances reflected by Niya Ancient Ruins, the later period of Shanpula in Luopu (Lop) County and the Lop Nor eastern-Han graves all show similarities as well. Third-period Zaghunluq culture clearly is related historically to what is known as the consolidation under the State of Shanshan, i.e., it was the result of the incursion of the State of Shanshan culture. At the same time, Zaghunluq culture was influenced by Central Plains culture, as well as the culture of the Gansu Hexi corridor as seen from the shape and style of excavated ceramics.

Agricultural implements found in Third-period culture graves were not significantly different from Second-period culture graves. Graves still had wooden shovels and stores of grain. However, the foodstuff excavated from Third-period culture graves was much finer and had various types of cakes made from flour. Strands of grapes were excavated, perhaps also oil, which implied that the life of Zaghunluq inhabitants was more settled and more agricultural.

From textiles excavated from Third-period culture graves, we can see that the material used for inhabitants' clothing had clearly changed. Silk and cotton fabrics now predominated while woolen cloth was rare.

From the silk textiles excavated, it is still hard to determine if there was more warp-faced *jin* or weft-faced *jin*. Weft-faced *jin* was represented by only one kind, however, while there were far more varieties of warp-faced *jin*. During the Third-period culture at Zaghunluq, the quality of cotton cloth had, moreover, clearly improved.

---

19 [Jin] Chen Shou (comp.), [Song] Pei Songzhi (comm.): *Sanguozhi [Record of the Three Kingdoms]*, 5 vols, Beijing: Zhonghua Shuju, 1964, vol. 3, p. 859 (chapter 30).
20 HHS 1973 (see note 16 above), vol. 10, p. 2909 (chapter 88).
21 HHS 1973 (see note 16 above), vol. 10, p. 2909 (chapter 88).

第二章　扎滚鲁克纺织品纺织技术观察

王明芳

　　自1985年扎滚鲁克墓地考古发掘以来，出土了大量的纺织品，初步统计有500多件。不过，大多数是破损严重的残片，保存较好（包括组织结构特殊和图案花纹保存较好的小残片）的有200件左右。主要是毛织物，其次是丝织物，还有少量的棉织物，麻制品只有麻绳一种。下面从纺织技术的角度，对它们进行介绍。

一　毛织物

　　扎滚鲁克古墓出土的毛织物，有平、斜纹毛布、毛纱、毛罗、毛绉、缂毛和栽绒毯等。从纺织技术的角度观察，这要讲到毛纱的捻向、染料、染色、羊毛品种、绞缬、晕繝、毛绣、挖花、织花等工艺，同时，也要介绍毡、编织物和牙线等。

捻毛线

　　羊毛纤维经过加捻变成了毛纱，而后才能织布。扎滚鲁克出土毛织物毛纱的捻向，分Z捻和S捻（图7），多数为Z捻毛纱。有的织物经纱是Z捻，而纬纱S捻，织布会有不同的效果，比较特殊。两根纱合捻称双捻，使Z捻纱变成S捻线，称S双捻。三根、四根或更多的纱属双捻性质的也称双捻，如三根、四根Z捻纱，一次捻合，变成了S捻线绳。另外，四根以上的纱捻合，一般是重复合捻，称重捻，如六根纱、八根纱，先由两根纱合捻成线，而后再由两根线合捻成线绳。重捻，是从Z捻到S捻，又从S捻到Z捻的过程。所以，以最后的捻合向来称呼，如S重捻或Z重捻。重捻线绳多用于编织或出现在织物的边穗上。

7 毛纱捻向　Twist direction of woolen yarn
左：Z捻向　Left: Z-spun yarn;
右：S捻向　Right: S-spun yarn

By Wang Mingfang

TECHNOLOGY OF ZAGHUNLUQ TEXTILES

A large number of textiles have been excavated from the Zaghunluq cemeteries since the start of excavations there in 1985. An initial count puts the number at more than 500, most of which, however, are fragments and damaged pieces. Around 200 pieces have been preserved in relatively good condition, including small pieces or fragments that have special weaves or particularly notable patterns. Most of these are woolen textiles; second in number are items made of silk; there are a small number of cotton textiles. Only one article was made from hemp, namely a hemp rope. The following describes the technology of these textiles.

WOOLEN TEXTILES

The woolen textiles excavated at Zaghunluq include tabby-weave woolens, twill woolens, gauze-like weaves, woolen gauze, woolen crepe (*zhou*), *kemao* tapestry, and pile carpets (*zairong tan*). Seen from the perspective of textile technology, we must address the question of the direction of twist of woolen yarns, the dyeing materials, the colors, the types of woolen fibers, resist dyeing, gradation of colors, woolen embroidery, brocading (*wa hua*), woven patterns and other techniques. At the same time, we will introduce felt, braiding (*bian zhi*), and edging with decorative threads (*yaxian*).

TWISTING WOOLEN THREADS

Sheep's wool has to undergo twisting or spinning in order to become woolen yarn, only after which it can be woven into cloth. Twists or spun threads are generally described as Z or S, depending on direction (fig. 7). Woolen yarn excavated from Zaghunluq was mostly made from Z-spun fibers. Some of the weavings were made from Z-spun warp and S-spun weft yarn, resulting in a quite different and rather special cloth. Two threads twisted together are called plied; two Z-spun threads are joined to form an S-twisted yarn, which is then called 'S-ply from two Z-spun ends.' Three or four threads, or even more, twisted together are also called plied. For example, twisting together three or four threads of Z-spun yarn results in an S-plied yarn. Twisting more than four threads together is generally done by repeated twisting, and is called a re-plied yarn. Four-, six-, and eight-plied threads are made by first combining two threads, and then combining these in groups of two again, and finally by recombining them into the final yarn. In terms of spinning direction, two Z-twisted yarns combine to form an S-twisted one, and two S-twisted yarns to a Z-twisted one. The ultimate name is given according to the final direction of the twist, whether that be S or Z. Re-plied threads were mostly used in interlacing or appeared on the fringes of woven items.

染料、染色与羊毛品种

扎滚鲁克古墓出土的毛纺织品材料，作过一些染料、染色与羊毛品种的鉴定，[1] 结果如下。

染料、染色　扎滚鲁克墓葬里出土了不少带有红、黄色颜料的角勺，在不少干尸脸面部能见到红、黄色的绘面纹饰，角勺的颜料与绘面的颜料是同一类颜料。经过颜料的测试，有雄黄、雌黄、铅黄及赤铁矿，都是石染颜料。赤铁矿又名赭石（Fe_2O_3），是红色颜料；雌黄（As_2S_3）、雄黄（AsS），是黄色颜料。不过，这些石染颜料是否用于毛纺织品的染色，还不是很清楚。

扎滚鲁克古墓出土毛织物的羊毛色，可以分两类，一类是染色，主色有蓝、红、黄、绿等；一类是羊毛原色，有白、黑、棕等。染色的深浅有些变化，如红色中有绯红、深红、浅红；黄色中有土黄、姜黄；蓝色中有天蓝、浅蓝等。同时，利用羊毛的原色也可以捻出有变化的色纱，如白和黑、白和棕色羊毛的混捻，因色毛所占的比例不同，纱色也会有所变化。

经过色谱分析等测试手段，认为扎滚鲁克毛织物的染料是植物，蓝色染料的主要成分是靛蓝素，即蓝草植物染料；红色的主要成分是茜素和紫茜素，即茜草植物染料。

一些学者对毛织物染色工艺进行分析、测定，认为测定的毛织物分别采用了四种染色工艺：直接染色、媒染染色、复染染色和套染染色。蓝色为直接染色；红色采用了媒染、复染工艺，绿色是由蓝色与黄色套染而成。黄色系绿色提取蓝色素后所得。红色是铝盐作媒染剂染色而成，铝盐含量与毛织品的色度呈相关性，浅青、青绿、黄绿等青绿色谱都需用靛蓝染料多次染色或套染而成。

羊毛品种　对扎滚鲁克古墓出土的 9 件毛织物纤维进行了品种鉴定，重点检定和分析了其中的六七件，应用的是扫描电镜分析羊毛纤维的组织结构、形态、纤维类型和细度。多数羊毛纤维较粗，是当地的绵羊毛，包括和田羊毛等，很少的有安哥拉山羊毛特征。

1.陈元生、贾应逸等：《山普拉墓群出土毛织品上蓝色染料的分析研究》，《文物保护与考古科学》第 12 卷第 1 期，2000 年 5 月，第 1～7 页；熊樱菲、解玉林，《周一汉毛织品的染色工艺探讨》，《文物保护与考古科学》第 14 卷第 1 期，2002 年 5 月，第 34～37 页；贾应逸、陈元生等，《新疆扎滚鲁克、山普拉墓葬出土（西周）毛织品的鉴定》，《文物保护与考古科学》第 20 卷第 1 期，2008 年 2 月，第 18～23 页。

DYEING WOOL: MATERIALS, COLORS, AND TYPES OF SHEEP'S WOOL

We evaluated Zaghunluq textiles for their dyeing processes, colors, and types of wool[1], and the results were as follows.

Dyestuffs and colors. Many horn ladles were excavated from the Zaghunluq cemeteries that had red and yellow dyestuffs or pigments in them, and many of the faces of corpses were seen to be painted in patterns using yellow and red. The pigments in ladles and those on faces were the same material. Analyzing these pigments, we determined that all of the various yellows and reds were mineral pigments. The red was made from Fe_2O_3, red iron ore or hematite, also called ochre. Orpiment, As_2S_3, and realgar or red orpiment, *xionghuang* AsS, were used for yellow. However, it is still unclear whether or not these mineral pigments were used for dyeing woolen textiles.

The colors of woolen textiles excavated at Zaghunluq can be divided into two types: one type was dyed, with the primary colors being blue, red, yellow, green, and so on. The other used the natural color of the wool, with the colors being white, black, brown, and so on. There was variation in the intensity of the colors of the dyed wool. For example, reds included dark red, light red, crimson red and others, yellows included earth-yellow, ginger-yellow, blues included sky blue, light blue, and so on. The natural colors of wool also varied depending on how the wool was spun and combined with fibers of other colors, for example white with black, white with yellow and so on. The final color of the yarn differed depending on percentages of different tones or shades of wool.

After undertaking chromatography, we believe that the Zaghunluq woolen textiles were dyed with vegetable dyes. The main component of the blue dyestuff is indigo, deriving from the indigo plant; the main components of red are alizarin and purpurin, deriving from Indian madder.

Scholars who have analyzed the woolen textile dyestuffs, and carried out testing, have determined that the makers of the woolens employed four kinds of dyeing techniques. One was direct dyeing, another was mordant dyeing, a third was duplicate dyeing or re-dyeing, and a fourth was over-dyeing. The direct dyeing technique was used for blue. The mordant and re-dyeing techniques were used for red. Green was dyed by combining blue and yellow, i.e., by over-dyeing. Red was accomplished by using aluminum salt as a mordant. The concentration of aluminum salt bore a direct relationship to the intensity of color. Light green, blue-green, yellow-green and so on all required the multiple use of indigo and over-dyeing.

Types of sheep's wool. We analyzed nine different kinds of fiber from woolen textiles excavated at Zaghunluq. The focus was on six or seven among these, using scanning electron microscope technology in order to look at the structure, composition, type of filament and degree of fineness. Most of the woolen filaments were relatively thick and were from locally raised sheep's wool, including fleeces from Hetian. Only rarely were the characteristics of Angora goat wool detected.

---

1 Cheng Yuansheng, Jia Yingyi et. al.: «Shanpula muqun chutu maozhipin shang lanse ranliao de fenxi yanjiu [Research on the analysis of blue dye on woolen weaves excavated from Shanpula cemetery]», *Wenwu baohu yu kaogu kexue* 12/1, May 2000, pp. 1–7. – Xiong Yingfei, Xie Yulin: «Zhou-Han maozhipin de ranse gongyi tantao [Investigation on the arts and crafts of wool dyeing in Zhou and Han dynasty]», *Wenwu baohu yu kaogu kexue* 14/1, May 2002, pp. 34–37. – Jia Yingyi, Cheng Yuansheng et. al.: «Xinjiang Zhagunluke, Shanpula muzang chutu (Xi Zhou) maozhipin de jianding [Evaluation of the woolen weaves (Western Zhou through Eastern Han dynasties) excavated from the graveyards of Zaghunluq and Shanpula in Xinjiang]», *Wenwu baohu yu kaogu kexue* 20/1, February 2008, pp. 18–23.

绞缬

扎滚鲁克古墓出土毛织物的绞缬染法，分缝绞法、绑扎法和夹缬法三种。

缝绞法　用针线穿缝及绞扎的办法，以作防染加工。扎滚鲁克缝绞染毛织物有2件（绞缬菱网纹毛布衣服残片96QZIM69：1-33［第四章图16］、绞缬枝叶纹毛布残片96QZIM99：1［第四章图16］）。

绑扎法　绞缬方格圆圈纹残毛布单（96QZIM65：24-20H，第四章图31）是通过绑扎、染色的织物，显方格、小圆圈纹。其中的小圆圈纹系用绑扎法染成。

夹缬法　夹缬齿纹残毛布裙（96QZIM64：20H，第四章图19），为一件夹缬染织物，是在带纹上夹板染色，夹板图案为波状的齿纹（图8）。

晕繝

扎滚鲁克古墓出土的晕繝毛织物比较多，主要表现在绦带式纹样的颜色变化，显现出由浅至深或由深变浅的效果，主要是纬线晕繝。花草纹绦毛带（98QZIM129：3-4，第四章图57），在中心和边缘之间是蓝、白色的绦式纹样，蓝、白之间色有些晕色效果，是白色毛和蓝色毛的混捻，白色毛相对多一些，由此织出来绦式纹样便有了晕色的效果。三角条纹绦毛残片（98QZIM129：3-8，第四章图60），蓝色向驼色渐变显晕繝效果。晕繝彩条纹毛布衣服残片（98QZIM129：3-15，第四章图63），经线为浅蓝色，纬线有浅蓝色、红色、蓝色和黄色，分区布置。其中浅蓝是地色，红色和蓝色之间分界明显，蓝色和黄色之间出现宝石蓝、藏蓝、浅绿的过渡色，同时在黄色上又可分出黄色和浅黄色。红和黄之间、蓝和黄之间分界不明显，呈一种过渡色形式。红和黄之间，红色有大红和紫红的区别。

8　夹缬齿纹毛布组织图（96QZIM64：20H，第四章图19）
Woolen striped cloth with clamp-dyed tooth pattern (96ZIM64:20H, cat. no. 19)

RESIST-DYEING

Three types of resist-dyeing techniques were used in excavated woolen textiles from Zaghunluq. These were stitching and gathering (*fengjiao fa*), binding and tying (*bangzha fa*), and clamp-resist dyeing (*jiaxie fa*).

Stitching and gathering. Two articles of woolen textiles from Zaghunluq used this method, a fragment of a garment with diamond-net pattern (96QZIM69:1-33, cat. no. 16) and a woolen cloth fragment with a pattern of branches with leaves (96QZIM99:1, cat. no. 17). A threaded needle was passed through the fabric to tie some of it together, to prevent dyeing in that part that was so stitched.

Binding and tying. 96QZIM65:24-20 (cat. no. 31), a fragment of a woolen cloth with a woven checker pattern and small circles used this method. The small circles were made using the tie-dyeing method.

Clamp-resist dyeing. 96QZIM64:20H (cat. no. 19), a fragmentary skirt with resist-dyed tooth pattern used this method. It was used on a cloth with woven stripes, and the pattern resulting from the use of the clamp boards was a soft wave edged with comb-like teeth (fig. 8).

COLOR GRADATION

A relatively large number of woolen textiles was excavated from Zaghunluq that used a technique of color gradation, mostly for patterns of bands or stripes. The result of this technique was a shift of colors from light to dark, or from dark to light. Usually it was the weft threads that were graded. A tapestry band with floral pattern (98QZIM129:3-4, cat. no. 57) used this method. In between the middle and the side bands one can see strips of blue and white, with the gradual change in hues between them. This was the result of twisting together white and blue wool with white becoming gradually dominant and therefore producing a lighter hue when woven. The result in piece 98QZIM129:3-8 (cat. no. 60), a tapestry fragment with a pattern of overlapping triangles, was blue shading into camel-hair color. A fragment of a garment made from wool cloth with bright stripes (98QZIM129:3-15, cat. no. 63) had warp threads that were light blue, and weft threads that were light blue, red, blue and yellow, used for different sections. The light blue was the color of the main field, with a clear line setting it off from red, and setting red off from blue. Azurite blue, blue-green, and light green appeared between the blue and the yellow, as transition colors. Similar transitions occurred between light and dark yellows, and between reds and yellows which included bright red and tangerine red.

毛绣

扎滚鲁克古墓出土不少毛绣。工艺有直针法、钉针绣、锁针绣和组合针绣。直针法，也叫缉针绣，是平针绣法，纹饰有平行曲折纹。钉针绣，是将其他的装饰线、装饰织物或是装饰物钉在织物表面，形成装饰效果的针法。可以分两种，一种钉线表露于外，是比较常见的穿绕方法；一种钉线从装饰线的侧面通过，没有露于表面，称隐伏方法。前者绣回菱纹（98QZIM124:8-6，第四章图71），后者绣平行线纹（96QZIM34:16-21，第四章图38）。锁针绣，是用绣线一圈一圈相叠套后形成线圈，效果像锁链而得名。扎滚鲁克古墓出土的锁针绣纹饰，有葡萄纹（98QZIM129:4，第四章图64和98QZIM141:2-2C，第四章图76）、涡旋三角纹（85QZM3:12，第四章图6）、螺旋三角纹。组合针绣是锁针绣和直针绣的组合，纹样残。长弧三角纹边饰是锁针绣，长弧三角纹内填的"米"字星纹是平针里的交针绣。

挖花

挖花，也叫嵌织花，呈"浮组织"效果。挖花部分本身不起地组织作用。扎滚鲁克古墓出土的挖花织物，一般是在平纹、2/2斜纹地上，以挖梭的方法在不同区间用各种色纱，挖织出纹样，属纬显花。纹样有曲线纹、菱格纹、羊纹、骆驼纹等（图9）。

9 挖花组织图（85QZM3:10，第四章图5）
Brocading (85QZM3:10, cat. no. 5)

EMBROIDERY

Quite a few examples of embroidery were found among Zaghunluq textiles. The techniques included running stitch (*zhizhen*), couching (*dingzhen*), chain stitch (*suozhen*), and composite techniques. The running- or straight-stitch technique is also called flat stitch (*qizhen xiu*) which uses a satin stitch (*pingzhen*), with the result being a curving pattern. The couching technique fixes other ornamental threads or pieces of fabric onto the surface of the primary piece of fabric. This technique has two varieties, one in which the stitching is visible on the outside, the comparatively often seen overcast technique, and the other in which the stitching is hidden, using so-called blind stitches. The first kind is used for a diamond pattern (98QZIM124:8-6, cat. no. 71); the latter for a pattern of parallel lines (96QZIM34:16-21, cat. no. 38). The chain-stitch technique allows the thread to make loop upon loop which results in a kind of chain along the fabric, hence the name of the technique. Among the embroideries excavated at Zaghunluq, this technique was used for grape patterns (98QZIM129:4, cat. no. 64 and 98QZIM141:2-2C, cat. no. 76), whorl and triangular patterns (85QZM3:12, cat. no. 6), as well as for spiral and triangular patterns. The composite embroidery technique combines chain stitch and running stitch. The pattern is incomplete, with long arched triangles executed in chain stitch, filled with eight-pointed stars executed in flat and cross-stitches.

BROCADING (WA HUA)

This results in a structure with floating pattern wefts, and it is also called an inlaid patterning (*qianzhi hua*). The elements of the fabric that are inlaid or brocaded are not part of the ground weave. Zaghunluq textiles that used this technique are generally brocaded on tabby or on 2/2 twill ground, using different colors of thread for the pattern, introduced according to the different pattern areas. In this technique, the pattern is exclusively formed by the weft. Patterns include: curving lines, diamonds, sheep, camels, and so on (fig. 9).

提花

提花，以变化组织显出比较明显的花纹。扎滚鲁克见到的提花，是在织物正面局部纬纱浮在经纱面上，纬纱显花纹，并起到地组织作用，延续到了两侧幅边。纹样有菱格、三角纹等（图 10）。

平、斜纹组织和平、斜纹的组合

扎滚鲁克古墓出土的毛织物中最多的是平纹组织，主要有白色平纹、黄色平纹、棕色平纹、红色平纹毛布等。其次是斜纹组织毛布，以 1/2 斜纹、2/2 斜纹为主，还有 1/3 斜纹、2/3 斜纹、3/3 斜纹，3/5 斜纹见于套头毛布小裙（96QZIM55：17G，第四章图 33）上的一块蓝、红条纹毛布，平纹地，1/5 组织显条纹。平纹组织毛布多较薄；1/2 斜纹、2/2 斜纹组织毛布中等薄厚；1/3 斜纹、2/3 斜纹、3/3 斜纹组织毛布比较厚。

平、斜纹的组合，指在一件织物上既有平纹也有斜纹组织的织物，在扎滚鲁克比较常见，如上文指出，平纹和 1/5 斜纹的组合，还有平纹和 1/3 斜纹、平纹和 3/5 斜纹的组合等。另外，还有就是在经头或经尾出现经线两根并股的现象，纬纱多变换颜色，起到边饰的作用。

10 提花组织图（98QZIM12 9：3-6，第四章图 59）
Self-patterning (98QZIM129：3-6, cat. no. 59)

SELF-PATTERNING (TIHUA)

This technique exhibits a clear pattern by changing the structure of the weave. The self-pattern or *tihua* seen at Zaghunluq are the result of weft threads floating over the warp threads thus forming the pattern, while they also serve as part of the ground weave of the fabric in areas that are not patterned. These weft picks run from selvage to selvage. Patterns include diamonds and triangles (fig. 10).

TABBY AND TWILL WEAVES, AND THEIR COMBINATION

Most of the woolen textiles found at Zaghunluq were tabby weave woolen cloths, using mainly the colors white, yellow, brown, and red. Second in quantity were twill-weave woolen cloth, mainly 1/2 and 2/2 but also 1/3, 2/3, 3/3, and 3/5 twill weaves. Twill in 3/5 weave was seen on the small woolen pullover dress 96QZIM55:17G (cat. no. 33). This was a woolen cloth with stripes of blue and red with tabby weave foundation, the stripes being formed by 5-span weft floats showing a stripe pattern. Most tabby weave woolen cloth was thin, 1/2 twill and 2/2 twill was of medium weight. Relatively heavy cloth included 1/3 twill, 2/3 twill, and 3/3 twill-weave woolens.

Combining tabby and twill weave means that both techniques are used in one piece of weaving. This was seen quite often at Zaghunluq. As noted above, tabby and 5-span weft floats, also tabby and 1/3 twill, tabby and 3/5 twill and so on fit this description. In addition, the phenomenon of warp threads grouped in pairs can be seen at either the head or tail of the warp; the weft threads then assume the function of border decoration and often introduce a different color.

毛纱

毛纱是借用了丝纺织品纱的名，指平纹组织中经、纬纱排列比较稀疏，显纱孔的织物。红色毛纱，见于百衲毛布套头裙衣（96QZIM55:17G，第四章图 33）上，是小片毛纱，由 15 行（宽 0.3 厘米）密纬组织和 4 行（宽 0.4 厘米）疏纬组织相间、互换分布，疏纬组织部分显方形纱孔。

赭红色毛纱服残片（96QZIM59:4，四章图 32）有毛纱，是 1/1 和 1/5 的组合。六条纬梭为一个编制单元，纬梭 1、2、4 和 6 为 1/1 的平纹织法，纬梭 3 和 5 则为 1/5 的显纬织法。毛纱是以此为单元而循环编织组成的。1/5 组织部分比较密，1/1 组织部分比较稀疏，给人以横向的暗条纹感觉，稀疏的地方显方纱孔（图 11）。

毛罗

毛罗是借用了丝织品罗的名，纬线平行排列，经线分绞经（起绞）和地经的毛织物。扎滚鲁克毛罗是两经绞罗，有的毛罗上既有罗组织，也有缂织组织。

11 赭红色毛纱组织图（96QZIM59:4，第四章图 32）
Ochre-red woolen gauze-like weave(96QZIM59:4, cat. no. 32)

WOOLEN GAUZE-LIKE WEAVES (SHA)

Adopting the Chinese term *sha* for woolen gauze-like weave borrows a word used generally to describe silk gauze. Here it is used for tabby weaves, with warp and weft threads relatively loosely or widely spaced, allowing holes to show through. A red woolen fabric, seen in the patchwork pullover garment 96QZIM55:17G (cat. no. 33), is a small fragment of such a weave. It is woven of alternating 15 picks (0.3 cm wide) of densely woven weft, and 4 picks (0.4 cm wide) of loosely woven weft. The loosely woven weft areas display the 'gauze' holes.

The fragment of a bright red garment 96QZIM59:4 (cat. no. 32) has another kind of woolen gauze-like weave, with the third and fifth out of six weft picks in 1/5 weave instead of the 1/1 weave of the other picks. This results in weft floats over five warp ends on the front of the fabric, and warp floats over five picks on the reverse. The 1/5 areas are relatively dense while the 1/1 part is quite sparse. In this way it imparts a sense of horizontality, with square holes showing through in the sparse areas (fig. 11).

WOOLEN GAUZE WEAVES (LUO)

Woolen *luo* also borrows a term from silk weaving. In contrast to *sha* however, its meaning here is also technically defined. In gauze weaves, weft threads are lined up in parallel while warp threads are divided into those that serve as crossing or doup warp ends and those that are fixed or ground warp ends. Zaghunluq's woolen gauze weave is a two-end simple gauze. Some woolen-gauze pieces combine gauze-weave structures and tapestry.

毛绉

毛绉是借用了丝织品绉（Crêpe）的名，是通过强加捻毛纱织成表面起绉的平纹织物，仅出土了一件。使用的羊毛较细，有绒毛，经纬线都是强捻，纬线捻度更强一些。

缂毛

缂毛是借用了丝织品缂丝的名，通经断纬的纺织工艺毛织物，日本人称作"缀织"，有的学者认为缂毛就是史书中记载的"罽"。扎滚鲁克古墓出土的缂毛分三种：一种是满幅缂织花纹的毛布；一种是在毛布上起装饰作用的绦式花纹缂毛布；还一种是缂毛绦。前两种皆称作缂毛或缂毛布，后者称作缂毛绦。

栽绒毯

栽绒毯是一种起绒的、能更好地防潮、防寒的织物。它将毛线绳拴在毛织物的经线，保留一定的长度，以增加织物厚度。同时，以彩色线绳栽绒能显现花纹。扎滚鲁克古墓出土栽绒毯有3件。目前，我们知道的最早的实物是阿尔泰山北麓巴泽雷克出土的栽绒毯，时代在公元前5～前4世纪。扎滚鲁克出土的栽绒毯，属第二期文化的晚段，即公元前3世纪末～公元3世纪中期。

WOOLEN CRÊPE (ZHOU)

This too borrows a term from silk weaving. It is a tabby weave that, through strongly twisted woolen threads allows the surface to exhibit a crêpe appearance. Only one piece was excavated. Fine wool was used, including cashmere, with warp and weft both strongly twisted but the weft slightly more than the warp.

WOOL TAPESTRY WOOLENS (KEMAO)

Tapestry woolens, in Chinese, likewise adapt a term from silk weaving. It has continuous warp and discontinuous weft, a technique known as *tsuzure-ori* in Japan. Some scholars believe that this technique is what was described as *ji* in historic writings. Examples excavated at Zaghunluq can be divided into three categories. One covers the entire woolen cloth with tapestry-woven patterns. Another is a tabby or twill woven cloth with the tapestry technique merely used for stripes or bands of patterns. The third category is narrow and could be called tapestry bands, while the first two are called simply tapestry.

CARPETS

Carpets are textiles with pile that give a better protection against the dampness and cold of the floor. Thick woolen threads are tied around the warp threads during weaving, preserving a certain length in order to increase the height of the pile and thus the thickness of the resulting textile. By using colored threads, carpets can exhibit beautiful patterns. Three pieces of carpets were excavated from Zaghunluq.

The earliest actual carpet known to date is one excavated from one of the Pazyryk tombs in the northern range of the Altai Mountains. It dates to 5th–4th centuries BCE. The carpets excavated from Zaghunluq belong to the late Second-period culture, that is, end-3rd century BCE to mid-3rd century CE.

编织帽、绦、带、鞘、绳

扎滚鲁克古墓出土的毛编织物，主要是五类：一类，毛编织帽；二类，服饰的边饰，称毛绦；三类，属系扎的带，称毛带；四类，编织的鞭鞘；五类，编织毛绳，截面呈圆形，用以捆扎。

毛编织帽　发现得比较多，皆为环编组织。[2]

毛绦和毛带　形式皆为扁宽的带，编织技术相似。一般来说，毛绦较窄，有的为长袍的襟边、底边、肩袖部分的饰边；有的套头上衣的领是宽毛绦，前胸饰窄毛绦；有的毛布单的边饰是窄毛绦；还有将窄毛绦或宽毛绦纵向连接，缝缀成直筒裙。毛带或宽或窄，也有些变化。毛绦和毛带多为 1/1、2/2 斜编绦，也有不少的 3、4、5 根线绳的绞编带。

编织绳　3 根粗线绞编呈绳状，即截面是圆形。出土 1 件棕色毛线鞭鞘，为 4 大股毛线绞编制成，截面呈长方体，鞭鞘头呈穗状。

毡

羊毛纤维在湿热、挤压或揉搓等作用下，产生缠结，称作羊毛的毡缩性。[3] 扎滚鲁克古墓出土的毡很少，有几件残片，发现一件毡衣。毡多为白色，也有红色毡，皆为单色。

牙线

牙线比一般的捻纱稍粗一些，是服饰的装饰线。扎滚鲁克古墓出土的袍、上衣、裤等服饰上发现有牙线，袍服的牙线多饰于袍身的前后中缝、领口或前襟边、袖口、肩袖部分，后背中缝，下摆底边。上衣的牙线饰于肩袖、领口、袖口或衣身两侧。裤服的牙线饰于裤身外侧、腿口。

牙线有红色、蓝色、棕色、黄色等，有单根牙线、拼股牙线和两根、多根的捻线等，单根牙线多 Z 捻，还有 4 根 Z 重捻线、8 根 S 重捻线、3 根 S 双捻线、18 根 S 重捻线等。

2. 赵丰：《中国古代的手编织物》，《丝绸》1990 年第 8 期，第 25~27 页。
3. 中国纺织品鉴定保护中心编著：《纺织品鉴定保护概论》，文物出版社，2002 年，第 30~32 页。

HATS, RIBBONS, BELTS, LASHES AND ROPES MADE WITH LOOPING AND INTERLACING TECHNIQUES

Five main types were excavated at Zaghunluq: woolen looped hats; the edging of clothes, called woolen ribbons or braids; belts for tying things up; braided lashes for whips; woolen ropes, round in cross-section, used for tying.

Woolen looped hats: Quite a few of these were discovered, all of an interconnected-looping structure.[2] Woolen ribbons or braids: All of these are flat, and also the interlacing techniques of all of these are similar. Generally speaking, ribbons are narrower than bands and they were found edging the front openings and hems of long gowns and decorating the shoulder and sleeve seams. Some of the pullover jackets had attached collars made from wide woolen braids and narrow ribbons to decorate the front part. Some of the woolen cloths had narrow ribbons along their edges. Narrow and wide ribbons were also sewn together lengthwise to form straight tubular skirts. Whether narrow or wide, there was great variation in the weave: most of the ribbons and bands were 1/1 and 2/2 twill oblique interlacing, but quite a few were made of twining with 3, 4, or 5 strands. Interlaced ropes: Twining three thick threads together and interlacing them into a rope results in a cross-section that is round. One woolen whip lash was excavated from Zaghunluq that had been made from four large strands of brown woolen threads. The cross-section was rectangular, and the top of the lash was fringed.

FELT (ZHAN)

Under treatments such as moistening, heating, pressing, and rolling, the fibers of sheep's wool shrink and interlock among themselves into what is known as felt.[3] Very little felt was excavated at Zaghunluq. There were a few fragmentary pieces and one piece of felt clothing. Most of the felt was white but there were also examples of red felt; all were of a single color.

ORNAMENTAL EDGING OR PIPING (YAXIAN)

Ornamental edging or piping uses thicker yarn than most spun yarns. Amongst the finds from Zaghunluq such edging was used frequently as decorative accents to clothing, especially on gowns, upper garments, and trousers. Piping on the gowns was placed at the waist seam, along the collar, or along the front edge of the gown, the sleeve cuffs, on the armhole and shoulder seams, and along the lower hem. Those on the upper garments or jackets were along the armhole, on the collars, the sleeve cuffs, or along the side seams. Trousers had piping also along the side seams and at the leg openings. Edging used red, blue, brown, yellow and other colors, made from single or multiple threads, including plied and re-plied yarns. Most of the single examples used a Z-twist, but there were also Z re-plied yarns from 4 ends, S re-plied yarns from 8 ends, S-plied yarns from 3 ends, or S re-plied yarns from 18 ends, and so on.

---

2 Zhao Feng: «Zhongguo gudai de shoubian zhiwu [Ancient Chinese hand braiding techniques]», *Sichou* 8/1990, pp. 25–27.

3 Zhongguo fangzhipin jianding baohu zhongxin bianzhao: *Fangzhipin jianding baohu gailun = Textile identification and conservation*], Beijing: Wenwu chubanshe 2002, pp. 30–32.

二 丝织物

扎滚鲁克古墓出土的丝织物有绢、绮、缣、缦、纨、锦和刺绣等。其中绢、锦和刺绣在第二期文化和第三期文化墓葬中皆有出土，而绮、缣、缦、纨仅出现于第三期文化墓葬。同时，绢的出土量较大，锦、刺绣也有不少的发现，绮、缣、缦、纨的出土比较少。

绢、缣、缦、纨

绢　一般是对平纹素丝织物的通称，里面又有一些细微的变化。扎滚鲁克古墓出土丝织物，经、纬线密度不是太大。同时将经、纬线两者之间的密度相差不是太大的素色丝织品归入了绢类。

缣　扎滚鲁克古墓出土的丝织物，称作缣的丝织物，经线密度较绢的经线明显要密，纬线则比较疏。白缣（98QZIM122:4-1），经密 70 根／厘米，纬密 22 根／厘米。

缦　扎滚鲁克古墓出土的缦，是经、纬线要比缣要更密的一种丝织物，显经畦纹。黄棕色缦残片96QZIM34:T50-1，经密 128 根／厘米，纬线 70 根／厘米，纬线相对要疏一些。

纨　这在平纹的丝织品中，应该是最细密的，比较光亮。扎滚鲁克墓地出土的一件绿色和一件土黄色平纹丝织品，定名为纨，其中绿色纨（96QZIM24:24-1），经密 146 根／厘米，纬密 63 根／厘米，也表现出纬线相对要疏一些。

SILK TEXTILES

Silk textiles excavated from Zaghunluq include: Normal silk tabby (*juan*), damask on tabby (*qi*), various silk qualities (*jian, man, wan*), compound weaves (*jin*), and embroidery (*cixiu*). Among these, normal silk tabby, compound weaves, and embroidery were all excavated from Second-period and Third-period graves, while damask on tabby (*qi*), and *jian, man,* and *wan* silks only appeared in Third-period culture graves.

The quantity of normal silk tabby (*juan*) was greatest, although considerable amounts of compound weave and embroidery were also discovered, while other silks including *qi, jian, man,* and *wan* were relatively scarce.

JUAN, JIAN, MAN, WAN

Juan. This is the general term for tabby-weave plain silk. There are minor variations within this category. The thread count of warp and weft in silks excavated from Zaghunluq graves was not very high, and the difference in thread count between warp and weft was also not great. All undyed silks in which the difference in density between warp and weft was not great were included in the group of textiles that we categorized as *juan*.

Jian. The warp thread count in *jian* silk textiles excavated at Zaghunluq was noticeably greater than that of normal silk tabby. The weft thread count, on the other hand, was not as great. A white *jian* (98QZIM122:4-1), for instance, had a thread count of 70 warp ends per cm and 22 weft picks per cm.

Man. The *man* textiles excavated from Zaghunluq had even higher warp and weft density than *jian*, and exhibited a plaid or checkered pattern. One fragment, of brownish-yellow color (96QZIM34:T50-1), had a thread count of 128 warp ends per cm and 70 weft picks per cm. Relatively speaking, the weft was looser.

Wan. Among tabby-weave silk textiles, *wan* can be considered the finest weave or that with the highest thread count. It is also relatively lustrous. Two pieces excavated from Zaghunluq were designated as *wan*, one a green color and the other earthen-yellow. The green *wan* (96QZIM24:24-1) had a warp thread count of 146 ends to the cm and a weft thread count of 63 picks to the cm. Again, the weft was relatively looser.

绮

《说文》: "绮,文缯也。"也就是平素纹显暗花组织的丝织物。扎滚鲁克古墓出土的绮,地纹皆为平纹,以 3/1、2/1 组织显花。

锦

织彩为文(纹)曰锦。扎滚鲁克古墓出土的织锦,大体可以分为平纹经锦和平纹纬锦两大类:锦经丝线不加捻;纬锦丝线加捻,即绵经绵纬。

刺绣

扎滚鲁克古墓出土的刺绣,发现的不多,但很精彩,皆为锁针绣,有五种:白绢地忍冬纹刺绣、胭脂红绮地花草纹刺绣残片、原白色缣地萄萄纹刺绣残片、绿绢地鸟纹刺绣残片和果绿色缣刺绣残片。

纹样以植物纹为主,还发现对鸟纹。用色明快、艳丽。

丝编织带

扎滚鲁克古墓出土两件,是比较特殊的丝编织带:一件是黄地蓝菱格纹丝编织带,3/3 斜编制成(98QZIM129:3-10,第四章图 61);一件是白地蓝网格纹丝编织带,4/4 斜编制成(98QZIM129:3-11,第四章图 62)。两件丝编织带皆显得比较厚,编织比较密。

QI

The ancient book called the *Shuowen* includes the phrase, «Qi, is termed *zeng*.» *Qi* is a silk textile that has a plain tabby ground with self-patterning (*anhua*). All *qi* excavated at Zaghunluq used a tabby ground, with pattern in 3/1 or 2/1 weave.

COMPOUND WEAVES (JIN)

Weaving colors into patterns is called *jin*. Technically they exhibit compound-weave structures. The *jin* silks excavated from Zaghunluq could generally be divided into warp-faced compound tabby and weft-faced compound tabby. The threads of warp-faced *jin* were not given a twist whereas both the warp and weft threads of weft-faced *jin* were spun.

EMBROIDERY

Not much silk embroidery was discovered at Zaghunluq, but what was excavated was very fine chain-stitch embroidery. There were five pieces:

White *juan* ground with embroidered honeysuckle pattern, fragment of red-colored *qi* with plants and flowers, fragment of originally white-colored *jian* with grapes embroidered on it, fragment of green *juan* with embroidered bird patterns, and fragment of fruit-green *jian* with embroidery. Most of the ornamentation or patterns were of vegetation but patterns with confronted birds were also discovered. The coloration was bright and striking.

SILK BRAIDS

Two of these were excavated at Zaghunluq, and they were quite special. One (98QZIM129:3-10, cat. no. 61) had a blue diamond pattern on a yellow ground and was worked in 3/3 twill oblique interlacing. The other (98QZIM129:3-11, cat. no. 62) had a blue netting pattern on a white ground and was worked in 4/4 twill oblique interlacing. Both pieces were quite thick and were braided quite densely.

三 棉织物和麻制品

棉织物

棉织物多数为白色平纹棉布，织得比较细密，在96QZIM18、96QZIM73、98QZIM133皆有出土，属扎滚鲁克第三期文化墓葬。在属于第二期文化晚段的96QZIIM2出土了一件红色平纹套头棉布上衣，纺织略为粗一些（96QZIIM2:10-1，第四章图28）。

麻制品

麻制品只出土了一件麻捻绳（96QZIIM2:73-7-1），是S双捻绳。

COTTON TEXTILES AND ARTICLES MADE OF HEMP

COTTON TEXTILES

Most of the cotton textiles were white tabby cloths, woven fairly tightly. Graves 96QZIM18, 96QZIM73, and 98QZIM133 all produced these textiles, which belonged to the Zaghunluq Third-period culture. From grave 96QZIIM2, belonging to late-Second-period culture, came a red cotton pullover jacket that was somewhat less fine (96QZIIM2:10-1, cat. no. 28).

ARTICLES MADE OF HEMP

One rope made of hemp was excavated (96QZIIM2:73-7-1). It was S-plied.

第三章　扎滚鲁克纺织品保护

木娜瓦尔·哈帕尔　郭金龙

　　扎滚鲁克墓地位于新疆南部的且末县。在自然环境上，南疆的气候相对干燥（新疆以天山为界，天山以南称南疆，以北称北疆），古代的纺织品长期埋藏在这样的气候条件下，出土时保存都较好。墓地出土的纺织品有毛织品、丝织品和棉织品等。毛织品占到了90% 以上，为服饰和生活用品，而且质地、纤维的强度和颜色都保存得比较好。然而，由于墓葬中的衣物与尸体的粘连，纺织品上残留有大量包括尸斑、血迹、生活污垢在内的污迹，个别还存在霉斑、金属锈斑以及地下矿物质沉淀、沙土灰尘等，出现了腐烂、炭化、褪色、破损等现象。同时，因受地下环境因素的影响，出土时有的变得十分脆弱，导致损害，纤维强度下降，发硬、变脆。有的经不起手拿，一碰即破，极难保护与保存。

　　多年来，随着文物保护科学工作的不断深入，国内外的文物保护专家在出土纺织品的保护、修复技术领域，进行了大量探索性研究，总结出不少宝贵的经验。由于被保护的纺织品残损程度不同及现有条件的限制，在扎滚鲁克纺织品的保护处理中，主要采用了清洗、消毒、有机玻璃夹持法等保护措施。

By Minawar Happar, Guo Jinlong
CONSERVATION OF ZAGHUNLUQ TEXTILES

The Zaghunluq cemeteries are located in the southern part of Xinjiang, in Qiemo County. In terms of the natural environment, southern Xinjiang's climate is relatively arid (the dividing line between north and south in Xinjiang is taken to be the Tianshan mountain range), and textiles that had been buried for a long time were therefore protected to a certain degree from damage. Excavated textiles included woolen, silk, and cotton weavings. Woolen weavings constituted over 90% of all textiles. They were used as clothing and as items for use in daily life, and the textures and the strength of the fibers, as well as the colors, were fairly well preserved.

Still, since clothing was adhering to corpses in graves, a large amount of damage was found in the form of blood stains and other stains due to the decomposition of the body, as well as dirt and other forms of damage that occurred while the person was alive. In some instances, there were also mildewed spots, rust spots due to proximity to metals, and spots or stains from underground mineral precipitates, sand and dust. The textiles therefore appeared deteriorated, carbonized, faded and generally damaged. Meanwhile, when the textiles were brought out of their underground environment they sometimes changed very quickly under new conditions. They hardened, became brittle, and some were even lost altogether as the strength of fibers deteriorated. Some could not withstand any handling – they would deteriorate at the slightest touch. It was extremely hard to protect and preserve these examples.

Scientific conservation of archaeological objects has seen much improvement over many years. Conservators both inside and outside China have brought valuable experience to bear on the field of conservation and restoration of excavated textiles. They have also carried out a tremendous amount of research. At Zaghunluq, the degree of damage to various textiles differed. Since conditions for textile conservation in Xinjiang are limited by uncontrollable factors, in preserving the Zaghunluq textiles we have mainly employed the three measures of cleaning, disinfecting, and pressure-mounting between perspex or Plexiglas sheets.

一 纺织品的清洗

清洗，是纺织品保护最常见的一种方法，也是一项比较复杂而细致的工作。除技术难度较大以外，还必须在认识上取得一致，建立起科学的清洗理念，严格遵循"整旧如旧"的基本宗旨，最大限度地保持毛纺织品的原貌，达到延长毛织品寿命的目的。

目前，国际上对古代纺织品的清洗有一定的要求，例如，对于纺织品上的血迹、金属锈斑，一般不主张清除，需要遗留这些具有研究价值的历史痕迹，强调了对纺织品保存环境的控制。但在新疆环境控制有相当大的难度，如果污染物不除去，纺织品有可能继续腐蚀，短期内就会完全损毁。因此，出土纺织品要经过清洗，才能入藏、研究或陈列。

纺织品的清洗与污垢的性质有直接的关系，也与织物纤维、保存情况等有密切关系，要了解织物的纤维成分、染料种类、污染物的种类及特性，不能只求操作速度和外表美观漂亮，应根据不同的情况，采用不同的清洗方法。

扎滚鲁克古墓出土的毛织品中有一部分为染色品，而且多使用的是不易掉色植物染料。但是，为了确定洗涤是否会让纺织品掉色，清洗前对纺织品进行了局部实验，并根据实验的结果再进行大面积的清洗。方法是将棉球蘸上相应的溶剂，涂抹在污垢处和带色处，大约 5~10 分钟后，观察污垢处是否发生变化。在有色织物上一般棉球要放于隐蔽位置，时间控制在 1 分钟左右，同样是观察色彩的变化问题。

CLEANING THE TEXTILES

Cleaning is one of the most commonly seen methods of conserving textiles, and yet it is a relatively complex and dedicated task. In addition to the technical difficulty there are different conceptual approaches: however, it is commonly agreed upon that we should proceed by scientific cleaning principles, strictly adhere to the basic principle of treating the old as old, preserving, to the greatest extent possible, the original aspect of the textile, and also achieving our primary purpose of extending the textile's life.

At present, there are specific international requirements with respect to cleaning ancient textiles. For example, removing blood stains or rust stains is not encouraged. One should leave these traces of a textile's past history to aid in scientific research. Instead, control of the environment surrounding the textile is emphasized. In Xinjiang, however, establishing a controlled environment is extremely difficult and, if the contaminating material on the textile is not removed, the textile may continue to deteriorate and in a short time be lost. Because of this, textiles must undergo a process of cleaning before they can be put into storage, be researched or exhibited.

The cleaning process bears a direct relationship to the type of contamination or damage, also to the type of fibers and their condition – how well they have been preserved. Before cleaning, one must first understand the chemical composition of the fibers and types of dyestuffs, as well as the nature of the contaminating agents. One must adopt different cleaning methods depending on the circumstances and not simply attempt to make the textile superficially beautiful, and in the shortest length of time.

A fair portion of the woolen textiles excavated from Zaghunluq had been dyed. The dyes used were vegetable dyestuffs that were quite color fast. Nonetheless, in order to ascertain whether or not colors might bleed, before cleaning the textile, a small portion was put through a partial or test-spot cleaning process. Only after results were known did we allow the entire textile to be cleaned. The method of testing was to use a cotton ball soaked in the appropriate solvent, and to daub this on a stained part of the textile or a part that had been dyed. After around 5–10 minutes, we observed whether or not the colors of the textile had changed. Usually this process was applied to a hidden part of or the underside of a textile and the process was carried out in one-minute periods in order to examine the possibility of bleeding.

（一） 毛织品的清洗

对毛织品的清洗主要是湿洗和干洗。

湿洗

毛织品纤维皆经加捻而成纱，毛纱粗细、疏密有些变化，大体可以分为粗毛纱、中毛纱和细毛纱等织物类。

粗毛纱织物的清洗。粗纱毛织物大多是毛毯及残片，毛纱粗且组织结构疏松，粘附沙土比较多。此类织物如果直接用水清洗，沙土不易冲干净，组织结构也容易被水冲散。所以，首先将毛织品展开，夹在尼龙纱网予以固定，而后用小型手提式吸尘器，将表面和背面的沙土吸干净，而后将尼龙纱网架子置于斜坡状的清洗台上进行水洗。清洗时，先用"去离子水"浸泡，然后用流动的自来水清洗。清洗织物反面时，将一件纱网平放在织物上面，将架子连同织物一起翻转，进行清洗，这样不易损坏织物。为了保证组织结构的完好，清洗的过程中要把水的压力控制到最小，最后再用去离子水清洗。中间使用自来水，是因为清洗对象比较厚，用水量大。一般情况下，清洗一遍就可以达到目的，不过有的毛织品的污垢用去离子水不易洗干净，因此，对它要进行第二遍的清洗。清洗时，采用了洗涤剂，洗涤剂的用量根据污垢的情况来定，清洗过程中洗涤剂的浓度控制在 10%~20%。需先配好洗涤液，少量滴在污垢处，待稍微浸润后，用软毛刷轻刷污垢，经 20 分钟左右，再用去离子水将毛织品漂洗干净，以免洗涤剂的酸、碱成分对毛织品产生影响。最后，织物上的水将要流尽的时候，用吸水性较好的毛巾或棉布将其水分吸干，再放在平面台上自然晾干。

CLEANING WOOLEN TEXTILES

Our two main cleaning processes for woolen textiles were wet cleaning and solvent cleaning.

WET CLEANING OR WASHING

The fibers of woolen textiles have all been twisted into yarn, which can be either thick or thin, depending on the fibers, and densely or loosely woven. In general, yarns can be divided into the three categories of heavy, medium-weight, and light woolen-yarn, in terms of how to clean them. Heavy woolen yarn. Most textiles using heavy yarn are either carpets or fragments of carpets. Not only is the yarn thick but the weave is loose and carries relatively more dirt and sand. If water is directly applied to this type of textile, not only is it not easy to wash it clean but the water is also liable to further loosen the weave. With the Zaghunluq textiles, it was therefore first necessary to spread the textile out and clamp it securely between sheets of nylon net before using a small handheld vacuum cleaner to get the worst of the dirt from both front and reverse sides. Then the nylon rack was placed on a slope for wet cleaning.

When cleaning, we first used deionized water to immerse and soak the fabric, then running tap water to clean it. In order to clean the reverse side of the textile, we put a net over the surface of the fabric and turned the whole thing upside down together in order not to damage the textile. The pressure of water had to be kept very low during the cleaning process in order not to affect the weave structure. In the final step, deionized water was once again used to clean. The reason for using tap water for most of the process lies in the thickness of the textile and the substantial amount of water used to rinse it. Usually, the desired result could be achieved with a single cleaning process, but in some cases, where deionized water was not enough to clean the wool textile, a second washing process was added. The amount of detergent used in cleaning had to be determined by the degree of soiling and by each specific situation, but the concentration of detergent was in no case more than 10–20%. The detergent was tested on a small area first, and watched to see the penetration while a soft woolen brush was gently used to aid in cleaning.

After around 20 minutes, deionized water was used once again to rinse, in order to avoid ongoing damage from the influence of acids and alkaline agents in the solvent. Finally, when the water was well drained from the textile, a highly absorbent towel or cotton cloth was used to take up moisture and then the article was placed on a flat rack to dry naturally in the air.

中毛纱毛织物的清洗。这类毛织品大都是上衣、裤子和编织腰带等，毛纱中等粗，组织结构相对要密一些。服饰大都是从干尸、骨架上脱下来的，所以残损程度不同（如仰身直肢葬者身下部位，由于尸体渗出的液体污染造成服饰严重腐蚀，有的衣服后背和裤子的腰臀部全部腐蚀）。中毛纱织物的清洗步骤与粗毛纱大体相似，不同的是它的清洗难度更大一些，因为清洗前需将衣服的形状摆出。发掘出土的纺织品送到清洗室时，一般都已打包，打开包时不易分辨服饰部位，即是前片、后片、领子，还是袖子等。操作时必须要慎重，若不小心服饰就会开裂，同时这种毛织品本身也比较厚，衣服的前后片及袖子会是两层重叠，所以不易去除里面的沙土。有的纺织品不仅有尸体分泌的污染物，还有生活污垢等，对此使用的洗涤剂也不尽相同（图12）。

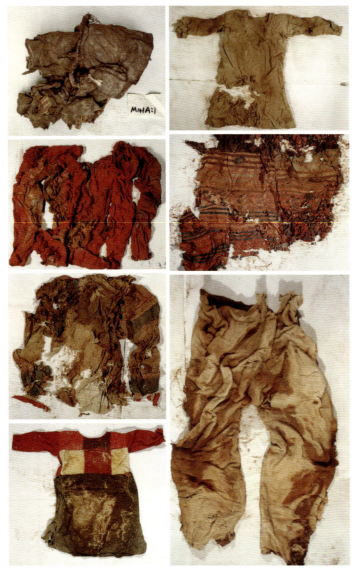

12　清洗前纺织品保存状况
State of preservation of the textiles before cleaning

Textiles made from medium-weight yarn. Most of these woolen textiles are jackets, pants, and braided belts. Since the yarn is slightly finer, the weave is also a little tighter than the above examples. Most of these garments were removed from mummies or skeletons, and had differing degrees of damage. In the case of corpses lying straight on their backs, for instance, the damage from bodily juices seeping downwards caused the backsides of fabrics to be more damaged than the front sides. Some backs of jackets, and the hip part of pants were completely rotten. The sequence of steps for cleaning medium-weight yarn textiles was the same as that for heavy-yarn textiles, the only difference being that cleaning medium-weight yarn textiles was more complicated because the textile must first be laid out flat. When excavated textiles are sent to the laboratory, they usually arrive in a packaged form. On opening the package, it is often not easy to distinguish the different parts of a garment, what is the front side, the back side, the collar, the sleeves and so on. One must be extremely careful in handling the textile during this process since it can so easily be torn. Moreover, these garments were generally fairly thick and, when lying flat, the double layers of front and back and of the sleeves hindered removing dirt from the garments' inside. Some of the textiles not only had contaminants from the corpse but had been dirtied and damaged to an extent by being worn during the life of the person. Cleaning agents were not necessarily the same for damage of different kinds (fig. 12).

细纱毛织物的清洗。所谓细纱毛织物多是较薄的毛布服饰和毛罗服饰及残片，组织结构相对也比较松疏，且很薄，大部分糟朽严重。此类毛织品不能摆在尼龙纱网架子上清洗，因尼龙纱较硬、粗糙，流动水压力会和毛织品与尼龙纱及毛纱之间产生摩擦，而这种摩擦会影响毛纱纤维的强度。所以这类毛织品的清洗要把它放在稍有倾斜度的光面清洗台上进行清洗。先用去离子水浸泡，然后用流动的去离子水慢慢冲洗，这样凝固在表面及组织里面的沙土和可溶性的盐都可以冲洗干净。一般情况下，冲洗一次就干净（案例处理前后的胶片）。

　　腐蚀比较严重毛织品的清洗。由于污染物的存在和自然因素的损害，有些毛织品腐蚀较严重，出现纤维强度下降、变脆、经不起手拿、一碰即碎等问题。在这种情况下不能采用任何清洗法，因受损的物品已无法承受清洗过程的机械力，所以我们对这类毛织品采用表面清洗法进行了处理。即把毛织品摊在平面台上，先用不同规格的小玻璃片，将皱叠的部位稍加湿润后进行压抚，然后用小气吹往同一方向轻轻吹除表面覆盖的灰尘，同时用棉布遮盖未处理部位，避免灰尘再次沉积，最后采用医用小型吸痰器吸除渗透在表面和组织里的毛杂、灰尘、污垢斑。采用这种做法也可以达到清洗纺织品的目的。从所取得的效果看，这种方法对于纺织品的局部清洗和易褪色织物的清洗十分有效（图 13）。

13　清洗后的纺织品
Textiles after cleaning

Cleaning fine-yarn woolen garments. So-called 'fine-yarn' includes garments made both of woolen cloth and woolen gauze as well as fragments of textiles. The weave of these was relatively loose and they were quite thin and mostly seriously rotted or deteriorated. It was not possible to put this type of textile on a nylon-net rack since the nylon threads are relatively hard and rough, so that the pressure of running water would create friction between them and the fabric. This would affect the strength of the wool fibers. This type of textile therefore had to be placed on a slightly inclined smooth rack for cleaning. It was first immersed in deionized water, then slowly rinsed in running deionized water in order to remove adhering dirt on the surface and in the weave of the textile, as well as any dissolvable salts. Generally, one such washing was enough to complete the cleaning process, otherwise the whole process would be repeated.

Cleaning textiles that were more severely soiled. Due to contaminating agents (for example, blood) as well as damage from natural causes, some of the textiles were more severely deteriorated with greatly diminished strength of the fibers. These were brittle and could not be handled without further damage. Water could not be used at all under these conditions. No mechanical process could be applied, so we did surface cleaning only on these textiles. We placed the textiles on a flat surface. Then, using different sizes of small glass plates, we smoothed out the wrinkles after applying a small amount of moisture. Then, using great caution we blew surface dirt off, always taking care to blow in the same direction. At the same time, we covered the portions currently not under treatment with cotton cloth to prevent dust from resettling on the fabric. Finally, using a small medical suction device, we drew off any stray yarn, dirt, and dust that was on the surface or in the weave. These methods generally allowed us to arrive at the goal of cleaning the textile. From the results, we feel these cleaning methods were effective in cleaning both fragmented textiles and those that had fugitive colors (fig. 13).

干洗

扎滚鲁克古墓出土了一些羊毛团、毛毡等没有组织结构的遗物，它们也带着生活污垢，若不及时处理，因环境的变化必然会滋生虫害，一旦发生病变则必定影响到其他织物的有效保护。这类遗物的污垢由于无法溶于水，须采用干洗处理。具体的做法是把一部分面积大、量多，清洗室无法干洗的物品送到了专门的干洗店进行处理。其余的遗物进行有机溶剂的处理，主要使用乙醇、丙酮、苯、三氯乙烯等。

超声波清洗

扎滚鲁克古墓有些毛织品出土时，因地下水为盐碱水，加之尸体分泌物和泥土的大量附着，出土时就已硬化。对于这些毛织品，我们采用了超声波清洗法。因为用普通方法清洗这些毛织品不但用时较长，而且也不易将异物去除，相反还会影响纤维的强度。而用超声波清洗法进行处理，在短时间内能使附着在毛织品上的污垢脱落，并且不影响纤维强度。

（二）丝织品的清洗

扎滚鲁克古墓出土的丝织品多为残片。虽然丝织品和毛织品都属动物纤维，不过丝织品较薄，表面较平，有光泽，强度较好，污垢停留在表面，比较容易清除。一般用蒸馏水浸泡、冲洗，就可以去除丝织品色彩和图案上的污斑。具体方法是将丝织品平摊于有机玻璃上，以有机玻璃的承托放置在斜面的清洗台上。先用蒸馏水浸泡，然后在丝织品上面覆盖一层塑料薄膜，停留 20 分钟左右，使一部分污垢溶解，再用缓流的蒸馏水清洗（正反两面分别清洗）。然后用柔软的小毛刷蘸 0.2% 的洗涤剂，轻轻地来回刷洗丝织品表面的污垢，以清洗残留的污垢。而后用吸水性较好的毛巾或棉布将剩下的水分吸干，放在平面台上自然晾干。

（三）棉织品的清洗

扎滚鲁克古墓出土的棉织品多是残片，仅有一件衣服保存得比较好。只是有大量地下水盐碱、尸体分泌物和泥土附着在衣物上，于是采用了适合它的超声波清洗方法。

SOLVENT CLEANING

Certain unwoven items made of wool were excavated from Zaghunluq that harbored living organisms. These included clumps of sheep's wool and felt. If these were not dealt with immediately, they would soon be infested with insects due to the sudden beneficial change in the insect's environment. They would then affect the preservation of the rest of the textiles. Since this kind of contaminant could not be dissolved through using water, solvent cleaning was the only method to adopt. Specifically, those large pieces and high quantity items that the laboratory had no facilities to deal with by itself were sent to a special dry-cleaning facility. The rest were handled in the lab using organic solvents, primarily ethanol, acetone, benzene, and trichloroethylene.

CLEANING BY USE OF ULTRASOUND WAVES

Due to saline-alkaline underground water as well as bodily secretions from the corpse and adhering dirt, many woolen textiles excavated from Zaghunluq would harden or stiffen when they were excavated. We used ultrasound techniques to clean these items. Using water took too long, was not effective in removing certain alien materials and also had the effect of lowering the strength of the fibers. Using ultrasound allowed us to clean these items quickly and effectively and it did not influence the fiber strength.

CLEANING SILK TEXTILES

Many of the silk textiles excavated from Zaghunluq were in fragments. Although silk and wool are both animal fibers, silks are finer and have a smoother surface, they are glossy and have preserved a better strength which makes it easier to remove dirt and contaminants from their surface. Generally, we immersed the silk textile in distilled water and rinsed it, which took out the stains on the colors and the patterns. Specifically, we spread the piece flat on plexiglass and, with this support, placed it on an inclined cleaning platform. First we soaked the textile in distilled water, and then covered it with a thin plastic membrane which we left for around twenty minutes to allow contaminants to dissolve. Then we washed with very gently running water (each side was done separately). We used a very soft woolen brush dipped in 0.2% detergent solution and lightly brushed the remaining contaminants off the surface of the silk. Finally, we used a highly absorbent towel or cotton cloth to take up excess moisture and then placed the textile on a flat board to dry naturally in the air.

CLEANING COTTON TEXTILES

Most of the cotton textiles excavated from Zaghunluq were in fragments. Only one item of clothing was relatively well preserved. It was, however, severely affected by saline-alkaline underground water, by secretions from the corpse, and by adhering mud and dirt, so we thought it appropriate to use ultrasound techniques.

二　纺织品的加固、消毒和平整

（一）纺织品的加固

对于扎滚鲁克古墓出土的纺织品，采用了夹持法和背衬法进行加固。

夹持法加固，就是对织物本身不施加任何直接的物质，只是将它夹持起来，起到固定的作用，这是最为原始和简单的加固方法。只要加持的表层采用呈透明状的物质，夹持后的残片可以直接用于陈列展览。对于扎滚鲁克古墓出土的部分纺织品我们就采用了有机玻璃夹持法。

背衬加固法是在纺织品背后用粘合、缝合等方法加上一层支撑物，以起到加固织物的作用。对于扎滚鲁克古墓出土的另一部分较残破和脆化的纺织品则采用背衬加固法中的托裱法（图14）。

（二）纺织品的消毒

消毒的主要目的是杀死微生物和害虫。因为新疆的气候干燥，一般微生物不容易滋生。即便如此，我们也不能忽略微生物对纺织品的危害，因为霉菌的孢子很小，初期不易被发现，一旦发现基本已到了晚期。从目前的情况看，在新疆对纺织品危害最大的是虫蛀问题。虽然清洗亦能起消毒作用，但由于属一般性处理，故不能达到彻底杀死虫卵、灭菌的效果。因此还需要进行专门的消毒处理，2002年以前我们对扎滚鲁克古墓出土的纺织品进行的消毒法是环氧乙烷熏蒸法，2002年以后采用低温冷冻消毒法。

1.环氧乙烷熏蒸法的具体操作方法：在没有环氧乙烷专用熏蒸器的情况下，将纺织品装入90厘米×180厘米聚乙烯塑料袋，然后放入100毫升的瓶装环氧乙烷，用烙铁烫封袋口，同时掐断玻璃瓶的尖头，环氧乙烷在其中自行挥发，熏蒸3~5天。我们做的这种方法虽然不完全符合环氧乙烷熏蒸法的要求，但是在现有的条件下，也起到了一定的消毒作用。

2.低温冷冻法的具体操作方法：在纺织品干燥的情况下，放入聚乙烯塑料袋，用真空泵将聚乙稀塑料袋中的空气抽去，封紧袋口，最后放入已经将温度降到−30℃的低温冷柜。在冷冻柜里放置两周后拿出来，等其恢复至室温后打开袋子取出毛织品。

CONSOLIDATING, DISINFECTING, AND ALIGNING TEXTILES

CONSOLIDATING TEXTILES

We used the two methods of pressure mounting, and backing with a support material, to consolidate textiles. The first is a simple method of consolidation and does not involve administering any extra material to the body of the textile. If the top layer of the pressure mount is transparent, the textile can be directly used in exhibitions without any further handling. We used perspex as material for the pressure mounts of some of the textiles excavated from Zaghunluq.

The second method of consolidation involved sewing or glueing a layer of supportive material to the back of the textile in order to consolidate it. For certain textiles that were either more damaged or in tiny pieces we used a supportive mount (fig. 14).

DISINFECTING TEXTILES

The purpose of disinfecting is to kill microorganisms and harmful insects. Since Xinjiang is arid, microorganisms do not thrive there but, nonetheless, we could not ignore the potential damage that they can do to textiles. Since the spores of mold are tiny and not easily detected in their early stages, once they are discovered it is often too late. At present, among all harmful agents, the one of greatest potential damage in Xinjiang to textiles is insects.

Washing also has a disinfecting function, but under most conditions it is not sufficient to kill insect eggs, or microbial spores. Other disinfecting methods are necessary. Before 2002, we used the method of fumigation by ethylene oxide for the textiles from Zaghunluq. After 2002, we used low-temperature freezing methods.

Our specific methods with regard to the first were as follows. Circumstances were such that we had no fumigation equipment for the ethylene oxide, therefore we devised our own treatment. We put the textiles into a polyethylene bag measuring 90 cm x 180 cm, and then put a 100 ml bottle of ethylene oxide inside this bag.

We used an iron to seal the bag shut while at the same time unsealing the mouth of the glass jar and allowing the gas to operate inside the bag. We fumigated for a period of three to five days. Although this method was not fully in line with proper usage of ethylene oxide, under the existing conditions it still could achieve certain results in disinfecting.

Our specific methods with regard to freezing were as follows. With the textiles in a dry condition, we placed them in a polyethylene bag and then used a vacuum pump to withdraw all the air. We sealed the bag and put it in a freezing cabinet that had been cooled down to –30 degrees Celsius. We left the textiles in the freezing cabinet for two weeks. When removing it from the cabinet, we allowed the polypropylene bag to come back to the ambient room temperature before removing the textiles.

(三) 纺织品的平整

在平整纺织品时，织物不同，方法上也有些变化。

1. 强度较弱的纺织品平整

清洗后的纺织品强度一般都会有比较大的下降，特别是纱、罗等薄型织物残片，难以用手移动。平整时，首先将它放在玻璃片上，利用细小流动水的帮助，仔细对齐经纬线，有图案的要拼对图案，最后用过滤纸做一次性吸水处理，待半干后进行平整。

2. 服饰类织物的平整

服饰类织物有两三层以上的厚度，因而吸水量较大，清洗后重量增大。因此，先用干毛巾进行吸水处理，待半干后移至平面工作台上进行平整（图 15）。

14 加固 Aligning of the textiles

ALIGNING TEXTILES

Stuctures of textiles vary, and so the methods used to align them also vary.

Aligning textiles that are substantially weakened: In general, fibers experience a steep decline in strength after being washed. This applies especially to fragments of sheer textiles such as gauze and gauze-like weaves. It is difficult to handle them. In the flattening process, we first placed them on a sheet of glass and, with the aid of a tiny stream of water, meticulously put warp and weft threads in order, aligning the patterns of the textile. Finally, we used filter paper to do a one-time absorption of water and, when the fibers were half dry, we definitely aligned the fragments.

Aligning articles of clothing: Clothing often has two or three layers of thickness and therefore absorbs more water and becomes much heavier during wet cleaning. Because of this, we first used a towel to blot up water. When the objects was half dry, we moved it to the work table used for flattening and carried out aligning (fig. 15).

15 平整 Consolidation of the textiles

三　清洗使用的洗涤剂和设备

（一）　清洗使用的洗涤剂

清洗扎滚鲁克古墓出土纺织品时，选用的洗涤剂是非离子表面活性剂。非离子表面活性剂在水溶液中，以非离子状态存在，稳定性高，不易受强电解质的影响，也不易受酸、碱的影响。在溶剂中为溶解性较好的洗涤剂，具有去污力强、抗静电、杀菌和保护胶体等多种性能，清洗古代纺织品比较安全。

（二）　设备

我们博物馆的处理设备主要是三种：

1. 吸尘设备有 ZL1500-1 型桶式吸尘器、NK-118 型手提式真空吸尘器和橡皮气球、YB・RX-1 小儿吸痰器等。

2. 水洗设备有木框尼龙网、wuc-D 型不同规格的超声波清洗漕，还有可移动、升降不锈钢清洗台面等（图16）。

3. 消毒设备有 MDF-792 和 MDF-392 型低温冷冻柜。

参加扎滚鲁克纺织品保护工作的除木娜瓦尔・哈帕尔和郭金龙外，还有张素珍和马金娥。

16　新疆博物馆清理室
The washing room at Xinjiang Museum

DETERGENTS AND EQUIPMENT USED IN CLEANING

DETERGENTS

In cleaning textiles excavated from Zaghunluq, the detergent used is a non-ionic surfactant. Dissolved in water, it exists in a highly stable non-ionic form with the ability to withstand the influence of electrolytes, as well as the influence of acids and alkaloids. Its cleaning capacity is relatively good, and it is well able to get rid of stains, resist static electricity, kill bacteria, and protect colloids. Moreover, it is a relatively safe way to clean ancient textiles.

EQUIPMENT

Our museum has three kinds of equipment for conservation:

Dust-collecting equipment includes: ZL1500-1 model drum-type vacuum cleaner, NK-118 model handheld vacuum cleaner, and rubber suction bulbs, YB-RX-1 child's phlegm suction unit.

Water-washing equipment includes: Wooden-framed nylon netting, WUC-D model ultrasonic cleaner with different specifications, also a movable stainless steel washing platform that can be raised and lowered (fig. 16).

Disinfecting equipment includes: MDF-792 and MDF-392 model, low-temperature freezing cabinet.

Conservation of the textiles from Zaghunluq was done by Minawar Happar and Guo Jinlong, with the help of Zhang Suzhen and Ma Jin'e.

17 拍摄前的平整工作 Arranging the textiles for after–conservation photography

第四章　扎滚鲁克纺织品珍宝

王明芳　王　博

　　在第二章中，从纺织技术的角度讲述了扎滚鲁克第二期和第三期文化墓葬出土的纺织品，主要是毛织品，还有丝织品和棉织品。为了能够清晰认识扎滚鲁克第二期和第三期文化出土纺织品的特点，选取了86件（第二期文化，1985年出土的13件、1996年出土的25件、1998年出土的35件；第三期文化，1996年出土的2件、1998年出土的11件），将它们分开以节的形式来介绍，即第一节介绍第二期文化墓葬出土的纺织品珍宝，第二节介绍第三期文化墓葬出土的纺织品珍宝。同时，又按发掘时间为序，即1985年、1996年、1998年发掘的墓葬，并且以墓葬为单元，以其早晚时间排序分别介绍。

一　第二期文化墓葬出土纺织品珍宝

　　在这里选取了第二期文化25座墓葬纺织品，墓葬分别是1985年发掘的3座墓葬（85QZM2~85QZM4）；1996年发掘的14座墓葬（96QZIM100、96QZIM71、96QZIM69、96QZIM99、96QZIM68、96QZIM64、96QZIM14、96QZIM4、96QZIIM2、96QZIM65、96QZIM59、96QZIM55、96QZIM54、96QZIM34）；1998年发掘的8座墓葬(98QZIM113、98QZIM136、98QZIM103、98QZIM114、98QZIM147、98QZIM139、98QZIM129、98QZIM124)。要介绍的纺织品有73件，其中毛织品66件，丝织品6件，棉织品1件。

By Wang Mingfang, Wang Bo

TEXTILE TREASURES OF ZAGHUNLUQ

In Chapter 2, we described the Zaghunluq textiles excavated from Second- and Third-period culture graves from a weaving-technology point of view. Most of them are woolen textiles, but there are also silk and cotton ones. In order to understand these textiles more fully, we have selected 86 items for presentation below. Of these, Second-period culture examples include 13 excavated in 1985, 25 excavated in 1996, and 35 excavated in 1998 (total of 73), while Third-period culture examples include 2 excavated in 1996, and 11 excavated in 1998 (total of 13).

We have divided the 86 representative textiles into two sections. The first describes Second-period culture textiles and the second describes Third-period culture textiles. We have ordered each section according to date of excavation, i.e., by graves excavated in 1985, 1996, and 1998. Textiles are then discussed according to the grave from which they were excavated, and the graves are listed in what we believe is chronological order.

TEXTILES EXCAVATED FROM SECOND-PERIOD CULTURE GRAVES

We selected textiles from 25 Second-period culture graves. Listed by the year they were excavated, the graves are as follows:

1985: 3 graves (85QZM2–85QZM4). 1996: 14 graves (96QZIM100, 96QZIM71, 96QZXIM69, 96QZIM99, 96QZIM68, 96QZIM64, 96QZIM14, 96QZIM4, 96QZIIM2, 96QZIM65, 96QZIM59, 96QZIM55, 96QZIM54, 96QZIM34). 1998: 8 graves (98QZIM113, 98QZIM136, 98QZIM103, 98QZIM114, 98QZIM147, 98QZIM139, 98QZIM129, 98QZIM124).

We describe 73 textiles from these graves, of which 66 are woolen textiles, 6 are made of silk, and 1 of cotton.

（一） 1985 年发掘墓葬出土纺织品珍宝（第四章图 1~13）

1985 年发掘的 5 座墓葬，皆位于 1996 年南西区第一发掘点，属第二期文化早段。其中 85QZM3~85QZM5 三座墓葬形制上没有大的变化，为长方形竖穴土坑墓。85QZM2 与 85QZM1 同处一个很大的墓圹，为双室墓。85QZM1 是一座婴儿墓室，小而浅。85QZM2 是长方形二层台墓室，室顶有棚盖，底部有腰坑，比较特殊。5 人葬，保存一男三女的干尸，其中两具干尸保存得相当完好。1 号为男尸，上身穿棕色开襟毛布长袍，下身穿棕色毛布裤。2 号女尸，上身穿红色套头毛布长袍。

这里介绍的 1985 年发掘的三座墓葬出土纺织品，皆为毛织物，共 13 件。其中 85QZM2 号墓 4 件，85QZM3 号墓 2 件，85QZM4 号墓 7 件。

85QZM2 墓曾取样进行 ^{14}C 年代测定，为公元前 1010±115 年；85QZM4 墓取样进行 ^{14}C 年代测定，年代为公元前 740±120 年。前者测年时间上有些偏早。

EXCAVATED IN 1985: 13 TEXTILES FROM 3 GRAVES (CAT. NOS 1–13)

The five graves excavated in 1985 were all in the 1996 southwest region's first excavation site. All belonged to the early phase of Zaghunluq Second-period culture.

Among them, graves 85QZM3 to 85QZM5 were similar in structure. All were rectangular vertical-shaft type earthen graves. 85QZM2 and 85QZM1 were located in a large grave area or precinct, and were in fact a double-chamber grave. 85QZM1 was the grave of a child, small and shallow. 85QZM2 was a rectangular two-tiered platform-type of grave, with covering and with a floor with a waisted pit, so it was somewhat special. Five people were buried in this grave. The mummies of one man and three women were preserved, among which two mummies were very well preserved. Person #1 was male, wearing a brown-colored long woolen robe that opened in front, and brown-colored woolen cloth pants. Person #2 was female, wearing a long pullover gown made of red woolen cloth.

The following describes thirteen textiles that came from three of the five graves mentioned above. All of these textiles were made of woolen cloth. Four were excavated from Grave 85QZM2, two from Grave 85QZM3, and seven from Grave 85QZM4.

Samples were taken from 85QZM2 for carbon-14 testing, which resulted in a date of 1010 BCE ± 115 years. Carbon-14 testing of samples from 85QZM4 yielded a date of 740 BCE ± 120 years. We feel that the first date may be on the early side.

蓝地红条带纹毛布单（85QZM2:5）

全长 126 厘米，宽 59 厘米。边穗长 7 厘米。

长方形。一幅毛布，保存两面幅边，幅宽 59 厘米。平纹组织，羊毛很细，经密 8 根／厘米，纬密 7 根／厘米。经纱 Z 捻，纬纱 S 捻。经纱蓝、红、棕三种色，分区，显蓝色地红、棕色条带纹。

另外，两经缘边[1]宽 0.7 厘米，经纱为并股纱，[2]显条带纹。红色条带纹，宽、窄有些变化，分别为 2.3、1.3 厘米。棕色条带纹，处于两侧幅边缘，宽 1.7 厘米。条带纹为红、蓝两种色的纬纱交织而成，蓝色为纱，红色为 2 根 S 双捻线。条带纹显蓝、红相间的短条纹饰（图 1）。

边穗，穗的粗细有些差别，粗的，为 6 根 Z 重捻；细的，4 根 Z 重捻。

1

1. 经边，指经头或经尾部分，多数织纺品无法区分经头和经尾。
2. 并股，皆指两根纱的并股。

1 组织图 Warp end band

WOOLEN CLOTH WITH BLUE GROUND AND RED STRIPES (85QZM2:5)

Full length 126 cm, width 59 cm. Fringe on ends 7 cm long.

Rectangular. The woolen cloth preserves both selvages, the loom width is 59 cm. The cloth is a tabby weave, made from fine wool with a warp thread count of 8 ends per cm; and a weft thread count of 7 picks per cm.

Warp threads are Z-spun, weft threads are S-spun. The warp yarn is blue, red, and brown, in sections, creating red and brown-colored stripes on a blue ground. The red stripes vary somewhat in width, from 2.3 to 1.3 cm. The brown stripes are at the two selvages and are 1.7 cm wide.

In addition, the two warp end bands are 0.7 cm wide each (fig. 1). It is impossible to distinguish which is the starting and which the finishing edge. For both edges, the warp ends are doubled. The blue and red pattern as shown by the weft is the result of a color-and-weave effect, resulting in alternatively blue and red, short vertical stripes. The blue weft is simple yarn, the red is S-plied from two Z-spun ends.

Fringe threads are of varying thickness. The heaviest consist of 6 single ends re-plied in Z direction, from S-plied yarns; the finest are made from 4 ends, S-plied and Z re-plied.

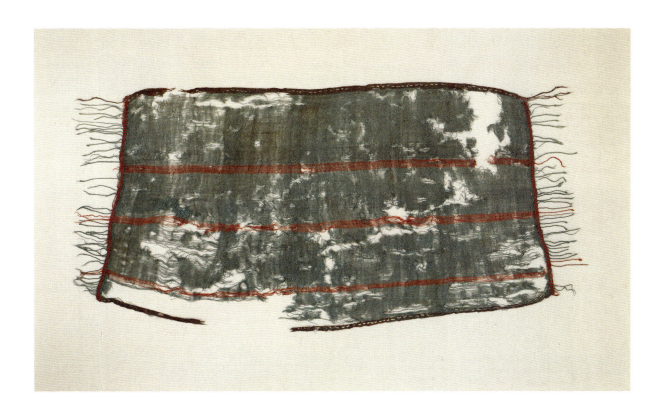

129

棕色开襟毛布长袍（85QZM2:10）

袍身长 142 厘米，肩袖通宽 167 厘米。[3] 袖长 44 厘米，袖口宽 12 厘米，肩袖口宽 25 厘米。[4] 肩宽 79~81 厘米，下摆宽 108 厘米。

袍身呈筒状，宽大，自胸部以下至下摆呈渐宽形式，开襟，为宽松式大袍服。袖呈梯形，肩袖较宽，袖口窄。

袍身左、右各为一幅毛布，前后对折，后背缝合，前面开襟。两袖各为一幅毛布，上下对折，下部缝合。毛布呈棕色，保存两面幅边，幅宽 54（袍身）、52.5（袖）厘米，袍身毛布全长 284 厘米。下摆前、后和袖口缘边，分别织出宽 15、8.5 厘米的红色边饰。袍身毛布为专门纺织的袍服布料，没有剪裁。缝制袍服，依据形制的需求，以向内折卷多少的变化去适宜服饰。袍身毛布在肩至胸的地方，略向内折卷，下摆则是毛布本身的幅宽。

窄袖，袖口部分向里折卷要多一些，肩袖口则比较少（图 1）。[5]

羊毛比较细，为 3/3 Z 斜纹毛布（图 2），经密 4 根／厘米，纬密 24 根／厘米。经纱 Z 捻，纬纱 S 捻。

襟边、后领和肩袖皆饰绞编绦（图 3），宽 0.5 厘米，在后领中部绞编绦折成"8"字形相交。下摆和袖口缘边皆为捻线绳饰边。

2

---

3 肩袖通宽，包括两袖的长和肩宽。
4 肩袖口宽，指肩部位置的袖口宽。
5 本书所用服装结构图皆由万芳绘制，在此表示感谢。

2 毛布 Woolen cloth

LONG GOWN WITH OPEN FRONT MADE FROM BROWN WOOLEN CLOTH (85QZM2:10)

The gown is 142 cm long, measuring 167 cm from the end of one sleeve across the chest to the end of the other sleeve (overall sleeve-and-shoulder width). The sleeves are 44 cm long, with 12-cm-wide cuffs, the armscyes are 25 cm high. The shoulder is between 79 and 81 cm wide, and the bottom border or hem width 108 cm.

The gown is tubular in shape, of comfortable width, and flaring out slightly from the chest to be somewhat wider at the bottom than at the top. It is open in the front and is a loose-fitting form of large robe. The sleeves have a trapezoid shape, wide at the shoulder and progressively narrower towards the cuff.

The left and right sides of the gown are each made of one piece of woven cloth, which was folded over the shoulder to form front and back. They are stitched together along the center back seam, the front is left open. Also each sleeve is made from one piece of woolen woven cloth, folded in half, with an underarm seam. The woolen cloth is brownish in color and preserves both selvages; the loom with varies from 54 cm (body sections) to 52.5 cm (sleeves). The full length of the fabric used for the gown's body is 284 cm. Red borders, 15 and 8.5 cm wide, were woven into the bottom of the gown and the bottom of the sleeves. The pieces of the robe had been woven specifically for the robe; there was no cutting. Robes of this purpose-woven nature had extra fabric folded in to the inside at sleeves to an appropriate degree depending on the shape of the garment. The cloth of the robe, from the shoulder to the chest, was folded slightly inwards whereas at the bottom of the gown the width corresponded to the full woven piece of cloth. Narrow sleeves and cuffs required that relatively more cloth had to be folded to the inside at cuffs and relatively less at the shoulder opening (fig. 1)[1].

2

---

1   All the diagrams in the book have been drawn by Ms Wan Fang to whom we would like to express our sincere thanks.

3 绞编带 Decorative braid

Fairly fine wool was used, woven in a 3/3 Z twill woolen cloth (fig. 2), with 4 warp ends per cm and 24 weft picks per cm. Warp yarn is Z-spun; weft is S-spun.

Along the front edges of the garment, along the back neckline, and along the armscye, there is a decorative braid, 0.5 cm wide (detail 3). At the center back of the neck it is folded to a figure-eight loop. The lower edge of the garment and the cuffs are adorned with twisted yarn piping.

2

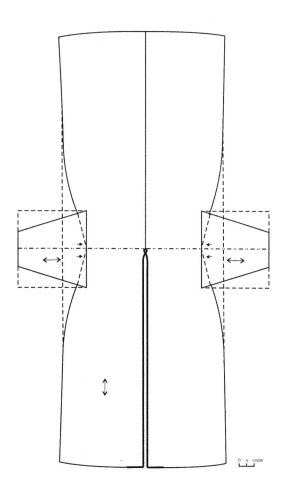

0 5 10cm

1 结构图 Cut and construction diagram

白色斜纹毛布直筒裤（85QZM2:33-1）

裤长 128 厘米，腰宽 60 厘米，腿口宽 29.5 厘米，裆高 31 厘米。

直筒裤。两条裤褪及腰各为一幅毛布，由外向内纵向对折，[6] 加裆缝制（图1）。

两幅毛布皆保存两面幅边，幅宽 60 厘米，看不到裁剪痕迹，是专门用来缝制裤服的毛布。毛布 1/2 Z 斜纹，羊毛中等粗。经、纬纱皆 Z 捻。经密 5 根／厘米，纬密 33 根／厘米（图2）。

裤腿口为捻线绳收边，裤腰口是毛边。

裤裆，残缺严重，对折呈阶梯式三角形，展开呈阶梯"十"字形毛布。长 62 厘米，宽不清。裆也是 1/2 Z 斜纹毛布，经、纬纱皆 Z 捻。经密 7 根／厘米、纬密 36 根／厘米，纬纱的疏密不稳定，与裤身毛布相比，密度有些变化。裤裆的毛布也是专门纺织。

3

STRAIGHT TUBULAR PANTS MADE FROM WHITE WOOLEN TWILL (85QZM2:33-1)

Length of pants 128 cm, width at waist 60 cm, width of trouser legs 29.5 cm, height of crotch 31 cm.

Each leg-and-waist part of these straight tubular pants is one piece of cloth, folded lengthwise, i.e. parallel to the warp, with a crotch sewn in between them (fig. 1). Both trouser legs preserve the two selvages. The fabric has a loom width of 60 cm. No traces of cutting can be seen, so the cloth was specifically made for the pants.

Woolen cloth: 1/2 Z twill, of medium-size yarn. Both warp and weft are Z-spun. The warp thread count is 5 ends per cm; the weft thread count is 33 picks per cm (fig. 2).

The trouser legs have twisted cords along the edge; the waist opening is left unfinished.

Damage to the crotch was severe. The fabric making up the crotch resembles a lozenge with stair-stepped edges, which was then folded into a triangular shape. The entire crotch piece is 62 cm long and of uncertain width, given the damage. The crotch is also 1/2 Z twill woolen cloth, Z-spun for both warp and weft threads. Its warp thread count is 7 ends per cm, weft is generally 36 picks per cm. The thread count for the weft of the crotch is variable, more variable than for that of the pants themselves. The cloth for the crotch was also woven specifically to shape.

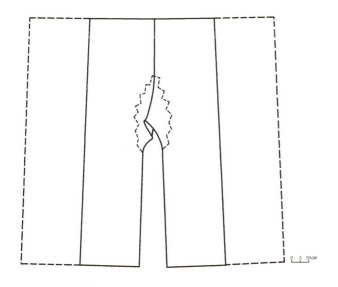

1 结构图
Cut and construction diagram

2 组织图
Detail: Woolen cloth and seam

3

135

编织毛绦裙（85QZM2:38）

展开，宽 120 厘米，长 29 厘米。

由 27 根编织毛绦横向缝缀连结而成，[7] 穿着时围绕在腰上即可。

自上而下（1 ~ 27 根）：其中第 1、3、5、7、9、11、13、15、17、19、21、23、25、27 根，共十四根编织绦，组织和用色相同，是红色斜编毛绦。由 3 根 Z 捻的并股纱线，2/2 斜编而成。毛绦宽、窄有些变化，宽 0.6、0.8、1 厘米不等。红色斜编毛绦数量多，处于菱格纹编织毛绦和波纹编织毛绦之间，起到一个连结的作用。

第 2、6、10、14、18、22、26 根，共七根编织绦，组织和用色相同，为菱格纹编织毛绦。毛绦宽、窄也有些变化，宽 1.3、1.4、1.5 厘米。用蓝、白、红三种色、2 根 S 双捻纱线，1/1 绞编而成（图 1）。

第 4、8、12、16、20、24 根，共六根编织绦，组织和用色相同，为波纹编织毛绦。毛绦的宽、窄也存在些变化，宽 1.3、1.2、1.4 厘米。用蓝、橘黄、红、酱紫四种色 2 根 S 双捻纱线，1/1 绞编（图 2）。

编织绦的羊毛中等粗。缝线是棕色，2 根 S 双捻纱，羊毛色有些杂。

7 横向缝缀，指顺纬纱方向缝缀。

1 菱格纹编织毛绦 Diamond-patterned woolen ribbed twining braid

2 波纹编织毛绦 Wave-patterned woolen ribbed twining braid

SKIRT MADE OF BRAIDED WOOLEN BANDS (85QZM2:38)

Width when opened out: 120 cm. Height 29 cm.

The skirt is made up of 27 braided woolen bands aligned horizontally and sewn together. It may have been worn by simply wrapping the garment around the waist.

There are 27 braids from top to bottom (1 to 27). Among these, 1, 3, 5, 7, 9, 11, 13, 15, 17, 19, 21, 23, 25, and 27, i.e. altogether fourteen bands, have similar structure and use of colors, namely twill oblique interlacing and red colored wool. They are made of tripled Z-spun threads, in a 2/2 twill structure, and their width varies, from 0.6 to 0.8 to 1 cm. The red bands are dominating in the skirt, they are placed in between braids with diamond patterns and others with wave patterns (see below), and serve a connecting function.

Braids 2, 6, 10, 14, 18, 22, and 26, altogether seven bands, also all employ the same structure and coloring and are diamond-patterned woolen braids. Their width also varies, from 1.3 to 1.4 to 1.5 cm. Three colors are used, blue, white, and red, and the yarn is S-plied from 2 Z-spun ends, worked in 1/1 ribbed twining (fig. 1).

Braids 4, 8, 12, 16, 20, and 24 (six bands altogether), are again similar to each other and use a wave pattern. Width varies from 1.2 to 1.3 to 1.4 cm. The coloration is blue, tangerine-orange, red, and dark purple. The S-plied threads, from 2 Z-spun ends, are worked in 1/1 ribbed twining (fig. 2).

The textile uses medium-weight woolen yarn. The thread used for sewing is S-plied from 2 ends, of varying shades of brown.

棕地挖花羊、骆驼纹残毛毯（85QZM3:10）

2片，长86厘米，残幅宽53厘米，边穗长9厘米。

经拼对，呈长方形。毛毯显棕红色，平纹组织，经、纬纱皆Z捻。经密6根／厘米，纬密4根／厘米。

纬纱主色是棕色，由红色和棕色羊毛混捻，其中红色羊毛较多，所以有些泛红色。棕色羊毛是原色，红色羊毛则是染色。所以，纬纱是先染后捻。经纱为棕色。

在毛毯的经边织有宽5厘米的红带纹，带纹处的经线为两根并股，纬纱为红色。

边穗残，为绞编带形式，由延伸下来的经线编织。带较窄，宽0.4厘米；保存完整的一条，长9厘米。绞编带里还夹杂着一股（2根纱）红色线。

在平纹地上纬向挖花，组织基本稳定，主要以1/3挖花（图1）：背面显示，一根经线下压2、3根挖花线。挖花有对三角纹、羚羊纹（七只，其中两只残）、骆驼纹等。对三角纹分布于毛毯的中间，因残缺严重，花纹拼对不很准确，似斜向排列，又似横向错位排列。对三角纹边框为白色和橘黄色，白色对三角纹内填红色，橘黄色对三角纹内填蓝色。羚羊纹主要分布于经缘边，高11厘米，宽7.5厘米，有白、红、橘黄等三色。羚羊的眼睛由蓝、红色作点缀。羊角大且呈曲弯状，腿作立式。

在毛布毯面上有两块补丁（29厘米×7.5厘米，27厘米×11.5厘米），一块补丁上有三排骆驼，每排两峰，共六峰骆驼，有一峰骆驼纹保存得比较好。昂首，前腿作跪状，后腿作立式，短尾下垂。骆驼也是三色，眼睛也是由蓝、红色点缀。驼峰显得比较高。一块补丁上皆为对三角纹。

BROWN WOOLEN CLOTH WITH BROCADED SHEEP AND CAMELS (85QZM3:10)

The fragment is in two pieces, full height 86 cm, width of remaining portions 53 cm, with fringe of 9 cm.

The fragments were pieced together in warp direction to result in a rectangular shape. The cloth is of reddish-brown color, woven in tabby, with both warp and weft Z-spun. The warp thread count is 6 ends per cm, weft is 4 picks per cm.

The primary color of the weft yarn was made by spinning reddish and brownish sheep's wool together. Red predominated so the overall impression was reddish. Brown (*zong*) is a natural wool color; red was the result of dyeing. Wool for the weft threads therefore was first dyed then spun. Warp threads used the natural brown color.

At one warp end of the cloth is a 5-cm-wide red woven band (fig. 1). The warp threads here are doubled, and weft threads are red.

The fringes are mostly gone, but were created by twining the warp threads extending over the edge of the fabric. The braid was fairly narrow – 0.4 cm in width. Only one strand of fringe is preserved in its entirety and is 9 cm long. Two red threads are introduced within the braid.

Brocaded supplementary weft threads (*wa hua*) display the pattern on a tabby foundation; the weave is basically steady and mainly uses three-span floats (1/3) to reveal the pattern (fig. 1). The reverse side shows that two or three pattern weft picks are passing under the same warp thread. The pattern consists of opposing triangles or hourglass shapes (a little like the ancient Chinese character for 'five'); antelopes (seven of them, among which two are fragmentary), camels, and so on. The hourglass shapes are distributed over the center area of the cloth. Due to loss of parts of the textile, the pattern elements do not meet up exactly. In some places, they seem arrayed in a slanting direction but in others they seem lined up in horizontal order. The hourglass shapes are outlined in white or tangerine-orange. Red fills the insides of the white triangles; blue fills the inside of tangerine-orange shapes. The antelope patterns are mainly distributed along the warp ends. They are 11 cm tall and 7.5 cm wide. They are woven in white, red, and tangerine-orange with eyes woven in blue and red. Their horns are large and wavy, and their legs are straight.

There are two patches on the woolen cloth (29 × 7.5 cm, 27 × 11.5 cm). Three rows of camels adorn one of the patches, each row having two camels in it. One of the camels is comparatively well preserved. Its head is raised and its two front legs seem to be kneeling while its back legs are straight. A short tail hangs downwards. The camels too are depicted in three colors and their eyes are also blue and red. The humps seem exaggeratedly tall. The other patch is composed completely of hourglass shapes.

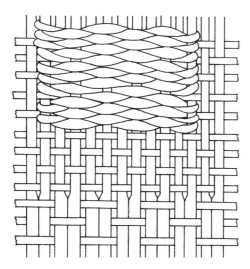

1 组织图
Warp–end band, tabby ground, brocaded pattern

棕地螺旋三角纹毛绣毯残片 (85QZM3:12)

　　大、小两片拼对：大片，长 30 厘米，宽 39.9 厘米；小片长 23 厘米，宽 23 厘米。大片是两幅毛布缝合，其中一幅保存两面幅边，幅宽 36 厘米。

　　毛毯残缺严重，地色为棕地和红地两种。有可能棕地部分是毯的缘边，而红地是毛毯的中间部分。

　　经纱白色，纬纱分棕和红两种色，分区。其中棕纱羊毛为酱紫和红色羊毛的混捻纱，其中酱紫色羊毛相对多一些，是在棕色羊毛上又染了红色。红色羊毛量少，由白色羊毛染红色而成。所以，整个棕色羊毛纱显酱紫色。

　　羊毛中等粗，经、纬纱皆 Z 捻。2/2 Z 斜纹毛布。经密 6 根 / 厘米，纬密 44 根 / 厘米。

　　刺绣处于棕地上，宽 8 厘米，为锁针绣，绣线有蓝、红、白、黄、棕黄等五色，为 S 双捻线（图 1）。

　　大、小片毛绣毯的刺绣图案，大体上都是螺旋三角纹，排列上略有些变化。大片上的图案，是两排平行的螺旋三角纹。上、下排纹样相似，由单个的三角纹和螺旋纹构成一个纹样单元，或中间是螺旋纹，两侧各有一个三角纹构成一个纹样单元，连续的平行排列。螺旋纹是两种色，色线的组合有红和黄、红和白、红和蓝、红和棕黄等。螺旋纹两侧的三角纹有些变化，分两种形式，一种是单色线的平行线纹，由长及短构成三角纹效果；一种是螺旋纹延伸出来的线，作为三角纹的外框线，内填竖向的平行短线而成。

　　小片毛绣的刺绣图案，也是两排纹样。上排，较宽，是由不同色线刺绣出的两个由一组螺旋三角纹构成的大三角纹，上下、反向重叠形成一个不很完整的纹样单元（在这里可以看成是螺旋三角纹和三角螺旋纹的重叠），再由下一个螺旋三角纹补缺，带有交错连续分布的效果。下排，则是以涡旋三角纹为单元纹样的连续排列，所以比较窄。

BROWN WOOLEN CLOTH WITH EMBROIDERED WHORLS AND TRIANGLES (85QZM3:12)

The fragment has been reconstructed from two pieces of different size. The large fragment is 30 cm high, 39.9 cm wide. The small is 23 cm high, 23 cm wide. The large piece is formed by sewing two woolen cloths together, of which one retains both selvages. The piece had a loom width of 36 cm.

The object is substantially damaged. Its ground is both brown and red, and it is possible that the brown areas formed the edges of the cloth while the red formed its center.

The warp yarn is white; weft is divided into brown and red sections. The brown is formed by spinning dark purple and red wool together. The dark purple color was created by dyeing naturally brown wool with a red dye while the red color was created by dyeing white wool with red dye. Dark purple fibers are predominating, and thus the overall color of the brown yarn is deep purple.

The wool of the cloth is of medium weight, with both warp and weft Z-spun, woven in a 2/2 Z twill. The warp thread count is 6 ends per cm, weft is 44 picks per cm.
The embroidery is on the brown areas only; it is 8 cm wide and done in chain stitch. Embroidery threads used come in five colors, blue, red, white, yellow, and brownish-yellow, all are S-plied from two ends (fig. 1).

6

143

Most of the design on both the large and small fragments of the textile is composed from whorls and triangles, but there are variations in the line-up. The pattern on the large piece includes two parallel rows of whorls and triangles. The pattern elements constituting the upper and lower rows are similar, with the first pattern unit formed by one whorl and one triangle, followed by pattern units formed by a whorl with triangles on either side, the latter units continuing along in parallel fashion. The whorls are in two colors, and the color combinations of threads include red and yellow, red and white, red and blue, red and brown, and so on. The triangles on either side of the whorls come in two shapes or forms. One is done in a continuous sequence of lines with increasing lengths making up the triangles. The other is made of extensions of threads from the whorl patterns, which are used as the outer framework of the triangle. Inside, short parallel vertical lines form the triangle.

The embroidery on the smaller fragment is also executed in two parallel rows. The upper row of motifs, slightly wider, shows a large triangular pattern worked in several colors that itself is composed of whorls and triangles. The upper and lower parts oppose each other in direction and overlap, forming a pattern unit that is not complete any more (but one can still see it is a pattern repeat consisting of a whorl-and-triangle element overlapping with a triangle-and-whorl). The next whorl-and-triangle element follows without a gap, resulting in a continuous intertwining pattern arrangement. The lower row is composed of whorl-and-triangle units following each other in a line, therefore it is comparatively narrow.

1 组织图 Chain stitch embroidery

红地羊角纹缂毛绦残毛布裙 (85QZM4:6)

展开，长 85 厘米，裙腰宽 91 厘米。

由四幅毛布、一幅缂织羊角纹毛绦和两条编织毛绦上、下拼接缝缀而成。依据裙腰部分较窄，下摆较宽看，可能是喇叭形毛布裙。布料，自上而下排列是：黄色毛布、缂织羊角纹毛绦、酱紫色编织毛绦、红色毛布、绿色毛布、红色毛布、红色编织毛绦。

黄色毛布，残，残长 26.5 厘米。保存一面幅边，残幅宽 6 厘米。2/2 Z 斜纹组织，经密 8 根／厘米，纬密 8 根／厘米。经纱 S 捻，纬纱 Z 捻，皆两根并股。毛布较厚。

红地缂织羊角纹毛绦，保存两面幅边，长 182 厘米，幅宽 12.4 厘米。

红地，平纹，缂织有白、蓝、绿、深蓝、黄等五色几何羊角纹。羊角由弯形角和三角组成。图案，由八只羊角纹，一正一反构成一个稍变形的"凸"字，呈横向连续排列。用色，交替变换。

酱紫色编织毛绦，为绞编，保存比较完整，宽 0.4 厘米。

红色毛布，残留了四片，中间有一个接缝，其中最大的一片，残长 48 厘米。保存两面幅边，幅宽 19.8 厘米。2/2 Z 斜纹，经密 14 根／厘米，纬密 16 根／厘米。经、纬纱皆 Z 捻，两根并股。斜纹纹路清晰。

绿色毛布，残留三片，其中最大的一片，长 29.5 厘米。保存两面幅边，幅宽 22 厘米。2/2 Z 斜纹，经密 16 根／厘米，纬密 14 根／厘米。经、纬纱皆 Z 捻，两根并股。斜纹纹路清晰。

红色毛布，残留三片，其中最大的一片长 94 厘米。保存两面幅边，幅宽 21.5 厘米。2/2 Z 斜纹，经密 14 根／厘米，纬密 15 根／厘米。经、纬纱皆 Z 捻，两根并股。

红色编织毛绦，残，Z 捻纱，两根拼股，2/2 斜编。毛绦宽 0.9 厘米，最长的一条 36 厘米。

毛布裙，以红为主，兼有绿色、黄色。用色较艳。

1 组织图 Tapestry weave

WOOLEN SKIRT FRAGMENT WITH MOUNTAIN GOAT-HORN TAPESTRY BAND (85QZM4:6)

Opened out, the garment is 85 cm high and 91 cm wide.

The skirt is sewn together from four pieces of woolen cloth, a woolen tapestry band with mountain goat-horn like patterns, and two strips of braiding. Since the waist part is quite narrow and the lower part quite wide, the original garment may have been an A-line skirt. From top to bottom, the material comprising the skirt is as follows: yellow woolen cloth, tapestry-woven cloth with mountain goat-horn pattern, dark purple-colored woolen braid, red woolen cloth, green woolen cloth, red woolen cloth, red woolen braid.

A bit of remaining yellow woolen cloth at the top, above the tapestry band, is fragmentary; it is 26.5 cm long along the selvage, and has a preserved maximum width of 6 cm. The cloth is a 2/2 Z twill weave, with warp thread count of 8 ends per cm and weft also of 8 picks per cm. Warp yarn is S-spun; weft yarn is Z-spun. Both are doubled. The cloth is fairly thick.

The tapestry-woven band has a pattern of mountain goat-horns on red ground. Both selvages are preserved, the band is 182 cm long and its loom width is 12.4 cm. On red ground, the tabby-woven tapestry uses five colors, white, blue, green, deep blue and yellow, to create stylized mountain goat-horns. These horns have the shape of a curve attached to a triangle, and they are arranged in V-shapes. Each V-shape is composed of eight horns set in opposition to each other – one right side up, one upside down. These are set crosswise continuously across the band. The use of colors creates the contrast.

The dark purple braided band that follows in the sequence is relatively complete. It is twined and 0.4 cm wide.

The next band is made of red woolen cloth and preserved in four fragments. Two of them are joined together with a vertical seam in the middle. The length of the largest fragment is 48 cm. Both selvages are preserved, so the loom width of the woven fabric can be measured and is 19.8 cm. This band is woven in 2/2 Z twill weave; with a warp thread count of 14 ends per cm and weft of 16 picks per cm. Both warp and weft are Z-spun and doubled. The twill pattern shows clearly.

The green woolen cloth is in three remaining fragments, among which the largest is 29.5 cm long. It retains both selvages and the loom width of the band is 22 cm. This strip is woven in 2/2 Z twill weave, with a warp thread count of 16 ends per cm and weft of 14 picks per cm. The warp and weft yarn is all Z-spun and doubled. The twill pattern shows clearly.

The red woolen cloth is in three remaining pieces, the largest of which is 94 cm long. It retains both selvages as well, and the loom width of the band is 21.5 cm. It is woven in 2/2 Z twill weave.

The warp thread count is 14 ends per cm, weft is 15 picks per cm. Warp and weft are both Z-spun and doubled.

The last band is a red braid, fragmentary, using Z-spun doubled yarn worked in 2/2 twill oblique interlacing. This braid is 0.9 cm wide and 36 cm long.

The skirt is predominantly red, with green and yellow used as supplementary colors. The use of colors is quite striking.

白地骆驼、野猪纹缋罽残片 (85QZM4:23)

长 37.5 厘米，宽 44 厘米。

保存两面幅边，幅宽 44 厘米。羊毛很细，手感软。2/2 Z 斜纹，经密 10 根／厘米，纬密 52 根／厘米。经、纬纱皆 Z 捻，经纱粗而疏，纬纱细而密（图 1）。幅边经线，为 2 根 S 双捻线。经边，为 4 根 S 双捻线，显线绳边效果。

仔细观察经、纬纱，感觉应该是白色，因表面有些污染而略显土黄色。在正面绘画，图案清晰。背面的彩，系渗染效果，模糊、图案不清。

绘画主要用红色，少有黄色，以线条勾勒。动物有骆驼和野猪两种，横向排列，残留四排。野猪和骆驼相间分布，给人一种行走的感觉，排与排之间的动物头向相反，即上一排向左，下一排则向右。野猪作直立状，嘴向下，呈尖或弧圆。眼睛圆，尾下垂，额部伸出一条短线，给人感觉有点像鬃。

野猪的肩部和腿上饰有红色线条，臀部绘画红色螺旋纹。同时，在野猪的身体、前后腿上也能看到用黄色画的线条，后蹄尖部位饰有黄彩。

骆驼为双峰驼，也作站立状，三角形头，也是尖嘴，短尾。骆驼的前胸和臀部绘螺旋纹和平行弧线纹，双峰上饰线条，在前、后峰和腿、臀部也能看到黄色的线条。

骆驼和野猪大小相近，都表现了前、后的一条腿，为侧面像，反映了扎滚鲁克居民早期动物绘画的艺术风格。

WHITE WOOLEN FRAGMENT WITH PAINTED CAMELS AND WILD BOARS (85QZM4:23)

Height 37.5 cm, width 44 cm.

The piece retains both selvages; the width of the woven fabric is 44 cm. The wool of this textile is very fine and feels soft to the touch. It is woven in 2/2 Z twill weave, with a warp thread count of 10 ends per cm, and weft of 52 picks per cm. Warp and weft both are Z-spun. The warp is heavy and sparse; the weft is fine and dense (fig. 1).

The outermost warp thread at the selvage is S-plied from 2 ends. The horizontal selvage is made from an S-plied thread made from four ends, with a cord-like aspect.

Careful examination of the warp and weft yarn shows that it was originally white but has been darkened to earth yellow by various kinds of stains. The pattern is painted on the right side of the fabric and very clear there. Because the color has seeped into the fabric the patterning is less clear on the reverse side.

The painting of the design is sketched in outline form and is executed primarily in red, with some yellow. It depicts two kinds of animals, camels and wild boar. They are lined up in horizontal rows, of which four remain. Camels and wild boar are distributed at regular distance, giving a sense of moving forward in a line. The direction in which the animals face alters in each row. Those in one row face left, the next one right, and so on. The wild boar stand erect, their snouts (either pointed or rounded) point downwards. Their eyes are round, their tails hang down, a short line comes from the forehead giving the impression of a short mane.

Red linear designs adorn the shoulders and legs of the wild boar and their hindquarters are accentuated with red whorls. One can also detect yellow linear painted designs on the front and back legs of the wild boar as well as yellow pigment on the rear hooves.

The camels are two-humped, and also shown standing, with triangular-shaped heads, pointed noses, and short tails. Whorl patterns are painted on their shoulders and hindquarters as well as parallel curved lines. The two humps are adorned with lines and one can again detect yellow lines on both front and back humps and legs, and on the hindquarters.

The size of the painted camels and wild boar is similar; each is shown in profile, with one front and one back leg depicted. This reflects the artistic style of the early phase of Zaghunluq animal painting.

8

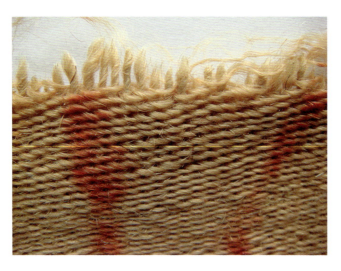

1 组织图 2/2 Z twill weave

黄地鱼纹缋罽裙残片 (85QZM4:23-1)

　　残，服饰形制不清。保存了大小不等的八片，最大的是上下横向缝合在一起的两片毛布，展开呈长方形，残长 115 厘米，残宽 56 厘米。其中上一片大，保存了两面幅边，幅宽 42 厘米。

　　这件缋罽裙残片，保存的还是比较大。从缝缀情况、纹样排列看，可能是横向围绕在腰间的筒裙。平纹，经密 12 根／厘米，纬密 11 根／厘米（图 2）。经、纬纱皆 Z 捻，羊毛较细。在两片缋罽相接处，饰有较粗的酱紫色牙线。在上片缋罽的外幅边，饰细的酱紫色牙线。细牙线，为 2 根 S 双捻线；粗牙线，为 4 根 Z 重捻线。

　　缋罽显土黄色，给人的感觉颜色比较重，应该是染色。绘画的是鱼纹，大体可以看出来是横向一字排列。保存完整两面幅边的一幅，绘四行，行与行之间的鱼身及头都呈相反方向。也就是说，中间的两排，鱼腹相对，头向相反。上下两边缘排列的鱼，则表现出鱼背相对、鱼头相反的形式（图 1）。

　　鱼纹略有些变形，鱼头大，似呈张嘴状。鱼身及尾呈弯曲状，鱼腹部绘向下凸出、连续弧线的鱼鳞纹，鱼背部也是用连续的弧线表现了鱼鳞或鱼翅的效果。鱼纹有大有小，鱼身轮廓由红线勾勒，勾勒线内的填色分两种，一是无填色，一是填酱紫色。这两种颜色的鱼纹相间排列，最大的鱼长 14 厘米，宽 8 厘米；小的长 11 厘米，宽 6 厘米。

　　在 1996 年发掘的扎滚鲁克二号墓地的 2 号墓中出土鱼骨饰珠，想来古代扎滚鲁克附近河水里应该有鱼，居民不仅捕捉鱼，而且将鱼纹应用到了服饰上。

FRAGMENT OF A YELLOW WOOLEN SKIRT PAINTED WITH FISH (85QZM4:23-1)

The piece is in eight fragments, of different sizes, but the total shape of the garment remains unclear. The two largest fragments are horizontal pieces of woolen cloth that have been sewn together to form top and bottom; opened out they have rectangular shape and extend 115 cm in length and 56 cm in height. The top piece preserves both selvages, the loom width was 42 cm.

9

Although damaged, a fairly large portion of the garment is preserved, and the seam and horizontal nature of the pattern would seem to indicate that this was perhaps a tubular skirt, worn wrapped around the waist. It is in tabby weave, with a warp thread count of 12 ends per cm, and a weft thread count of 11 picks per cm (fig. 2). Both warp and weft yarns are Z-spun and the yarn is fairly fine. A rather heavy dark purple piping thread is sewn into the seam where the pieces meet. Finer dark purple piping also adorns the upper piece of the painted cloth, on its external or outside selvage. This edging is S-plied from 2 ends. The thicker edging thread is Z re-plied from 2 S-plied yarns made from 2 ends each.

The coloring of the painted fabric is earth yellow, giving a sense of weight, and it is probably dyed. Fish patterns are painted on this, each laying horizontally. Four rows of such fish can be seen on the fragment that retains both selvages. Each row's fish are arrayed facing in opposite direction to the next row. In addition, the fish themselves are alternatingly given with either stomachs or backs up (fig. 1).

1 鱼纹局部 Fish pattern

The fish patterns vary, some being larger with seemingly open mouths. Bodies and tails are curved and curved lines scallop along their stomachs like fish scales; similar lines along the inside of the backs may be either scales or fins. There are larger and smaller fish, and all are sketched in outline form in red lines, inside which are two different treatments. One has no filling color, the other fills the outline with dark purple pigment. These two kinds of differently colored fish alternate with each other in each line. The largest fish are 14 cm long and 8 cm wide. The small ones are 11 cm long and 6 cm wide.

In 1996, decorative beads made of fish bones were found in the course of excavating grave number 2 in Cemetery #2 (96QZIIM2). It seems possible that, in ancient times, fish was dwelling in the rivers in the neighborhood of Zaghunluq. Inhabitants of Zaghunluq appear not only to have caught fish but to have used fish patterns on their clothing.

2 组织图 Painted tabby weave

白地棕条纹毛布开襟上衣 (85QZM4:26)

衣身长 73~76 厘米，肩袖通宽 143 厘米，下摆宽 88 厘米。袖长右 29 厘米，左 30 厘米；袖口宽 16.5 厘米；肩袖口宽 19.5 厘米。肩宽 84 厘米。

衣身呈直筒状，开前襟、立领、直筒、长袖。

衣身共三幅毛布：后身中间是一幅毛布，保存两面幅边，幅宽 60 厘米。后背下部有两处开叉，其距左边宽 13.5 厘米，距右边宽 14.5 厘米。前襟是两幅毛布，皆保存两面幅边，幅宽 58、57.5 厘米。左前襟宽 43.5 厘米，右前襟宽 41.5 厘米，肩部系相拼接缝合，两侧边是对折缝缀，下摆卷边。也就是说，用作前襟的左、右两幅毛布从侧面向后背纵向折过去。前襟缘边内折 1.5 厘米，加厚了襟边。其一侧襟缘边中部残留系绳，绳为 Z 捻白毛纱。

直筒袖，袖口略收。条纹呈纵向，应该是横向的对折。幅边在肩袖口部，袖口是剪裁边。袖子下面加了一块平纹三角形毛布。

立领，由一长方形的毡片缝制，毡的外表呈土黄色，里面呈深棕色。立领长 11 厘米，高 4 厘米（图 1）。

衣身为白地棕色竖条纹毛布，平纹，经、纬纱皆 Z 捻，经纱紧密，纬纱疏松。经密 10 根 / 厘米，纬密 6 根 / 厘米。纬纱白色，经纱分棕、白两种色，分区布置。条纹间宽：白色 3、4.5 厘米，棕色 0.5、2.3 厘米（图 2）。一般接近幅边是窄条纹，中间都是条带纹。

这件上衣虽然保持了不裁剪的一些特点，但是局部还是有一些变化。如领作立状，后背与前襟用三幅毛布，袖子下面加了一块平纹三角形毛布等。

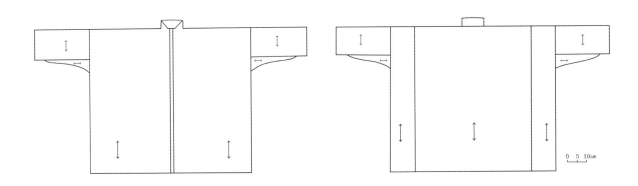

1 结构图 Cut and construction diagram

JACKET WITH OPEN FRONT MADE OF WHITE WOOLEN CLOTH WITH BROWN STRIPES (85QZM4:26)

The body of the garment is between 73 and 76 cm long, and measures 143 cm across the shoulders and both sleeves. The lower edge is 88 cm wide, the sleeves are 29 (right) and 30 (left) cm long. The cuffs are 16.5 cm wide, and the armscye is 19.5 cm high. The chest is 84 cm wide.

This jacket is a straight tubular form, open in the front, with upstanding collar and long straight sleeves. The body part is made of three pieces of woolen cloth. The middle of the back is one piece, which retains both selvages showing the fabric to be 60 cm wide. The two side back seams are at 13.5 cm distance from the left and at 14.5 cm distance from the right. The open front is made of two pieces of woolen cloth, both retaining both selvages, 58 cm in loom width for one and 57.5 cm in loom width for the other. The left side of the front is 43.5 cm wide and the right side is 41.5 cm wide. The shoulder seam is stitched closed with both sides folded in. Or, in other words, the right and left pieces of woolen cloth used for the front are folded to the back along the sides and sewn lengthwise to the center back piece, with the armscye cut into them. The bottom edge is folded in as well. The front opening is folded to the inside 1.5 cm, making it thicker. On one side of the opening is the remains of a tie, which is made of white Z-spun yarn.

10

The sleeves are straight and tubular in form, with cuffs slightly pulled in. The pattern of stripes goes vertically, because the piece is folded horizontally. The selvage is at the seam of the sleeve where it joins the body. The cuff has a cut edge. A triangular piece of woolen tabby has been inserted below the sleeve.

The standing collar is made of a rectangular piece of felt. The outside of this collar is earth yellow and the inside is deep brown. It is 11 cm long and 4 cm high (fig. 1).

The body of the jacket is striped woolen cloth with brown vertical stripes on a white ground. It is tabby weave with both warp and weft Z-spun, strong for the warp and more loosely for the weft. Warp thread count is 10 ends per cm; weft is 6 picks per cm. Weft yarn is white; warp yarn is two colors, white and brown, in different areas or stripes. The white stripes are 3 and 4.5 cm wide; the brown are 0.5 and 2.3 cm wide (fig. 2). The width of the stripes is usually narrower near the selvages and broader in the middle part of the cloth.

Although this garment still shows the characteristics of a purpose-woven garment, in places it has some variations. For example, the collar is upright, the front and back use three pieces of cloth, triangular pieces of tabby cloth have been added under the sleeves, and so on.

2 组织图 Striped tabby weave and seam

蓝色缂毛直筒裤 (85QZM4:50)

裤长 124 厘米，腰宽 55 厘米，腿口宽 19 厘米。裆高 18 厘米，宽 26.5 厘米。

近直筒裤。两条裤褪及腰各为一幅毛布，由外向内纵向对折，加裆缝制。腰部是拼对缝合。与直筒裤相比，裤腿局部有些变化。自裆以下 14 厘米处，将幅缘边向内折，并逐渐加大内折宽度，至裤腿口处内折了约 8 厘米宽。这样一来，毛布裤呈直腰、渐窄的裤腿形式。

裤腿及腰的两幅毛布，保存两面幅边，幅宽 54 厘米。2/2 斜纹，经密 7 根 / 厘米，纬密 44 根 / 厘米。经、纬纱皆 Z 捻，经纱强捻、纬纱弱捻。毛布的经边，都是两根经纱 S 双捻的线绳效果。这样，不仅使边缘结实，而且有很好的装饰效果。

毛布长 121~124 厘米。毛布中部是蓝色，长 95.5 厘米。上、下两经边缘是红色的宽带纹：腰部带纹宽 7.5 厘米，腿部带纹宽 11.5 厘米。在腿部和腰部红色宽带纹的上部，缂织出了红地的绦式纹样，宽 2.5~3 厘米。经纱棕色，较粗，纬纱红、蓝两色，分区布置，有些变化。蓝色的纬纱羊毛较细、软，缂织用毛也很细。

在红带纹处，纬纱是红色，故显出红的宽带纹。缂织花纹用色有蓝、红、棕、姜黄等四色，花纹为组合式图案，地色红色，显菱回纹和斜长方格纹，斜长方格纹内饰锯齿纹（图 1）。

裤裆毛布是独立的一片，呈阶梯十字形毛布，对折呈阶梯式三角形，长 36 厘米，宽 26.5 厘米。也是 2/2 Z 斜纹毛布，保存两面幅边，经密 9 根 / 厘米，纬密 52 根 / 厘米。较裤腿用毛布稍细一些，经边都进行了处理，即将纱头穿插在了组织里面。裤裆经纱，为黄色；纬纱，为蓝色。

1 组织图 Twill tapestry weave

STRAIGHT TUBULAR PANTS MADE OF BLUE TAPESTRY-WEAVE WOOLEN CLOTH (85QZM4:50)

Length of the pants 124 cm, width of waist 55 cm, width of trouser leg 19 cm, height of crotch 18 cm, width of crotch piece 26.5 cm.

The tubular form is nearly straight. Each of the trouser legs-cum-waist is one piece of cloth, folded lengthwise from outside to inside, with crotch sewn in. The waist simply sews the pieces together.

Compared to other straight tubular pants, here the trouser legs are slightly different. Fourteen cm down from the crotch, the selvage of the fabric is folded inwards and the size of the fold is gradually increased going down the leg. Down at the cuff, the folded-in part is 8 cm wide. Therefore, the pants have a straight waist part but the legs of gradually become narrower towards the cuffs.

The two pieces of woolen cloth that make up the legs and waist of the pants retain both selvages, the loom width is 54 cm. The cloth is woven in a 2/2 twill weave, with a warp thread count of 7 ends per cm and weft thread count of 44 picks per cm. Both warp and weft are Z-spun, the warp strongly, the weft more gently. Along both horizontal selvages the warp ends are twisted into two S-plied cord edgings. This strengthens the edges but also gives a pleasing decorative effect.

The woolen cloth is between 121 and 124 cm long. The middle part, blue, is 95.5 cm long. Above and below this are red bands: the one at the waist is 7.5 cm wide, that at the lower edge of the pants is 11.5 cm wide. Along each red band is a 2.5–3 cm wide strip of tapestry-woven decorative patterning. The warp yarn is brown and rather coarse; the weft yarn is red and blue in separate areas. The weft yarn in the blue areas is fine and soft; the yarn used for the tapestry-weave is also very fine.

The weft yarn is red in the bands, making the band look red. Yarn used for the tapestry-weave strip is blue, red, brown, and ginger-yellow; the pattern is a composite form with red ground and patterning shown in diamonds and slanted rectangles, inside which are sawtooth patterns (fig. 1).

The crotch fabric is a separate piece, shaped like a cross with stair-stepped edges. Folded over, it becomes a stair-stepped triangle on either side, 36 cm long and 26.5 cm wide. It too is a 2/2 Z twill weave woolen piece retaining both selvages. Its warp thread count is 9 ends per cm; the weft is 52 picks per cm. The cloth used for the crotch is slightly finer than that for the trouser legs; its horizontal selvages are finished by tucking the warp yarn ends back into the weave. The warp yarn of the crotch is yellow; the weft yarn is blue.

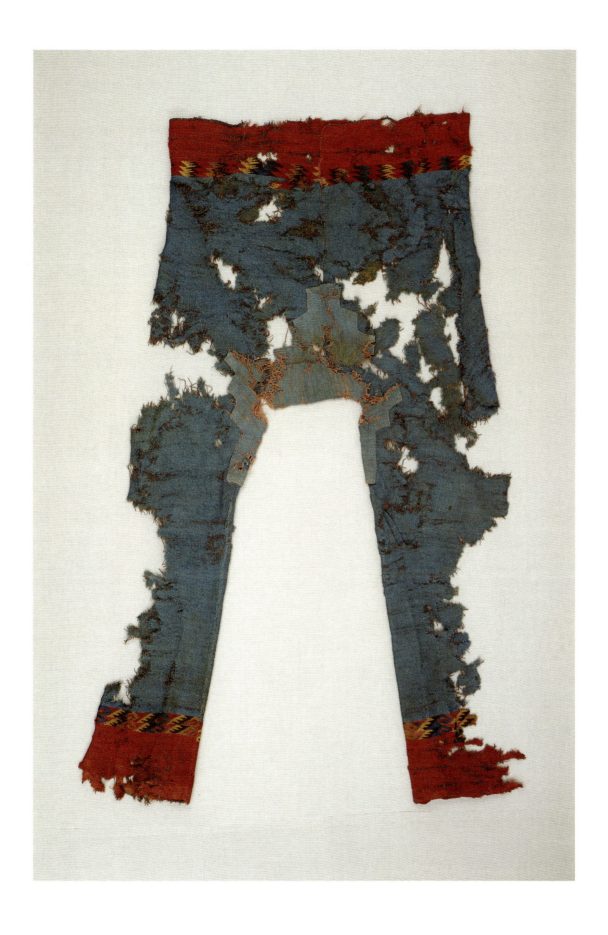

159

黄地虎、野猪纹缂罽袜残片 (85QZM4:56)

残存四片：a. 长 35 厘米，宽 11.5 厘米；b. 长 13.5 厘米，宽 28.5 厘米；c. 长 39 厘米，宽 17.5 厘米；d. 长 18 厘米，宽 18.5 厘米。

经过拼对大体呈长方形，残长 75 厘米，可以复原出两面的幅边，幅宽约 40 厘米。

在缂罽一侧幅边的局部，织出阶梯状的效果，保留了三级阶梯，有可能是袜的专用织布。

袜的形制已不清楚，分面和衬里。衬里是白色毡，表面是黄地虎、野猪纹缂罽。保护处理时剥取了毛毡。缂罽的经、纬纱皆 Z 捻，2/2 Z 斜纹。经密 10 根 / 厘米，纬密 72 根 / 厘米。经纱紧、粗，纬纱松、细。保存了经过处理的一面经边，为经纱的捻线绳边。毛很细，有点像羊绒。

毛布显黄色，感觉是染色。在缂罽正面以红色粗线条绘画动物纹样，保存了总共是九排，八排是虎纹（图 1），残留了一只野猪纹（图 2）。动物的排列，排与排之间呈反向行走状。向左行走的一排，向右行走的一排，一正一反排列很整齐。虎纹与白地骆驼、野猪纹缂罽残片（85QZM4:23，第四章图 8）上的虎纹有些相似，一排 3 只，尖状头，椭圆形眼；两条腿，腿较短，腿的肩、臀部饰螺旋纹；细长尾。用色以红彩为主，在虎的嘴、眼睛和腿爪部位，饰姜黄色（图 1）。绘画线条较均匀。织物面上有的地方有红色小点，可能是用笔过程中滴上去的，或能作为缂罽的根据之一。这从背面的颜色是渗透过去的，也可以得到说明。

野猪纹，处于缂罽的左上角，残。野猪特征比较明显，嘴较方（图 2）。

12

FRAGMENT OF A YELLOW WOOLEN SOCK WITH PAINTED TIGERS AND WILD BOARS (85QZM4:56)

The fragment is in four pieces: a. height 35 cm, width 11.5 cm; b. height 13.5 cm, width 28.5 cm; c. height 39 cm, width 17.5 cm; d. height 18 cm, width 18.5 cm.

After reconstructing and putting the pieces together, they form roughly a rectangular shape. The incomplete length is 75 cm, while, from remaining selvages, the loom width could be reconstructed to be 40 cm. Woven into the bottom right-hand corner of the piece are three 'stairsteps' or successive indentations in the fabric, which may indicate that the piece was woven specifically to be a sock.

The shape of the sock is unclear. The piece originally had a surface fabric and a lining. The lining was made of white felt. The surface fabric is yellow woolen cloth with painted tiger and wild-boar patterns. In conserving the piece, the felt was removed. Both warp and weft yarn of the wool are Z-spun, they are woven in 2/2 Z twill. The warp thread count is 10 ends per cm; weft is 72 picks per cm. The warp is tight and heavy; the weft is loose and thin. One warp edge has the warp ends twisted into a cord edging. The wool is very soft, somewhat like cashmere.

The woolen cloth is yellow and appears to have been dyed. A total of nine rows of painted wild-animal patterns have been preserved, drawn in thick lines. Eight of these rows show tigers (fig. 1), and a fragment of one wild boar remains (fig. 2). The animals give the appearance of walking along; each row is arrayed with heads in opposite direction to the row of animals above, and all are very orderly. The tigers resemble the ones on the woolen fragment with camels and wild boar painted on white ground (85QZM4:23, cat. no. 8). There are three in each row; they have pointed noses, oblong-shaped eyes, and straight short legs; the shoulders and hindquarters are decorated with whorl patterns, and they have narrow long tails. The painting is done mostly with red pigment, in smooth and regular lines. The tigers' mouths, eyes, and claws are all daubed with ginger-yellow paint (fig. 1). Small red dots appear at places on the fabric, which may have been dropped there in the course of painting. This could be evidence of the decoration having indeed been painted. Furthermore, the color seeps through to the reverse side of the fabric, which also enhances such an interpretation.

The wild boar pattern is in the upper left corner of the weaving. It is fragmentary but its qualification as wild boar is apparent, given its rather square snout (fig. 2).

1 虎纹 Tiger

2 野猪纹 Wild boar

黄地螺旋三角纹缋罽单 (85QZM4:79)

长 61 厘米，宽 59.5~56 厘米。

一幅毛布制成，保存完整的两面幅边，幅边不整齐，幅宽 59.5~56 厘米。

经边，一侧是残边，一侧残留卷边缝缀的部分。羊毛较细，经、纬纱皆 Z 捻，2/2 Z 斜纹，属纬斜纹。经疏、纬密，经密 12 根／厘米，纬密 80 根／厘米（图 1）。

缋罽表面显黄色，色比较深，应该是染色效果。绘画用色主要是红色，局部使用了红紫色彩。花纹颜色不太均匀，织物面上有红色的滴珠，应该是绘画所致。

图案呈纵向排列，主要是螺旋三角纹。由曲波线条为隔线框，应该有九排，除靠左边的一排曲波纹线条显三角弧线纹外，其余的都是线条式的曲波纹。

螺旋三角纹，将一个螺旋纹和两个三角纹组合在一起，呈一曲波式宽带。

这件缋罽的纹样繁琐，多用红彩，紫红采用的比较少。在构图上，感觉用色没有规律，紫红彩绘小、大三角纹，用红彩绘螺旋纹，也绘大、小三角纹等。有的三角纹带有小钩，纹样大小也有一些变化。

13

YELLOW WOOLEN CLOTH PAINTED IN RED WITH TRIANGULAR AND WHORL

PATTERNS (85QZM4:79)

Height 61 cm, width 59.5–56 cm.

This textile is made of one piece of woolen cloth which preserves both selvages. The selvages are uneven and the width varies from 59.5 to 56 cm. One warp end is damaged; the other retains a portion of a rolled-up hemmed edge. The wool is fairly fine; both warp and weft are Z-spun and woven in a 2/2 Z weft-faced twill weave. The warp is loose, and the weft tight: the warp thread count is 12 ends per cm; the weft thread count is 80 picks per cm (fig. 1).

The surface of the painted fabric is a fairly deep yellow which appears to be the result of dyeing. The color used in painting the pattern is mainly red with parts in red purple. The coloring of the pattern is uneven and there are spots of red color on the fabric, probably dropped there during painting.

The pattern is displayed lengthwise and is mainly whorls and triangles. Wavy lines form the boundaries of the vertical pattern rows, of which there are nine. Except for the line on the left, which has triangular arcs, all the rest of the wave patterns are continuous wavy lines. The whorl-and-triangle pattern combine always one whorl and two triangles into one unit, to form a wavy belt.

The color used for the patterning is mostly red, with only a little purple-red. In the composition, the color appears to have been used without any set regularity, purple-red was used for small and large triangles while red was used for whorls, large and small triangles. Some of the triangles have small hooks and the size of triangles is quite variable.

1 组织图 Painted woolen cloth

（二）1996年发掘墓葬出土纺织品珍宝

1996年在一、二号墓地发掘墓葬中，有92座墓属于第二期文化。这里要介绍的是14座墓葬出土的25件纺织品，推测墓葬年代的顺序是：96QZIM100、96QZIM71、96QZIM4、96QZIM65、96QZIM69、96QZIM99、96QZIM68、96QZIM64、96QZIM14、96QZIIM2、96QZIM59、96QZIM55、96QZIM54和96QZIM34。

96QZIM100墓葬（第四章图14）

位于1996年南东区发掘点。长方形竖穴土坑墓，墓向呈南北向。属第二期文化早段墓葬。

墓口长2.4米，宽1.7米。墓深1.2米。

5人葬。骨架集中在墓室的南半部。A个体，处于墓室中部，头向东正对着墓室东壁，面朝北，侧身左屈肢，两手臂屈于腹部。头戴帽，身上穿毛布衣服，脚上穿毛布鞋。B个体，处于墓室的中部偏西位置，侧身左屈肢葬。C个体，处于墓室的西南部，侧身右屈肢，头伸向D个体的身下，两手屈于腹部，上身穿红色毛布衣服。D个体，处于墓室的东南部，俯身左屈肢，身上穿着衣和裤。E个体，处于墓室的南角。墓葬填土中出土陶钵。

96QZIM71墓葬（第四章图15）

位于1996年南东区发掘点。长方形竖穴土坑墓，墓向东北—西南向。属第二期文化早段墓葬。

墓口，近圆角长方形，长3米，宽1米。

2人葬。皆仰身屈肢，双手置于腹部。A个体为男性，处于南面，头向西南。B个体为女性，处于北面。随葬器物有陶钵、角勺，出土服饰有裤、裙、上衣等。

EXCAVATED IN 1996: 25 TEXTILES FROM 14 GRAVES

Ninety-two of the graves excavated in 1996 in Cemeteries #1 and #2 belonged to Second-period culture. Below, we describe 25 textiles excavated from 14 of these graves. We propose the following order of dating of the graves: 96QZIM100, 96QZIM71, 96QZIM4, 96QZIM65, 96QZIM69, 96QZIM99, 96QZIM68, 96QZIM64, 96QZIM14, 96QZIIM2, 96QZIM59, 96QZIM55, 96QZIM54 and 96QZIM34.

GRAVE 96QZIM100 (CAT. NO. 14)

Located in the 1996 southeast region's excavation site, this was a rectangular vertical-shaft type earthen grave with north-south orientation. It belongs to the early phase of Second-period culture. The entryway was 2.4 m long, 1.7 m wide, and the grave was 1.2 m deep.

Five people were buried in it. Skeletons were concentrated in the southern half of the grave chamber. Person A was in the central part of the grave chamber with head towards the east, directly pointing in the direction of the east wall. The face was looking towards the north, the body was on its side with legs in flexed position to the left and with the two arms folded over the belly. The head wore a hat, the body wore woolen clothing, and the feet were in woolen cloth boots.

Person B was located slightly to the west of the middle of the chamber. It too was on the side with legs flexed to the left. Person C was in the southwest part of the chamber, on its right side with flexed legs, the head was pointing in the direction of Person D. Its two hands were over the belly; its upper body was wearing a red-colored woolen garment. Person D was in the southeast part of the chamber, lying prostrate with legs flexed to the left. It was wearing both gown and pants. Person E was in the south corner of the grave. A ceramic bowl or *bo* was unearthed from the disturbed earth of the grave.

GRAVE 96QZIM71 (CAT. NO. 15)

Located in the 1996 southeast region's excavation site, this was a rectangular vertical-shaft type earthen grave. The grave was oriented northeast-southwest. It belongs to the early phase of Second-period culture.

The grave opening was rectangular with rounded corners, 3 meters long and 1 meter wide.

Two people were buried in this grave. Both were on their backs with legs flexed and hands folded over their bellies. Person A was male, located in the southern part of the grave, with head towards the southwest. Person B was female, located in the north. Accompanying burial items included a ceramic bowl *bo*, a horn ladle; excavated textiles included pants, a skirt, a jacket, and so on.

96QZIM69 墓葬（第四章图 16）

位于 1996 年南东区发掘点。长方形竖穴土坑墓，墓向近南北向。属第二期文化早段墓葬。

墓口长 2.55 米，宽 1.5 米。墓深 0.83 米。

单人葬。墓主人为青年男性，头向北，仰身直肢，两手臂屈于腹部，两脚腕上有系带，保存着残毛布衣服和裤。葬具为羊毛毡，平铺在尸体下面。

96QZIM99 墓葬（第四章图 17）

位于 1996 年南东区发掘点。长方形竖穴土坑墓，近东西向。属第二期文化早段墓葬。

墓口长 2.4 米，宽 1.5 米。墓深 0.8 米。

在墓室填土中出土少量毛织物和散乱的人骨架。

96QZIM68 墓葬（第四章图 18）

位于 1996 年南东区发掘点。长方形竖穴土坑墓，墓向东南—西北向。属第二期文化早段墓葬。

墓口长 2.85 米，宽 3.2 米。墓深 1.07 米。

2 人葬。A 个体处于西南，为成年男性，仰身屈肢，两手臂屈于腹部，头向东南。B 个体处于东北，为成年女性。保存有残服饰，裤、袍、上衣等，随葬器物有角勺、刻纹骨板。

GRAVE 96QZIM69 (CAT. NO. 16)

Located in the 1996 southeast region's excavation site, this was a rectangular vertical-shaft type earthen grave, with grave orientation nearly north–south. It belongs to the early phase of Second-period culture.

The entryway of the grave was 2.55 meters long, and its width was 1.5 meters. The depth of the grave was 0.83 meters.

One person was buried in this grave, a young male. He lay on his back with legs stretched out, head towards the north, hands folded over the belly, and he wore strings on his ankles. He still wore fragments of woolen clothing and pants. Grave goods included a felt piece made of sheep's wool, spread out under the person's body.

GRAVE 96QZIM99 (CAT. NO. 17)

Located in the 1996 southeastern region's excavation site. This was a rectangular vertical-shaft type earthen grave with a nearly east–west orientation. It belongs to the early period of Second-period culture. The grave opening was 2.4 meters long and 1.5 meters wide, and the grave was 0.8 meters deep.

A few woolen fragments and scattered bones were found in the disturbed earth filling the grave chamber.

GRAVE 96QZIM68 (CAT. NO. 18)

Located in the 1996 southeast region's excavation site, this grave was a rectangular vertical-pit type earthen grave, with a southeast–northwest orientation. It belongs to the early phase of Second-period culture.

The grave opening was 2.85 cm long and 3.2 m wide, and the grave was 1.07 m deep.

Two people were buried in this grave. Person A was in the southwest and was a male adult. He was lying on his back with flexed legs and arms folded over his belly, with head facing southeast. Person B was located in the northeast and was an adult woman. Fragments of clothing have been preserved: pants, a gown, and a jacket. Grave goods included a horn ladle and a bone 'board' carved with designs.

96QZIM64 墓葬（第四章图 19~20）

位于 1996 年南西区第二发掘点。单墓道长方形竖穴棚架墓，墓向呈东西向。

墓室呈长方形，墓道处于墓室的北角，与墓室的北壁平齐，形成了直柄的刀形。墓道有二层台，分三级依次下降，并在墓室壁上挖了一个脚窝。

墓室东西长 3 米，宽 2.5 米。墓深 2.28 米。室底中部有粗立柱，东北角有一个小棚架。在小棚架下，发现砺石、陶瓶、角杯、残弓、木盖、钻木、捕鸭器、木带扣、铁块、木盘及一些织物。

17 人葬。这里选用了 H 个体的服饰，H 个体为成年男性。属第二期文化早段墓葬。

96QZIM14 墓葬（第四章图 21~22）

位于南西区 1996 年第二发掘点。单墓道长方形竖穴棚架墓，墓向呈东西向。

墓室长 5 米，宽 3.6 米。深 1.4 米。

19 人葬。其中中年 15 人，男性 4 人，女性 11 人。另有 2 个小孩，其余 2 人性别不明。随葬器物有单耳罐、砺石、木弓、打纬木刀、木竖箜篌、弓囊附件、木梳、木腰牌、长齿木梳、木纺轮、木拐杖、木碗、长方形木盒、绊马毛索、漆木棒等。另外，还有石珠、玻璃珠、铜环、加工木件、苇秆束捆、帽、毛布袋。

取红柳枝 ^{14}C 样本测年，公元前 761±61 年。属第二期文化早段墓葬。

GRAVE 96QZIM64 (CAT. NOS 19–20)

Located in the 1996 southwest region's second excavation site, this was a rectangular vertical-pit grave with single entryway and with a canopy in it; the orientation of the grave was east-west.

The grave chamber was rectangular with the entryway located in the northern corner, in line with the northern wall of the chamber. It formed the shape of a straight-handled knife. The entryway had two platforms so that one descended successively down three levels. In addition, a hollow spot for feet had been dug out of the wall.

The grave chamber was 3 meters long from east to west, 2.5 m wide, and the grave was 2.28 m deep. In the center of the bottom of the chamber was a rough vertical pillar; and there was a small platform or rack in the northeast corner.

The following items were discovered under this platform: a whetstone, a ceramic bottle, a horn cup, a damaged bow, a wooden cover, a wooden drill for making fire, a device for catching duck, a wooden belt buckle, a piece of iron, a wooden basin, and also some textiles.

Seventeen people were buried in this grave. The following describes the clothing of Person H, who was an adult male.

This grave belonged to the early phase of Second-period culture.

GRAVE 96QZIM14 (CAT. NOS 21–22)

Situated in the 1996 southwest region's first excavation site, this was a rectangular vertical-pit type grave with single entryway and platform or rack, orientation east-west. The grave chamber was 5 meters long and 3.6 m wide, and the grave was 1.4 m deep.

Nineteen people were buried in this grave. Among them, fifteen were 'middle-aged,' four of whom were male and eleven of whom were female. There were also two children; the age and gender of the remaining two is unknown. Accompanying grave items included: a single-handle jar, whetstones, a wooden bow, a wooden sword for beating the weft, two wooden upright *konghou* instruments, a bow case, wooden combs, wooden waist plaques, a long-toothed wooden comb, wooden spindles, wooden walking sticks, a wooden bowl, a rectangular wooden box, horse hobbles, a lacquered wooden stick, and so on. There were also stone beads, glass beads, a copper ring, worked or processed wooden pieces, a bundle of thatch, hats, a woolen cloth bag.

Samples of willow were taken for carbon-14 dating which resulted in a date of 761 ± 61 BCE. This grave belongs to the early phase of Second-period culture.

96QZIM4 墓葬（第四章图 23~27）

位于 1996 年南西区第一发掘点。单墓道长方形竖穴棚架墓，墓向东西向。

墓葬有墓道、墓口和墓室三部分组成，墓道位于墓室的西角，呈斜柄的刀形。墓口呈长方形，长 5 米，宽 4 米。墓深 2.2 米。

19 人葬，分上、下两层，保存了不少的服饰及织物。上层有 15 人。A 个体为成年男性，处于墓室的西壁一侧，头向南。M 个体为成年女性，处于北壁一侧，头向西。K 个体为壮年男性，头向东，顺北壁平躺。N 个体为男性，处于南壁一侧，头向南壁。他的东边是 B 和 C 两个体，B 个体仅剩头骨，C 个体为小孩。处于墓室南壁一侧，中部有 E、F、D、P 和 O 个体，E 个体为青年女性、F 个体为青年女性、D 个体为壮年女性、P 个体为成年女性、O 个体为男性。处于墓室南壁一侧东部的个体有 G、H、J 和 L4 个个体，G 个体仅剩头骨，H 个体为青年男性，L 个体为成年女性。下层有 4 个个体，处于墓室东壁一侧，从南向北排列，头向皆朝东。I 个体为成年男性，R 个体为壮年女性，S 个体为青年男性，Q 个体为青年女性。

在墓室填土中发现毛织物残片、皮刀鞘、砺石、木带扣等。

GRAVE 96QZIM4 (CAT. NOS 23–27)

Located in the 1996 southwest region's first excavation site, this was a rectangular vertical-pit type grave with single entryway and with a platform or rack; the orientation of the grave was east-west.

The grave was composed of three parts: entryway, grave opening, and grave chamber. The entryway was located in the southern corner of the grave chamber, protruding from it like a knife with a slanting handle. The grave opening was rectangular, 5 meters long, 4 m wide, and the grave itself was 2.2 m deep.

Nineteen people were buried in this grave, in two layers, one on top of the other. Many items of clothing and textiles were preserved. The upper layer had 15 people. Person A was an adult male located alongside the western wall of the grave chamber, with head towards the south. Person M was an adult female, located by the northern wall, head pointing west. Person K was a male in his prime, head facing east, lying alongside the northern wall. Person N was male, located by the south wall, head pointing toward the south wall. On his east side were Persons B and C. Only the skull remained of Person B. Person C was a child. Located beside the middle section of the south wall of the grave chamber were Persons E, F, D, P, and O. Persons E and F were young women, D was a woman in her prime, P was an adult woman, O was a male. On the eastern section of the south wall of the grave chamber were Persons G, H, J, and L. Only Person G's skull remained. Person H was a young male, L was an adult female. The lower level held four persons, located alongside the east wall. They were lined up all with heads facing east, in a row that was aligned north-south. Person I was an adult male; R was a female in her prime; S was a young male, and Q was a young female. Fragments of textiles, a leather knife sheath, a whetstone, and a wooden belt buckle were found in the earth filling the grave.

96QZIIM2 墓葬（第四章图 28~29）

位于扎滚鲁克二号墓地。单墓道长方形竖穴棚架墓，墓道位于墓口的南角，墓向正南。属第二期文化晚段墓葬。

墓室长方形，口长 7.4 米，宽 5.2 米。墓室深 1.4 米。在墓室靠西南壁的中部发现一个尸床，东西长 3 米，南北宽 1.3 米。

墓室填土及尸床上共发现 27 个个体。填土中出土 9 个个体，除 3 具年龄不明者，成年人骨架 4 具，小孩骨架 2 具。墓底有 18 个个体，3 具骨架性别、年龄不明，小孩骨架 7 具，女性架骨 3 具，男性骨架 5 具（4 具成年，1 具壮年）。

随葬器物，可以看出器形的 129 件，有石器、陶器、木器、骨角器、藤编器、铜器、铁器和装饰品等。墓葬出土不少的纺织品，主要是毛织品，也发现少量的棉织品。

96QZIM65 墓葬（第四章图 30~31）

位于 1996 年南西区第四发掘点。单墓道长方形竖穴棚架墓，墓向呈东西向。

墓室长方形，墓口长 5.6 米，宽 3.44 米。墓深 2.14 米。

16 个个体，其中 N、O、P3 个个体在墓室南壁一侧，N 个体在墓室的南西位置，R 个体在西壁一侧，W、V 和 U3 个体处于东壁一侧，M 个体处于北壁一侧偏东的位置，T 个体处于北壁一侧，S 个体在墓室的西北角。属第二期文化晚段墓葬。

96QZIM59 墓葬（第四章图 32）

位于 1996 年南东区发掘点。长方形竖穴土坑墓，墓向呈北南向。墓口长 3.2 米，宽 2.48 米。墓深 1.34 米。

7 人葬，在墓室及填土中出土了木纺轮、角勺和角杯等。属第二期文化晚段墓葬。

GRAVE 96QZIIM2 (CAT. NOS 28–29)

Located in Zaghunluq Cemetery #2. This was a single entryway rectangular vertical-pit type grave with canopy, and with the entryway situated on the southern corner of the grave opening. The grave faces due south. It belongs to the late phase of Second-period culture.

The grave chamber was rectangular, with an opening 7.4 meters long and 5.2 meters wide, and the grave chamber was 1.4 meters deep. A corpse rack or bed was discovered in the central part of the south-west wall of the chamber. It was 3 meters in length from east to west and 1.3 meters in width from north to south.

Twenty-seven individuals were discovered in the earth that had refilled the chamber and on the rack or bed. Nine individuals were excavated from the refilled earth. Among these were four adult skeletons and two skeletons of children, three were of uncertain age. On the bottom of the grave were another 18 individuals. Among these, three skeletons were of uncertain age and gender; the rest included the skeletons of seven children, three females, and five males, thereof four adult and one in his prime.

Grave goods included 129 pieces that were of recognizable form. These included items made of stone, ceramic, wood, bone and horn, basketry, copper, iron, and arious adornments. Many textiles were excavated from this grave, primarily woolens but also a small number of cotton textiles.

GRAVE 96QZIM65 (CAT. NOS 30–31)

Located in the 1996 southwest region's fourth excavation site. This grave had a single entryway and was a rectangular vertical pit-type grave with canopy, in east-west orientation.

The grave opening was 5.6 meters long and 3.44 meters wide. The depth of the grave was 2.14 meters.

Sixteen people were buried in this grave. Among them, Persons N, O, and P were along the south wall of the chamber. Person N was in the southwest part of the chamber, R was on the west wall, W W, V, and U were on the east wall, M was towards the east side along the north wall, T was on the north wall, S was in the northwest corner of the chamber. This grave belonged to the late phase of Second-period culture.

GRAVE 96QZIM59 (CAT. NO. 32)

Located in the 1996 southeast region's excavation site. This grave was a rectangular vertical-pit type grave, with north-south orientation. The grave opening was 3.2 meters long, 2.48 meters wide. The grave was 1.34 meters deep.

Seven people were buried in this grave. Items excavated from the grave chamber as well as the disturbed earth included: a wooden spindle, horn ladle, and horn cup, among others. The grave belongs to the late phase of Second-period culture.

96QZIM55 墓葬（第四章图 33~34 ）

位于 1996 年南西区第三发掘点。单墓道长方形竖穴棚架墓，墓向北南向。

墓室为长方形，墓道处于北部偏东的位置。墓口长 5.36 米，宽 3 米。墓深 2.02 米。

墓室东南角发现一小孩（G），仰身直肢，头向南。小孩身下铺长方形白毛毡，头戴帽，身上依次盖着芨芨草、柽柳盖、皮衣、套头裙衣等。在墓底发现木纺轮、圜底罐、单耳罐等。属第二期文化晚段墓葬。

96QZIM54 墓葬（第四章图 35 ）

位于 1996 年南西区第二发掘点。单墓道长方形竖穴棚架墓，墓向为正北方向。

墓室呈长方形，墓道处于墓室的北角位置。墓口长 5.5 米，宽 4.2 米。墓深 2.9 米。

2 人葬。出土器物有带柄木碗、木盘、木梳、木刀、木板、木扣、小木件、石球、铁块、毛织物、丝织品等。墓葬中还发现有马头骨。属第二期文化晚段墓葬。

96QZIM34 墓葬（第四章图 36~38 ）

位于 1996 年南西区第二发掘点。单墓道长方形土坑棚架墓，墓向西南—东北向。墓道处于墓室的东南角。墓口长 4.5 米，宽 3.5 米。墓深 2.8 米。出土文物中有许多纺织品。属第二期文化晚段墓葬。

GRAVE 96QZIM55 (CAT. NOS 33–34)

Located in the 1996 southwest region's third excavation site. This was a single-entryway, rectangular, vertical pit-type grave with canopy, and with a north-south orientation.

The grave chamber was rectangular, with entryway located on the north-eastern side. The grave opening was 5.36 meters long, 3 meters wide, and the grave was 2.02 meters deep.

At the southeast corner of the chamber was a child (G), lying on his back with limbs extended, head facing south. A rectangular white piece of woolen felt had been placed under his body. He wore a hat and had been covered in a succession of materials: from outside to inside, they included: *jiji* grass, a willow covering, a leather garment or clothing, and finally a skirted dress-like pullover garment. On the bottom of the grave were discovered a wooden spindle, a round-bottomed jar, a single-handle jar, and so on. This grave belonged to the late phase of Second-period culture.

GRAVE 96QZIM54 (CAT. NO. 35)

Located in the 1996 southwest region's second excavation site. This grave had a single entryway, was rectangular with vertical pit and canopy, and the grave orientation was due north.

The grave chamber was rectangular with the opening located at the northern corner. The grave opening was 5.5 meters long and 4.2 meters wide. The grave was 2.9 meters deep.

Two people were buried in this grave. Excavated items included: a wooden bowl with handle, wooden basin, wooden comb, wooden knife, wooden board, wooden buttons, small wooden pieces, stone balls, iron pieces, woolen textiles, and silk textiles. The bones of a horse's head were also found in the grave. This grave belongs to the late phase of Second-period culture.

GRAVE 96QZIM34 (CAT. NOS 36–38)

Located in the 1996 southwest region's second excavation site. This was a single-entryway rectangular earthen pit-type grave with canopy, in southwest – northeast orientation. The entryway was in the southeast corner of the grave chamber. The grave opening was 4.5 meters long, 3.5 meters wide, and the grave was 2.8 meters deep. Among excavated items were many textiles. The grave belonged to the late phase of Second-period culture.

红色毛布套头长袍 <small>(96QZIM100:2C)</small>

袍身长 122 厘米，肩袖通宽 128 厘米。袖长 37 厘米，41 厘米，袖口和肩袖口宽皆为 17 厘米。肩宽 50 厘米，下摆宽 71 厘米。

长袍，窄肩、直身、套头、对领、直筒袖，饰牙线和毛绦。

袍身由两幅平纹毛布，前、后对折缝制。毛布保存两面幅边，幅宽 36 厘米。肩至下摆呈渐宽形式，宽 50~71 厘米。肩部左、右内折，多少有些变化。

领部，前面开口。领口缘边，略向内折，呈对领状，领口长 32 厘米。

袖，各用一幅毛布，上、下对折而成（图 1）。

袍身和袖的毛布，平纹，先织后染。经、纬纱皆 Z 捻，经密 13 根 / 厘米、纬密 11 根 / 厘米（图 2）。

牙线为蓝色，饰于袍身前、后中缝。

毛绦，2/2 斜编，宽 4.5 厘米。饰于下摆缘边。

另外，在长袍的腰际系扎着一根姜黄色腰带。腰带（98QZIM100：2-1C），系 6 根 Z 重捻线，棕、黄色线 2/2 斜编而成。带长 155 厘米，宽 1.5 厘米。

C 个体身为女性，红色毛布套头长袍为典型的女性袍服。

14

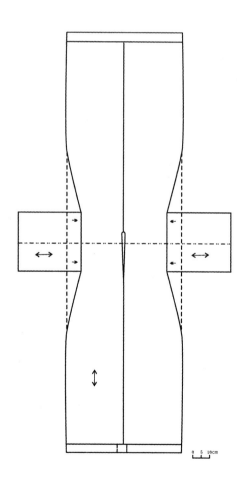

1 结构图 Cut and construction diagram

LONG PULLOVER GOWN OF RED-COLORED WOOLEN CLOTH (96QZIM100:2C)

The gown is 122 cm long, with an overall sleeve-and-shoulder width of 128 cm. The sleeves are 37 and 41 cm long; the cuffs and armscyes are both 17 cm wide. The width across the shoulders is 50 cm, at the lower hem it is 71 cm.

This is a long gown with narrow shoulders and straight body, put on over the head. It has an edge-to-edge front, straight tubular sleeves, and is decorated with piping and a woolen braid.

The gown is made from two pieces of woolen tabby cloth, folded over the shoulders to form front and back, and stitched together. The cloth retains both selvages, it has a loom width of 36 cm. The garment flares out slightly from shoulders to lower hem; its width goes from 50 to 71 cm. At both shoulders, the fabric is folded to the inside with some variation in width of the fold. The front part of the neckline is left open and the edges are folded slightly to the inside, making an edge-to-edge front; the neck opening is 32 cm long. Each sleeve is made from a piece of woolen cloth formed by folding top and bottom together, and closed with an underarm seam (fig. 1).

The woolen cloth of the body and sleeves is a tabby weave, woven first and then piece-dyed. Both warp and weft threads are Z-spun; the thread count of the warp is 13 ends per cm; of the weft, it is 11 picks per cm (fig. 2).

The piping threads are blue and adorn the front and back central seams of the gown. The woolen braid is worked in 2/2 twill oblique interlacing, it is 4.5 cm wide and stitched to the lower hem.

In addition, a ginger-yellow belt is fastened to the body of the gown at the waist. The belt (98QZIM100:2-1C) is made from wool yarn, Z re-plied from 6 ends. It is 155 cm long and 1.5 cm wide, and is worked in brown and yellow threads in 2/2 twill oblique interlacing.

Person C was female, and the long red woolen gown, put on over the head, is a typical form of female attire.

2 组织图 Woolen cloth

白色毛绢套头上衣 (96QZIM71:6A)

衣身长72厘米,肩袖通宽135厘米。袖长33.5厘米,35厘米,袖口宽12厘米,肩袖口宽17.5厘米。肩宽64厘米,下摆残缺严重,复原宽67厘米。

直筒衣身,窄袖口、对领。衣身为两幅毛绢拼对,前后对折而成。皆保存两面幅边,幅宽:右30.5厘米,左33厘米。

袖,各为一幅毛绢,上、下对折制成。肩袖口内折的少一点,较宽;袖口内折的多一些,窄(图1)。右袖保存基本完好,左袖残。皆保存两面幅边,幅宽36厘米。

对领,开口长28.5厘米。领边有一组紫色系领的毛线绳,[8] 保存有结扣。

毛绢,布面多显经向的褶绉,毛纱强捻:经纱Z捻,纬纱S捻。羊毛较细,有绒。平纹,经密26根/厘米,纬密12根/厘米(图2)。

A个体为男性,白色毛绢套头上衣为男服。

---

8 领部的系线绳,起扎系领口的作用。

PULLOVER JACKET OF WHITE-COLORED WOOLEN CRÊPE (ZHOU) (96QZIM71:6A)

The body of the garment is 72 cm long; the overall sleeve-and-shoulder width is 135 cm. Length of sleeves: 33.5 and 35 cm respectively, width of cuff: 12 cm, breadth at shoulders: 64 cm, width of armscyes: 17.5 cm. The lower edge of this jacket has been severely damaged; reconstructed, it is 67 cm wide.

15

The body is in tubular form, with narrow sleeves and edge-to-edge front. The jacket was made from two pieces of woolen crêpe put together, folded over the shoulder and sewn. Both pieces retain two selvages; the loom width of the right side piece is 30.5 cm, of the left side piece 33 cm. Each of the sleeves is made from one piece of woolen crêpe, with top and bottom folded together and sewn with an underarm seam. The seam allowance is only narrow at the armhole, while the material at the cuffs is folded in more. Thus, the sleeve gradually becomes more narrow (fig. 1). The right sleeve is still quite complete; the left sleeve is damaged. Both sleeves retain two selvages; the loom width is 36 cm.

The edge-to-edge neck opening is 28.5 cm long. At the edge of the neckline, a purple woolen string is fastened, used to tie the neckline closed, with the knot still preserved.

Woolen crêpe is a fabric with marked crinkles in warp direction. The yarn is strongly twisted; warp threads are Z-spun, weft threads are S-spun. The sheep's wool is rather fine, and includes cashmere. It is woven in tabby, and the warp thread count is 26 ends per cm; weft 12 picks per cm (fig. 2).

Person A was male; this white woolen crêpe jacket, put on over the head, is a garment typically worn by men.

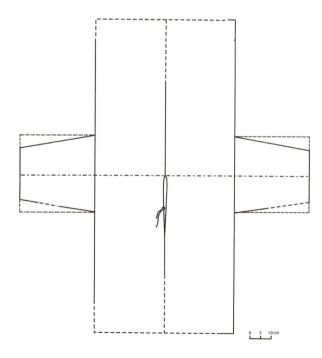

1 结构图 Cut and construction diagram

2 组织图 Woolen tabby

绞缬菱网纹毛布衣服残片 (96QZIM69:1-33)

长 56 厘米，宽 53 厘米。

衣服残片，可能是袖或下摆的一个角，呈不规则形状。保存一面幅边，残幅宽 37 厘米。

羊毛中等粗，经、纬纱皆 Z 捻，经纱捻得较紧。平纹，经密 22 根／厘米，纬密 14 根／厘米。

缝绞染毛织物，扎系的地方经、纬纱为白色（图 2）。背面显直线菱格纹，正面显连点菱格纹。应该是扎染效果。

毛布的拼接处，保存有棕色牙线。为两根拼股，比较细。

16

FRAGMENTS OF WOOLEN CLOTHING WITH TIE-DYED DIAMOND-NETWORK PATTERN (96QZIM69:1-33)

Height 56 cm, width 53 cm.

This fragment of clothing was perhaps a sleeve or perhaps a corner of a lower hem. It is in an irregular shape. One selvage remains; the preserved width of the fabric is 37 cm. The wool is of medium thickness and both warp and weft have been Z-spun. Warp threads are twisted more tightly than weft threads. The piece is woven in tabby weave, with a warp thread count of 22 ends per cm, and a weft thread count of 14 picks per cm.

The warp and weft of this stitch-resist dyed woolen textile stayed white where they were tied during the dyeing (fig. 2). The back of the fabric shows straight-line diamond patterns; the front shows aligned-dot diamond patterns, which is the result of tie-resist dyeing.

Brown-colored piping remains along the seams. It is made from doubled strands of fairly fine yarn.

1 组织图 Woolen tabby with selvage

2 组织图 Tie-dyed pattern

绞缬枝叶纹毛布残片 (96QZIMQ9:1)

长 43 厘米，宽 39.8 厘米。

衣服残片，保存右侧的一面幅边，残幅宽 39.8 厘米。平纹，经、纬纱皆 Z 捻，经密、纬疏，经密 19 根／厘米，纬密 12 根／厘米。

缝绞染，花纹呈对生叶状，像一根枝上的对生叶，叶纹呈小圆形。

枝叶纹分布有些变化，大体分两类，一类间隔较远，约 5、5.5、6.5 厘米，共三条，分布在 18 厘米宽的范围内；一类间隔近，分布在 21 厘米宽的范围内，共七条，叶瓣间几乎相连或近乎重叠（图 1）。

最长的一条枝叶残长 43 厘米，有 29 对叶，呈交互生状。叶瓣直径也有些变化，一般直径在 1 厘米间，最大的 1.3 厘米，小的 0.8 厘米。

应该是顺纵斜向折叠，折叠数应与叶瓣数相同，最长的应有 29 叠。从叶瓣的大小可以看出来折叠的宽窄有些变化。折叠断面呈连续的"M"字效果，应该是以叶瓣中心为中轴，直线缝缀。而后需作浸水处理，是为了防止干燥织物投入染液时会造成染色不均现象。同时预湿后能使纤维膨化而利于上染。

在毛布上织一条蓝色横条带纹，1/2 Z 斜纹组织，经纱两根并股，宽 0.8 厘米。蓝色带纹有些泛红色，推想应该是先织后缝绞缬染所致。

1 组织图 Woolen stitch resist–dyed tabby, reverse

FRAGMENT OF WOOLEN CLOTH WITH STITCH-RESIST DYED BRANCHES WITH LEAVES (96QZIM99:1)

Height 43 cm, width 39.8 cm.

This fragment of a garment retains one selvage on the right side, its remaining width is 39.8 cm. It is woven in tabby weave, with both warp and weft Z-spun. The warp is fairly dense and the weft comparatively sparse; thread count of the warp is 19 ends per cm, of the weft it is 12 picks per cm.

Stitch-resist dyed along a line or a 'seam', the pattern results in opposing leaves, seemingly along a branch. The leaves are depicted as small roundels. There are variations in the distribution of the pattern. In general, it is of two types: in one, the distance between branches is great and in the other the distance between branches is small. In the first type, the distance varies from 5 to 5.5 to 6.5 cm in between rows of leaves. This type shows three rows of leaves across a span of 18 cm. The second type has closer patterns spread across 21 cm. Altogether there are seven branches or lines of opposing leaves in this section. The leaves almost touch or seem to be almost overlapping (fig. 1). The longest branch with its leaves is still incomplete, but 43 cm long. It has 29 pairs of opposing leaves, growing out opposite from one another. There is also some variation in the diameter of the leaf petals, mostly 1 cm but some 1.3 cm, the smallest 0.8 cm.

In order to do the resist-dyeing, the cloth appears to have been folded along vertical diagonals, and the number of stitches or tucks in that fold corresponds to the number of pairs of leaf roundels. The longest branch must have had 29 stitches or tucks. From the size of leaf roundels, we can see that there was considerable variation in the process of stitching. The result was a series of neat folds on the surface of the cloth that looked like a continuous row of 'M' letters. This was to form the central axis in the center of the leaves, stitched as a straight line. After stitching, the process was to soak the cloth in water, to allow dry fibers to expand with water to facilitate the dye's penetration and to assure even dyeing of the fabric.

A blue horizontal stripe was woven into the cloth, made in a 1/2 Z twill weave. For this, the warp threads were doubled, and the stripe is 0.8 cm wide. The blue was somewhat suffused with red, so we surmise that the resist-dyeing was done after the weaving.

黄地网格纹缋罽裤残片 (96QZIM68:2A)

展开：长 141.5 厘米，宽 82 厘米。

残裤腿，裆缺失。为两幅毛布拼对缝缀，幅边经纱两根并股。羊毛中等粗，以平纹组织为主，经、纬纱皆 Z 捻，捻得比较紧，经密 20 根／厘米，纬密 14 根／厘米。

经纱，为黄色。纬纱有两色：黄和蓝。纬纱分区，蓝色纬纱以 1/3 织出 3 行（仅有一组是 5 行的）很窄的条纹，条纹间宽 3.1、3.3、4.5 厘米不等（图 1）。

裤腰经边缘，有 0.7 厘米宽、18 行的蓝条纹，向内折缝。蓝条纹的第一行是 1/3 斜织，第二行将一根经纱抽去，使其不与纬纱交织，随之以下都变成了平纹组织。

毛布正面显绘画的网纹，清晰。背面是染色渗透的效果，有的花纹明显，有的则模糊。同时，网格大小有别，不很整齐；形状也有变化，有菱形格、椭圆格等（图 2）。

牙线，为蓝色，饰于裤身外侧、裤腿口。裤外侧上部是单根纱，下部则是两根并股。裤腿口的牙线是两根并股。

1 组织图 Woolen tabby with blue stripes, painted

2 组织图 Painted net pattern

FRAGMENT OF YELLOW PANTS PAINTED WITH NETWORK DESIGN (96QZIM68:2A)

Opened out, the textile is 141.5 cm high and 82 cm wide.

The fragment is the leg part of the pants, the crotch is missing. It consists of two lengths of cloth sewn together. The outermost warp thread at the selvages is doubled. The wool is of medium thickness. The predominant weave is tabby. Both warp and weft threads are relatively strongly Z-spun, with a warp thread count of 20 ends per cm and a weft thread count of 14 picks per cm.

The warp yarn is yellow. The weft yarn is in two colors, yellow and blue, divided into sections. The blue sections are woven in very narrow stripes of three picks each (there is one single stripe of five picks), with staggered 1/3 weft-floats, with the spacing between the strips being 3.1, 3.3, and 4.5 cm (fig. 1).

The waist is the end of the warp and has a 0.7-cm-wide blue stripe (18 picks) that was folded and sewn to the inside. The first pick of the stripe is 1/3 weft floats; the second uses only warp threads not interwoven by the first pick; the third is repeating the first, and so on. The result is a tabby weave with half of the warp threads only.

The proper side of the cloth was painted in a netting pattern that is very clear. The dye penetrated through to the back of the cloth where some of the pattern is visible while other parts are indistinct. Meanwhile, the size of the netting varies: its shapes are sometimes more triangular, sometimes more oblong (fig. 2). The piping threads are blue. They adorn the outer side of the pants and the cuffs. Those on the outer side are single strand in the upper part, but in the lower part, as well as on the cuffs, they are doubled.

18

夹缬齿纹残毛布裙 (96QZIM64:20H)

展开：长 95 厘米，残宽 172 厘米。

长方形，饰牙线。毛布裙由裙身和裙摆组成，裙身和裙摆上、下卷边拼接缝合而成，穿着时围绕在腰上即可。裙身和裙摆上皆有补丁，补丁上以平针缝缀，显菱格纹。

裙身为红色锯齿纹缂毛，5 幅毛布拼接。两幅保存两面幅边，一幅保存一面幅边。幅宽 34.5 厘米。身长 50 厘米，残宽 130 厘米。裙腰缘边有宽 5 厘米的缂织长锯齿纹，齿纹边缘斜直、清晰。羊毛很细，经纱为白色，纬纱是红色，红色是染色。平纹，经、纬纱皆 Z 捻，经密 13 根／厘米，纬密 34 根／厘米（图 1）。

裙摆为夹缬齿纹毛布，9 幅毛布拼接。仅一幅保存两面幅边，余皆保存一面幅边。幅宽 41 厘米。摆长 45 厘米，残宽 172 厘米。夹缬齿纹毛布，羊毛中等细，经、纬纱皆 Z 捻，平纹，经密 22 根／厘米，纬密 12 根／厘米。纬纱是白色，经纱是白和绿色两种，分白、绿两区。首先织出白、绿带纹。宽、窄相差不大，多在 2.3、2.4、2.5、3、3.2 厘米不等，幅边缘 1.6 厘米，而后夹缬齿纹。

夹板是一个带有弧线三角、齿纹的板。板的宽度大概是 3.2 厘米，一个三角纹的长度 14.6 厘米。推测是夹板印花，其主要根据是正、背两面的花纹完全相同，齿纹边缘平齐。夹板弧顶的齿较长，长为 1.4 厘米；凹处的齿短，长 0.5 厘米。夹板后，涂红色，形成了现在的颜色效果，即在白、绿色纬纱上，都能看到红彩的痕迹。夹板图案是波状锯齿纹，白带纹上显红的波状锯齿纹，绿带纹上显深绿色波状锯齿纹（图 2）。

牙线，绿色。处于裙身和下摆的接缝处。

另外，残留一件粗毛绳，残为两截：长 62、29 厘米，直径 3 厘米。由红、白、蓝三色毛线合捻。

1 缂织花纹 Tapestry-woven pattern

2 夹缬花纹 Clamp resist-dyed pattern

FRAGMENT OF A WOOLEN SKIRT, WITH CLAMP-DYED TOOTH PATTERNS (96QZIM64:20H)

Opened out, the fragment is 95 cm high and 172 cm wide.

The fragment is rectangular and adorned with piping. The woolen skirt is composed of a main part and a hem part, both of which were folded in and stitched together to make the garment. The skirt was worn by wrapping it around the waist. Both the body of the skirt and the hem part have patches, which are stitched on with a diamond pattern in satin stitch.

The body of the skirt is made of red wool, with a tapestry-woven sawtooth pattern. Five lengths of cloth are sewn together. Two of the pieces retain both selvages, and one more piece retains one selvage. The loom width is 34.5 cm. The body of the skirt is 50 cm high and, although fragmentary, it is still 130 cm wide. Along the waist edge of the skirt is a 5-cm high strip of tapestry-woven sawtooth patterning, with vertical teeth and very clearly executed. The wool is very fine, the warp yarn is white, and the weft yarn is white and red, of which the red only was dyed. The fabric is woven in tabby weave, with warp and weft threads both Z-spun. The thread count of the warp is 13 ends per cm, of the weft it is 34 picks per cm (fig. 1).

The bottom of the skirt is made of clamp-dyed woolen cloth with tooth patterns. It is assembled from nine pieces of cloth. Only one of these retains both selvages, the rest all have one selvage. The loom width of the whole piece is 41 cm. The hem part of the skirt is 45 cm high, and 172 cm wide. Its clamp-dyed woolen cloth is made out of medium-weight fibers with both warp and weft threads Z-spun and woven in tabby weave. The thread count of the warp is 22 ends per cm, and of the weft it is 12 picks per cm. The weft yarn is white, the warp was white and green, divided into discrete sections. First, white and green stripes were woven, fairly uniform in width, 2.3, 2.4, 2.5, 3.0 and 3.2 cm, with 1.6 cm at the edges. Then the clamp-dyeing of the tooth pattern was done.

The clamp was a piece of wood with a rounded triangle with teeth. The width of the boards was probably 3.2 cm. The length of one triangle pattern was 14.6 cm. We surmise that the pattern was clamp-dyed, the evidence being that the right side and backside of the fabric have patterns that are completely congruent, with the teeth edges lined up exactly. The teeth at the top of the arc on the wooden clamps were long, their length being 1.4 cm. The teeth at the recess edges were shorter, 0.5 cm. Red dye was applied on the clamped textile, resulting in the current coloring. The wooden clamp left curved toothed waves on the fabric. They appear brightly red on the white stripes and deep green on the green stripes (fig. 2).

19

The edging cord is green. It is stitched along the seam between the body of the skirt and the hem part.

In addition, fragments of a thick woolen cord were found, in two sections, measuring 62 and 29 cm in length and 3 cm in diameter. This was made of red, white, and blue woolen thread twisted together.

棕灰地条纹毛布圆领套头上衣 (96QZIM64:19H)

衣身长 69.5 厘米，肩袖通宽 144 厘米。袖长 38、39.5 厘米，袖口宽 11 厘米，肩宽 62 厘米。

衣为窄肩、宽下摆衣身，圆领，窄袖口，饰牙线。

衣身，为一幅毛布，前、后对折，开圆形领口，衣身两侧加三角。袖，各为一幅毛布，上、下对折缝合（图 1）。

毛布为平纹，经、纬纱皆 Z 捻，经密 11 根／厘米，纬密 9 根／厘米。经、纬纱皆由白、棕色羊毛混捻，显棕灰色。同时，经纱分深棕色和浅棕色两种，分区布置。深棕色经纱显条纹，含白色羊毛少、棕色羊毛多。浅棕色经纱为地色，则是白色羊毛多、棕色羊毛少（图 2）。

牙线，红色，Z 捻。饰于肩袖缝合袖口处。

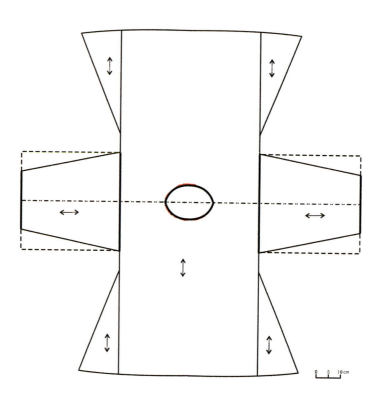

1 结构图 Cut and construction diagram

WOOLEN PULLOVER JACKET, IN GREY-AND-BROWN STRIPED PATTERN (96QZIM64:19H)

The garment is 69.5 cm long, its overall sleeve-and-shoulder width is 144 cm. The sleeves are 38 and 39.5 cm long. The cuffs are 11 cm wide. The measurement across the shoulders is 62 cm.

The garment is narrower at the shoulders than at the hem. It has a round neck, narrow cuffs, and is decorated with piping.

The body of the garment is made of one piece of cloth, folded to form front and back. The neck is a round cut-out, and four triangular gussets are added at the side seams. Each of the sleeves is one piece of cloth, folded and stitched with an underarm seam (fig. 1).

20

The woolen cloth is tabby weave with both warp and weft threads Z-spun; the warp thread count is 11 ends per cm, of the weft it is 9 picks per cm. Both warp and weft yarn are composed of white and brown fibers spun together, to result in a greyish-brown hue. At the same time, the warp threads are divided into those spun with dark-brown and those with light-brown fibers, which are arranged into discrete sections. The dark-brown warp creates stripes in the cloth that hold less of the white fibers and more of the brown. The lighter-brown warp yarn serves as the ground and has more of the white fibers and less of the brown (fig. 2).

The piping cord is Z-spun red wool. It adorns the seam between shoulder and sleeve, and the cuffs.

2 组织图 Woolen tabby

星纹、波纹缂毛残裙 (96QZIM14:63D)

展开，长 126 厘米，宽 157 厘米。

三幅平纹毛布横向拼接缝缀，其中两幅保存两面幅边，一幅保存了一面幅边，幅宽有些变化，分别为 60 厘米（中间）、49 厘米。保存一面幅边的毛布，残幅宽 48 厘米。

出土时，裙盖在 D 个体的腿部，怀疑是裙，以缠绕的方式穿着即可。裙腰和下摆部分皆残，局部还有补丁。

毛布为平纹，经、纬纱皆 Z 捻。经密 6 根 / 厘米，纬密 24 根 / 厘米（图 1）。

纱以白纱为主，还有白色羊毛和棕色羊毛、白色羊毛和黄色羊毛的混捻纱，粗细不匀，羊毛也有粗细的差别。纬纱有蓝、棕、土黄、绿、红、橘黄、姜黄、茶色等八种色，分区布置，织出成组的条带纹。三幅毛布的条带纹组合各有些变化，有宽有窄，蓝和茶色条带纹比较窄，宽 1 厘米。宽条带纹中，除没有蓝色外，其他各色都有，宽 1.5 厘米。另外，还有一种宽 10 厘米的宽带纹。在三组蓝条带纹（包括宽带纹）之间、上下条带纹上缂织有星纹和连续的短波纹（图 2）。星纹有三组，四种色，即白、橘黄、蓝和姜黄，中间饰棕、红色。有一组连续的短线波纹，用色为白、酱紫、红、姜黄、橘黄、蓝、土黄等七色相间分布。

SKIRT FRAGMENT OF TAPESTRY-WOVEN CLOTH WITH STAR AND WAVE PATTERNS (96QZIM14:63D)

Opened out, the height of the fragment is 126 cm, the width is 157 cm.

Three pieces of tabby-weave woolen cloth were sewn together side by side to make the skirt. Two of these retain both selvages, one preserves only one selvage. The loom width shows variation: 60 cm for the length of cloth in the middle, and 49 cm for the one on the side. The woolen cloth which retains one selvage is 48 cm wide.

1 组织图 Striped tapestry weave

When excavated, the skirt was covering the legs of Person D, and there is some doubt about its being a skirt although one could have worn it wrapped around the body. Both the waist and hem parts of the garment are missing; parts of the fabric were patched.

The woolen cloth is tabby weave, with both warp and weft threads Z-spun. The warp thread count is 6 ends per cm; the weft thread count is 24 picks per cm (fig. 1). White yarn predominates in the warp, although there are also threads of white and brown, or white and yellow wool spun together. The yarn is of varying thickness and the wool fibers were also of varying thickness. The weft yarn included eight colors: blue, brown, earth yellow, green, red, tangerine yellow, ginger-yellow, and tea-color. These were woven in discrete sections of bands decorating the fabric. Each of the groups of stripes on the three different pieces of woolen cloth had its own combination: some with narrow, some with wide bands. There were groups of narrow, blue or tea-colored bands, around 1 cm in width, while other groups had wider bands, 1.5 cm in width, that could be of any color, except for blue. In addition, there were striped areas, 10 cm in width, that were placed in between groups of three blue stripes. These areas carried bands with continuous short wave patterns or stars. The stars (fig. 2) were vertically aligned in groups of three and came in four colors: white, tangerine-yellow, blue, and ginger-yellow. The center area of each star was woven in either brown or red. The colors in the continuous strips of short waves included: white, dark purple, red, ginger-yellow, tangerine-yellow, blue, and earth yellow, in regularly alternating sections.

21

2 组织图 Star pattern in tapestry weave

白地棕条纹毛布圆领套头上衣 (96QZIM14:75C)

衣身长 79 厘米,肩袖通宽 138 厘米。袖长 37.5 厘米,袖口宽 14 厘米,肩袖口宽 16.5 厘米。肩宽 63 厘米。领口宽 21.5 厘米,领深 5 厘米。下摆宽 95 厘米。

衣残。衣身左侧下部缺失较多。窄肩、宽下摆、圆领,直筒袖,饰牙线和编织绦。

衣身是一幅毛布,保存两面幅边,幅宽 65 厘米。前、后对折,剪出圆领口缝缀而成(图 1)。

毛布为平纹,经、纬纱皆 Z 捻,经纱细、纬纱粗。经密 12 根／厘米,纬密 7 根／厘米。纬纱白色。经纱分白和棕色两种,分区,显白地棕条纹。棕条纹集中在衣身的左侧,宽 34 厘米。条纹三条为一组,一宽二窄(图 2)。衣身右侧显白色,宽 31 厘米。衣身两侧加三角,其长 40 厘米,底宽 14 厘米。

袖,用布与衣身相似,不过经过了刀裁。袖子主要利用了毛布的条纹部分,仅发现一面幅边。条纹也有些变化,为四条一组,一宽三窄。

牙线,两种。红色牙线,饰于肩袖。领口牙线为棕、红色 S 双捻。

编织绦,红色,饰于袖口,为 2/2 斜编,用两根并股纱编织。

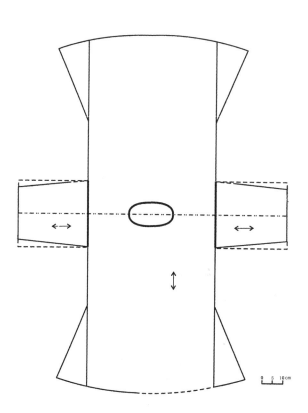

1 结构图 Cut and construction diagram

WOOLEN CLOTH PULLOVER JACKET, WITH BROWN STRIPES ON A WHITE GROUND (96QZIM14:75C)

The length of the body of the garment is 79 cm; the overall sleeve-and-shoulder width is 138 cm. The sleeves are 37.5 cm in length; cuffs are 14 cm wide. The height of the armscyes is 16.5 cm. The measurement across the shoulder is 63 cm. The neck opening is 21.5 cm wide, and the neckline is 5 cm deep. The lower hem is 95 cm wide.

The garment has sustained some damage, particularly on its lower left side. It has narrower shoulders and is wider at the lower edge, has a round neckline, straight tubular sleeves, and is adorned with piping and narrow braids.

The body of the garment is one piece of cloth. It retains both selvages; the fabric has a loom-width of 65 cm. It was folded over at the shoulder, a neckline was cut out, and the sides were then sewn together (fig. 1).

The woolen cloth is tabby weave with both warp and weft threads Z-spun, the warp thread more tightly, the weft more loosely. The warp thread count is 12 ends per cm; the weft thread count is 7 picks per cm. The weft yarn is white. The warp yarn is divided into the two colors white and brown, woven in different sections to display brown bands or stripes on white ground. The brown striped pattern is concentrated on the left-hand side of the garment and is 34 cm wide. In this section, each three stripes make up a group which includes one wide and two narrow lines of color (fig. 2). The right side of the garment is white and is 31 cm wide. Both sides of the garment have had triangle-shaped gussets added to the bottom outside edges; they are 40 cm long and 14 cm wide at the bottom.

The cloth of the sleeves is the same as that used for the body but it has been cut with a knife. The sleeves are mainly made up of the striped part of the cloth; only one selvage was discovered. The sleeve pattern is slightly different in that four stripes make up each group, with one wide and three narrow lines of color.

The edging cords come in two types. Red-colored piping threads are found at the armhole seam. The piping at the neckline is S-plied from one brown and one red end.

Red braided bands adorn the cuffs and are 2/2 twill oblique interlacing, made with doubled yarn.

2 组织图 Striped woollen tabby

浅棕色直筒毛布裙 (96QZIM4:73)

　　裙长 100 厘米，腰宽 65 厘米，臀部宽 62 厘米，下摆宽 73.5 厘米。

　　裙分裙腰和下摆两部分。裙腰，直，呈筒形。由一幅毛布横折缝合而成，接口在右侧边。毛布保存两面幅边，幅宽 45.5~48.5 厘米。裙腰的前身，左、右两边都有打褶，使得裙腰呈上略窄、下略宽的形式。打褶部分用蓝、姜黄、橘红毛线捆扎。

　　裙腰毛布，白色经纱，纬纱以白色纱为主，有少量的棕色纱，毛布面微微显出棕色竖条纹。在裙腰前的中部有一条宽带纹，呈很浅的米红色，宽 11~12.5 厘米。毛布，平纹，经、纬纱皆 Z 捻，羊毛中等粗，经密 5 根／厘米，纬密 8 根／厘米。

　　裙摆基本上呈筒状，也是由一幅毛布缝缀，保存两面幅边，横折缝合而成，接口在右侧。幅宽 50~55 厘米。

　　下摆只是在腰际略有些打褶，至下部完全打开。毛布为 2/2 S 斜纹组织，经纱 Z 捻，纬纱 S 捻。经密 3 根／厘米，纬密 20 根／厘米（图 1）。经、纬纱多是白色羊毛，纬纱也有棕色和米红色的羊毛混捻纱，使下摆显宽窄不匀的浅色条带纹。

1 组织图：正、反面 Woolen twill front and back side

STRAIGHT TUBULAR WOOLEN SKIRT IN A LIGHT BROWN COLOR (96QZIM4:73)

The skirt is 100 cm long, the waist is 65 cm wide. Around the hips it is 62 cm wide, and at the lower hem it is 73.5 cm wide.

23

The skirt is divided into the waist or upper part and a lower part. The upper part is straight and tubular, made from one piece of cloth that has been folded and sewn along one seam, which is on the right side of the garment. The woolen cloth retains both selvages; the fabric is between 45.5 and 48.5 cm wide. There are tucks in the front right and left sides, making the waist slightly smaller and the bottom slightly wider. The tucks are stitched with woolen threads that are blue, ginger-yellow, and tangerine-red in color.

The cloth of the waist part of the skirt is made from white warp yarn, while the weft yarn is mainly white but also mixed with a small amount of brown. A very finely striped look is the result. In the center front there is a wide band that is woven in a very faint light red color. It varies from 11 to 12.5 cm wide. The woolen cloth is tabby weave with both warp and weft Z-spun. It is woven of medium-weight wool, with a warp thread count of 5 ends per cm and a weft thread count of 8 picks per cm.

The lower part of the skirt is basically tubular and is also sewn together out of one piece of cloth. It retains both selvages and is folded with the seam on the garment's right side. The loom width of the fabric is between 50 and 55 cm. The lower part of the skirt also has tucks on the waist end of the fabric, but is completely open at the lower end. The woolen cloth is 2/2 S twill weave with warp threads Z-spun and weft S-spun. The warp thread count is 3 ends per cm; weft is 20 picks per cm (fig. 1). The warp and weft are both mostly white, although the weft yarn has been mottled with some brown and some light red wool, giving the lower part of the skirt an uneven and blurred striped appearance.

棕色地格纹毛布开襟残上衣 (96QZIM4:87)

衣身长 65 厘米，肩袖通宽 107 厘米。袖长：左 30 厘米，右残长 27 厘米；袖口宽 17 厘米，肩袖口宽 22 厘米。肩宽 52 厘米，下摆宽 51 厘米。

上衣残，后背中间断开。直身，开襟，对领，窄袖口，饰牙线。衣身左后背下摆饰边穗，比较特殊（图 1）。

衣身为两幅毛布，前、后对折拼接缝合而成，皆保存一面幅边，幅边处于衣身外侧，后背中缝呈折边缝合状。

袖，用布与衣身相近，保存了两面幅边，幅宽 46 厘米，上、下对折缝合。袖口窄，肩袖口宽。

毛布为平纹，经、纬纱皆 Z 捻。经密 6 根／厘米，纬密 6 根／厘米（图 2）。衣身左后背下摆的边穗，为 5 根经纱的捻绳。纬纱有棕、橘红、黄等三种色，经纱则有棕、橘红、黄和蓝等四种色，蓝色纱退色严重。经、纬纱三条一区，均匀分布，显格纹。

牙线，红色，饰于前襟缘边、肩袖和袖口。

FRAGMENT OF A BROWN JACKET WITH OPEN FRONT, WITH PLAID PATTERN (96QZIM4:87)

The body of the garment is 65 cm long, and has an overall sleeve-and-shoulder width of 107 cm. The left sleeve is 30 cm long; the right sleeve is fragmentary and 27 cm long. Cuffs are 17 cm in width, armscyes are 22 cm high. The shoulder width is 42 cm, the bottom edge is 51 cm wide.

The jacket is in fragments, with the center part of the back torn open. It has a straight body, with an open edge-to-edge front, and narrow cuffs, and it is adorned with piping. The left side of the lower back hem has decorative fringes, which is rather special (fig. 1).

The body of the garment is made from two pieces of cloth. Front and back were folded over at the shoulder and stitched together at side seams and center back. Both pieces retain one selvage, which is located at the side of the garment. The back is sewn together with a tuck in the center. The sleeves use a similar cloth to what is used for the body; here it retains both selvages, showing the loom width to be 46 cm. Top and bottom were folded together and sewn into a seam. Cuffs are narrower than the armscyes.

24

The woolen cloth is tabby weave with both warp and weft Z-spun. The thread count of the warp is 6 ends per cm, of weft it is 6 picks per cm (fig. 2). The fringe on the bottom of the left side of the back is made of 5 warp threads twisted together. Weft yarn includes the three colors brown, tangerine-red, and yellow. Warp thread has four colors: brown, tangerine-red, yellow, and blue. The blue has severely faded. The warp and weft each employ three stripes in one 'area' or square, and the spacing is quite even, resulting in the plaid pattern.

The piping is red and adorns the front edges of the jacket as well as the armhole seams and the cuffs.

24

1 左后背下摆的饰穗
Fringe decorating the back hem at the lower left

2 组织图 Woolen tabby

棕色波纹缂毛单 (96QZIM4:92)

全长 189 厘米，宽 159 厘米。穗长 14.5 厘米。

长方形，由两幅毛布纵向拼对缝合。毛布皆保存两面幅边，幅宽 76.5 厘米。羊毛中等细，平纹，经、纬纱皆 Z 捻。经密 16 根／厘米，纬密 9 根／厘米（图 2）。经、纬纱皆为棕色，为羊毛原色。

毛单的经边缘，由红色纬纱织出带纹边缘饰，带纹宽 4.6 厘米。在这里，经纱是两根并股，同时，在红带纹上缂织出宽 2.5 厘米的绦式水波纹，显红地，蓝、橘红、白和黄等四种色的花纹。纹样由波状短线组成，平行连续，构成了长长的绦式水波纹（图 1）。

穗为 6 根经纱的 Z 重捻线，穗头有结。

毛单两侧缘边，饰宽 0.9 厘米、红色 Z 双捻线 1/1 斜编织绦。

1 缂织花纹 Tapestry-woven pattern

BROWN WOOLEN CLOTH WOVEN WITH TAPESTRY-WOVEN WAVE PATTERNS (96QZIM4:92)

The entire length of the textile is 189 cm, the width is 159 cm. The fringe is 14.5 cm long.

The cloth is rectangular, and made by stitching two pieces of cloth together lengthwise. Both pieces retain two selvages; their fabric width is 76.5 cm. The woolen fibers are of medium weight, the cloth is woven in tabby weave, with both warp and weft yarn Z-spun. The thread count of the warp is 16 ends per cm; of the weft it is 9 picks per cm (fig. 2). Both warp and weft are brown-colored, the natural color of the wool.

The warp end of the woolen cloth is adorned with a border woven of red-colored weft yarn. The whole border is 4.6 cm wide and worked in tapestry weave on doubled warp ends. The wave-patterns form a band 2.5 cm wide and are woven into the red border in four colors: blue, tangerine-red, white and yellow. The patterning is executed in short parallel lines forming a long continuous wave pattern (fig. 1).

The fringe is Z re-plied from three S-plied threads consisting of two warp ends each, and knotted on the ends.

A woolen braid, 0.9 cm wide, is stitched to the side edges of the cloth. It is made from Z-plied red yarn in 1/1 oblique interlacing.

2 组织图 Woolen tabby

红地紫条纹毛布单 (96QZIM4:94-1E)

全长 142 厘米，宽 140 厘米。穗长 6 厘米。

长方形，残。由两幅平纹毛布纵向拼对缝合而成，皆保存两面幅边，幅宽 70 厘米。纬纱，红色。经纱分红和紫两种色，分区布置，织出红地紫色条纹。条纹宽 0.5 厘米。羊毛较细，经纱捻得较紧，纬纱 S 捻，经纱 Z 捻。经密 9 根／厘米，纬密 8 根／厘米（图 1）。

经边，由棕红色纬纱织出宽 1.1~1.9 厘米的横条带纹，条带纹的宽窄变化与纬纱的松紧有密切关系。在这里，经纱都是两根并股，6 根经纱 Z 重捻为线绳穗，穗头打有穗结（图 2）。

毛单的两侧缘边，饰有棕色绞编绦，宽 0.8 厘米。

毛布染红色，系先织后染。纬纱原应该是白色纱，经纱应该是白、棕两种色纱，染完后再加两侧缘的绞编绦。所以，白纱显红色，棕纱显紫色，而绞编绦仍然保持棕色。

毛布的局部有缝补，以平针缝绣出菱回纹。

1 组织图 Striped woollen tabby

26

213

WOOLEN CLOTH WITH PURPLE LINES ON A RED GROUND (96QZIM4:94-1E)

The entire length of this textile is 142 cm; its width is 140 cm, the fringe is 6 cm long.

This rectangular cloth is fragmentary. It was made by sewing two pieces of woolen tabby together lengthwise. Both pieces have two selvages; the loom width is 70 cm. The weft yarn is red. The warp yarn is red and purple, with the purple in narrow stripes 0.5 cm wide, so that the effect is purple lines on a red ground. The wool is relatively thin and the warp yarn is given a fairly strong twist; weft has been S-spun, warp Z-spun. The thread count of the warp is 9 ends per cm; of the weft it is 8 picks per cm (fig. 1).

The warp ends have a woven band of brownish-red weft threads that is between 1.1 and 1.9 cm wide. The variation in width is related to the varying weft density. In this area, the warp ends are doubled. Groups of six warp ends are Z re-plied to form the fringe cords. The ends of the fringe have been knotted (fig. 2).

Either side of the cloth is adorned with a brown-colored twined braid that is 0.8 cm wide.

The cloth was first woven, then dyed red. The weft yarn was originally white while the warp was two colors, white and brown. After dyeing, the two side-braids were added. In the process of dyeing, the white yarn turned red, the brown yarn turned purple, while the side braids remained their original brown.

The cloth has been mended in several places. This was done with satin stitches arranged in concentric lozenges.

2 经边穗 Warp end band and fringe

几何羊纹缂毛裤残片 (96QZIM4:65Q)

拼对展开，长 82 厘米，残幅宽 50 厘米。

残为 4 片，没有幅边。发掘时处于 Q 个体的腿部，为裤的残片。裤样不清。通幅毛布缂织有几何羊纹，平纹，经、纬纱皆 Z 捻，经密 7 根／厘米，纬密 36 根／厘米（图 1）。

经纱为棕色，纬纱分红、蓝、土黄、浅黄等四色。显红地，蓝、土黄、浅黄色几何羊纹。

羊纹纵向排列，比较密集，一正一反，略有些错位。羊纹为单色，蓝、浅黄和土黄色羊纹分行布置。

FRAGMENT OF TAPESTRY-WOVEN WOOLEN PANTS WITH STYLIZED MOUNTAIN GOAT (96QZIM4:65Q)

Reconstructed and spread out (with the warp running horizontally), the height is 82 cm, the remaining width is 50 cm.

This fragment is in four pieces, none of which retains a selvage. The piece was found on the legs of Person Q when excavated and is what remains of a pair of pants. The appearance of pants is no longer possible to make out. The entire width of fabric is tapestry-woven in stylized mountain goat designs. The weave is tabby-based tapestry, with warp and weft both Z-spun, warp thread count 7 ends per cm, weft thread count 36 picks per cm (fig. 1).

The warp yarn is brown; the weft is divided into four colors: red, blue, earth yellow, and light yellow. The combination displays stylized mountain goat patterns in blue, earth yellow and light yellow on a red ground. The patterns are lined up lengthwise and the arrangement is fairly dense. The animals alternate in direction, one is in one direction, the next in the opposite direction. The mountain goat are arrayed in a succession of single colors, blue, light yellow, and earth yellow.

1 组织图 Tapestry weave

土红色开襟棉布上衣 (96QZIIM2:10-1)

衣身长88.5厘米，肩袖通宽188厘米。袖长：右60厘米，左（残）50厘米。袖口宽：右14.3厘米，左残宽16厘米。肩袖口宽27厘米，肩宽82厘米。下摆复原宽104厘米（残宽93.5厘米）。

衣为立领，窄肩，开襟，宽下摆，窄袖口，饰毛布绦。

衣身为两幅棉布，右侧一幅保存一面幅边，残幅宽45厘米。前、后对折，下摆加三角。三角高52厘米，底边宽10.5厘米。

在衣身的前襟缘边、肩袖，背面下摆底缘，皆饰蓝色毛布绦。绦宽4厘米。肩袖间的蓝色毛布绦，还保存了一面幅边。棉布的前襟和下摆边缘，皆向外折边，由蓝色毛绦覆盖。

袖，各一幅棉布，皆保存一面幅边，残幅宽35厘米。袖子近衣身处也加有三角，三角由前、后两片组成，长21厘米，底宽11.5厘米。

棉布为平纹组织，经、纬纱皆Z捻，经密21根／厘米，纬密12根／厘米（图1）。

牙线，为姜黄色3根S双捻线。饰于衣身加三角的前后接缝，后背衣与领的连接处。

立领，残，为两层棉布，由两片纵向缝合，一片较完整，一片残缺严重。后面饰蓝色毛布，领长16厘米，高6.3厘米。

蓝色毛布绦，宽4厘米。平纹，经、纬纱皆Z捻，经密16根／厘米，纬密17根／厘米。

1 组织图 Cotton tabby and selvage

JACKET WOVEN OF EARTHEN-RED COTTON, WITH OPEN FRONT (96QZIIM2:10-1)

The garment is 88.5 cm long and the overall-sleeve-and-shoulder width is 188 cm. The sleeve lengths are 60 cm (right) and 50 cm (left, fragmentary), the width of the right cuff is 14.3 cm, the fragmentary left sleeve is 16 cm wide at its end. The armscyes are 27 cm high. The shoulder width is 82 cm, and the width at the lower hem, reconstructed, is 104 cm (the remaining width is 93.5 cm).

28

The garment has a standing collar and narrow shoulders, it is open down the front, has a wide lower hem, narrow cuffs, and is decorated with woolen braids.

The body of the garment is made from two pieces of cotton cloth. The right side preserves one selvage; the fragment is 45 cm wide. The front and rear were folded over the shoulder and sewn together with four triangular pieces fitted into the lower hem. These are 52 cm high and 10.5 cm wide across the bottom. Along both sides of the front opening, the armscyes, and along the bottom of the back, woolen bands were added that are blue in color. They are 4 cm wide. The band at the armscye retains a selvage. The edges of the cotton fabric of the jacket front and the lower hem are folded to the outside and finished with the blue woolen bands. The sleeves were each made from one piece of cotton cloth, and both retain one selvage, the remaining width is 35 cm. The sleeves also have triangular pieces of cloth fitted in on the body side of the sleeves. The triangle is formed of two pieces, front and back. The length is 21 cm, with a lower width of 11.5 cm.

The cotton cloth is tabby weave with both warp and weft Z-spun. The thread count of the warp is 21 ends per cm, the thread count of weft is 12 picks per cm (fig. 1).

The edging is ginger-yellow S-plied threads from three single ends. It is found on the front and back seam of the triangles on the body of the fabric, as well as on the seams at the center back of the jacket, and on the rear of the jacket where collar and back come together.

The standing collar is fragmentary and made of two layers of cotton cloth, which have been sewn together lengthwise. One piece is fairly complete, the other has severe damage. The rear is adorned with blue-colored woolen cloth; the length of the collar is 16 cm and its height is 6.3 cm.

The blue woolen-cloth bands are 4 cm wide. They are woven in tabby with warp and weft all Z-spun. The thread count of warp is 16 ends per cm, of weft it is 17 picks per cm.

28

白地棕色花纹栽绒毛毯 (96QZIIM2:9)

长 84 厘米，宽 73 厘米。

呈长方形，保存了两面幅边，宽 73 厘米。地组织，为 2/2 斜纹。经、纬纱皆白色，经纱 Z 捻，纬纱 S 捻，捻得较紧。

栽绒纱为白、棕两种色，以白色为主，皆 S 捻，捻得比较松。隔六行栽一行绒线，绒线为五根并股纱。结扣为波斯扣，也称生纳扣（图 1）。

在毛毯的局部可以看到棕色栽绒线的显花，但图案不清。

WOOLEN PILE CARPET WITH WHITE GROUND AND BROWN-COLORED PATTERN (96QZIIM2:9)

Length 84 cm, width 73 cm.

The fragment is rectangular, retaining both selvages that show the width of the woven fabric to be 73 cm. The foundation weave is 2/2 S twill. The warp and weft yarn are white, with warp Z-spun and weft S-spun, both relatively strongly.

The pile yarn is white and brown, with white predominating. Both are comparatively loosely S-spun. Every six picks there is a line of pile weft, which is a fivefold yarn. Persian knots are used, also known as Senna knots (fig. 1).

From parts of the carpet we can see the pattern originally displayed by the brown pile threads, however the patterning is very indistinct.

1 背面 Reverse side of blanket　　　　　　　　　2 组织图 Diagram of pile knot

白地棕条纹毛布肚兜 (96QZIM65:18-1D)

全长 46 厘米，肩宽 36 厘米，下摆宽 38 厘米。边穗长 6.5 厘米。

一幅毛布制作，表面有些残洞，保存两面幅边，幅宽 40.5 厘米。毛布肚兜经过刀裁缝制。兜身上缘中间开领口，领口呈方折的凹形，卷边缝制。在两侧相当于肩袖的位置，刀裁出缺口，卷边缝制，使得肚兜呈"凸"字形。其中右侧保存较好，呈方折效果；左侧残，呈溜边缘状。

平纹毛布，经、纬纱皆 Z 捻，捻得比较紧。经纱有白、棕两种色，分区布置，显白地棕条纹效果。棕条纹宽 0.3 厘米，间宽 3 厘米。经密 12 根 / 厘米，纬密 9 根 / 厘米。

纬纱有白、红两种色，布面用白色纱，红色纱作下摆缘边，为一道红色条带纹，宽 0.7 厘米。这里的经线是两根并股，显得比较密（图 1）。

在领口两头各有一根捻绳，用作系绳。另外，在右肩部位也保存一根捻绳，左侧缺失，都是一根线，从毛布边穿过去，而后捻合在一起。毛线系绳长 12、13、20 厘米。

1 组织图 Brown stripe and horizontal red band

UNDERGARMENT (BREAST COVER) OF WHITE WOOLEN CLOTH WITH BROWN STRIPES (96QZIM65:18-1D)

Entire length 46 cm, 36 cm wide at shoulders, lower hem 38 cm wide. Fringe 6.5 cm long.

This garment was made from one piece of woolen cloth. It is somewhat damaged and has holes in it, but retains both selvages; the loom width is 40.5 cm. The apron was cut with a knife and sewn into its present shape. The upper edge was cut in the middle to form a neck opening, which is square shaped and hemmed at all sides. On either side of the upper part of the body are knife-cut indentations which were again rolled and hemmed so that the entire garment has the shape of the Chinese character 凸 . The right side of the garment is better preserved. There, the angle of the arm opening retains its original square shape while the other side is deformed.

The textile is a tabby-weave woolen cloth with warp and weft both relatively strongly Z-spun. The warp is composed of both white and brown yarn, arrayed in sections so that a pattern of brown stripes is displayed against a white ground. The width of the stripes is 0.3 cm; separated from one another by 3 cm. The thread count of the warp is 12 ends per cm, of the weft it is 9 picks per cm. The weft yarn includes the two colors, white and red. The white is used for the body of the garment with red used for the lower edge so that it shows up as a 0.7 cm wide band at the bottom. Warp threads here are doubled and the weave is more tightly (fig. 1).

Two strings are attached to either side of the neckline, for tying the garment. In addition, a string is retained on the right shoulder; the left is missing. All are made from a single thread, pulled through the woolen cloth and the two ends then twisted together. The strings are 12, 13, and 20 cm long.

30

绞缬方格圆圈纹残毛布单 (96QZIM65:24-20)

长 110 厘米，宽 96 厘米。

长方形，残。一侧边（幅边）饰编织绦，经边有缂织花纹和穗。由两幅毛布横向拼接，皆保存一面幅边，残幅宽 67 厘米。

毛布单主体是平纹，经、纬纱皆 Z 捻，经、纬密度相近。经密 9 根／厘米，纬密 7 根／厘米。从现有的颜色看，经、纬纱皆分紫和红两种色，分区布置，显方格纹。为此，方格纹出现三种色，一是酱红，二是红，第三种是酱红纱和红纱重叠的方格纹。方格纹长 2.5 厘米，宽 2.2 厘米。小圆环纹是在红色方格内扎染而成，显白色。同时，酱红色毛纱表面的色有些变化，大部分羊毛显酱红，少部分羊毛显红色。感觉它们在扎染红色之前，酱红色羊毛应该是棕色羊毛，而红色羊毛是白色羊毛。

最初羊毛纱分白和棕两种色，棕色纱系棕色羊毛和白色羊毛的混捻。白纱和棕纱经、纬分区，织出方格纹也出现三种色：白（白色经纱和白色纬纱的重叠）、棕（棕经、纬纱的重叠）和棕白（棕色经、纬纱与白色经、纬纱互换的重叠）。而后，在白色方格里进行系扎，染红色。这样一来，白色纱显红色，棕色纱显酱红色，棕白纱则显酱红纱和红纱的重叠效果（图 2）。

毛布单的底边有一条 3.5 厘米的红宽带纹，在红宽带纹与方格纹之间是 2.5 厘米宽的绦式缂织花纹。缂织花纹呈波状，由蓝、红、橘黄、棕红、黄、白等六色小波曲纹组成（图 1）。缂织花纹是扎染后再织的，所以花纹没有受到扎染的影响。同时，方格纹进入缂织花纹时，经线成了两根并股。

残留了很少的穗，皆是三根纱 Z 双捻线绳，尾部系结。

编织毛绦，残长 53 厘米，宽 0.9 厘米。为 1/1 斜编绦，纱分棕红、红、白三种色，都是 S 双捻线。图案显红和白、棕红的右斜条纹，白、棕红两色相间分布，又显出小的长方格纹。

1 缂织纹样 Tapestry-woven band　　2 绞缬圆圈纹 Tie-dyed circle

WOOLEN CLOTH FRAGMENT WITH TIE-DYED CIRCLES IN A SQUARE

PATTERN (96QZIM65:24-20)

Height 110 cm, width 96 cm.

The cloth is in fragments but generally rectangular. A braided band is attached on one side (the selvage side). At the warp end there is a tapestry-woven band and fringe. The cloth was made by putting two pieces of woolen fabric together horizontally, both of which retain one selvage. The incomplete loom width is 67 cm.

The main body of the woolen cloth is tabby weave with both warp and weft Z-spun and with a similar thread count for warp and weft. The warp thread count is 9 ends per cm, the weft is 7 picks per cm. From colors as they appear today, both warp and weft are striped in purple and red, which results in a woven square pattern, or a kind of plaid. The squares appear in three colors: dark red, red, and dark red and red threads woven together. The length of each square is 2.5 cm, the width is 2.2. cm. Inside the red squares, small circles have been created through tie-dyeing, and so allow some of the original white of the yarn to show through. The dark red-colored yarn shows variation. Most of it is dark red, but a small portion of the fibers is red. The interpretation of this is that before tie-dyeing with red dye, what is now dark red was brown-colored wool, and what is now red was white-colored wool.

At the outset, therefore, the yarn was white and brown. The brown wool was composed of white and brown wool that had been spun together. When woven, the result was three different colors: white (white warp interlaced with white weft), brown (brown warp interlaced with brown weft), and brown-white (brown or white warp interlaced with white or brown weft). After weaving, the fabric was resist-tied in the white squares. Then the whole piece was dyed with red, so that the white threads now appear red in the blanket and the brown appear dark red, while the brown-white appears as mixed from dark red and red (fig. 2).

At the warp edge of the woolen cloth is a 3.5-cm-wide red band. Between this red band and the squares is a 2.5-cm-wide strip of tapestry-woven patterning. The pattern is in a wave form made up of six colors, blue, red, tangerine-yellow, brown-red, yellow, and white (fig. 1). The tapestry-patterned band was only woven after the cloth was dyed red so that the pattern does not show mixing of colors. At the line, where the check pattern changes to the tapestry-woven pattern, the warp threads are grouped in pairs and continue as double threads.

The very small remaining amount of fringe is all Z-ply threads from 3 ends, with knots tied on the ends.

The woven woolen braid fragment is 53 cm in length and 0.9 cm wide. It is a 1/1 oblique twining ribbon, divided into three colors, brown-red, red, and white, all S-ply. The pattern appears as a design of Z-slanted red, white, and brown-red lines. White and brown-red alternate and the effect is that of small squares.

31

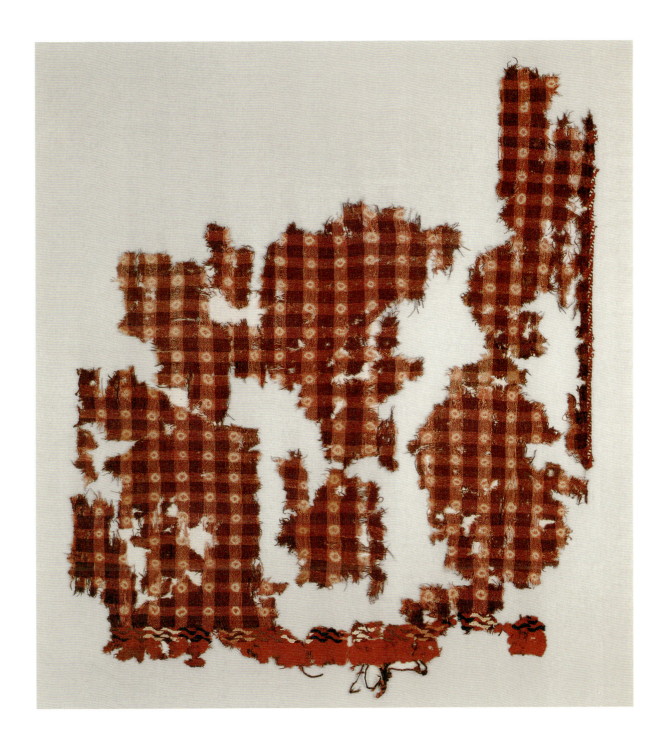

赭红色毛纱残片 (96QZIM59:4)

长 16.5 厘米，宽 27.5 厘米。

不规则长方形，为衣服残片。毛纱没有保存幅边，在一边缘上缝缀蓝色编织毛绦。

毛纱的组织比较复杂，是 1/1 和 1/5 的组合。六条纬梭为一个编制单元，纬梭 1、2、4 和 6 为 1/1 的平纹织法，纬梭 3 和 5 则为 1/5 的显纬织法。毛纱是以此为单元而循环编织组成的。1/5 组织部分比较密，1/1 组织部分比较稀疏。这样一来，显横向的暗条纹，稀疏的地方显方孔纱眼（图 1）。

羊毛较细，捻得比较紧，经、纬纱皆 Z 捻，经密 26 根／厘米，纬密 19 根／厘米。

编织毛绦有些退色，显黄色，为 2/2 斜编绦。绦长 26 厘米，宽 0.8 厘米。

1 组织图：左，反面；右，正面
Back (left) and front side (right) of gauze-like weave

FRAGMENT OF BRIGHT RED WOOLEN GAUZE-LIKE WEAVE (96QZIM59:4)

Length 16.5 cm, width 27.5 cm.

This is a fragment of clothing and has now an irregular rectangular shape. The gauze-like weave does not retain a selvage. A blue-colored woolen braid is sewn to one side.

The gauze-like weave of the piece is somewhat complex: it is a combination of 1/1 and 1/5 weave. In a weaving unit of six weft picks, picks 1, 2, 4, and 6 are woven in 1/1 tabby, picks 3 and 5 in 1/5 weft floats; this cycle is continued throughout the textile. The 1/5 weave parts are fairly dense, the 1/1 weave parts are fairly loose. In this fashion, a subtle pattern shows in cross-wise direction, with small square holes being formed in the sparse parts (fig. 1). The wool is rather fine, with warp and weft both relatively strongly Z-spun. The thread count of the warp is 26 ends per cm, of the weft it is 19 picks per cm.

The color of the braided band is somewhat faded and has turned yellow. The band is worked in 2/2 twill oblique interlacing, it measures 26 cm in length and 0.8 cm in width.

32

百衲毛布套头裙衣 (96QZIM55:17G)

通长 63 厘米：裙身长 23.7，裙摆长 39.3 厘米。通袖宽 81.5 厘米，肩宽 34.5 厘米，领径 13.5 厘米。袖长 23.5 厘米，袖口宽 9 厘米，肩袖宽 12.2、10.5 厘米。裙摆残宽 50 厘米。

裙衣分裙身和裙摆两部分，裙身部分是由 6 片长方形小毛布拼缀而成。[9] 圆领，直筒袖，饰牙线。除裙摆左侧部位开口、加三角部分缺失外，其余部分保存完好。大概是 4~5 岁小孩的裙服。

裙摆呈喇叭状，上窄下宽。上宽 37.5 厘米，下摆残宽 50 厘米。

袖，大体呈直筒形，袖口略窄，肩袖口略宽。各由两幅红条纹毛布缝合，毛布皆没有幅边。

裙衣用毛布共六种：棕色平纹毛布、白色平纹毛布、蓝红条纹毛布、红条纹毛布、红色平纹毛布和红色毛纱。

棕色平纹毛布，用于下摆及加三角部分。保存两面幅边，幅宽 44 厘米。经、纬纱皆 Z 捻，经密 13 根 / 厘米，纬密 16 根 / 厘米。

白色平纹毛布，用于前、后裙身的小片毛布，保存有一面幅边，残幅宽 14.3 厘米。经、纬纱皆 Z 捻，经密 14 根 / 厘米，纬密 14 根 / 厘米。

蓝、红条纹毛布，是用于前、后裙身的小片毛布，没有发现幅边，残幅宽 13 厘米。纬向条纹。地组织为平纹，以 3/5 斜纹显条纹。经、纬纱分蓝、红两种，分区。在平纹组织部分，红、蓝纱各五行，显红色、蓝红色方格纹和蓝红色条纹。同时，红、蓝色纬纱又以 3/5 斜纹显条纹，布于平纹组织的格纹之间，一般是四行斜纹显一条纹，红、蓝色互换。经、纬纱皆 Z 捻，经密 18 根 / 厘米，纬密 26 根 / 厘米（图 1）。

红条纹毛布，用于两袖，没有发现幅边，残幅宽 6.2 厘米。它以组织变化显纬向条纹，即平纹和 1/3 斜纹组织的组合，形成条纹。三行平纹和五行 1/3 斜纹组织的循环。经、纬纱皆 Z 捻，经密 24 根 / 厘米，纬密 34 根 / 厘米（图 2）。

红色毛纱，用于裙身的小片毛布，没有保存幅边，残幅宽 12 厘米。经、纬纱皆 Z 捻，密度有些变化。其中 14~15 行（宽 0.3 厘米）纬纱较密，4 行（宽 0.4 厘米）则较疏，疏的地显方形纱孔（图 3）。

红色平纹毛布，是用于裙身的小片毛布，没有保存幅边，残幅宽 13 厘米。经、纬纱皆 Z 捻，经密 16 根 / 厘米，纬密 18 根 / 厘米。

牙线饰于领口、袖口和肩袖处，分两种，一种是 S 双捻的并股，一种是单根的毛纱。

33

9 百衲衣，因许多小片毛布拼缀缝合而得名。

231

SKIRTED PATCHWORK PULLOVER GARMENT MADE OF WOOLEN CLOTH (96QZIM55:17G)

Overall length 63 cm: height of bodice part 23.7 cm, length of skirt 39.3 cm. Overall sleeve-and-shoulder width 81.5 cm. Width across the shoulders 34.5 cm, neckline diameter 13.5 cm, length of sleeves 23.5 cm, width of cuffs 9 cm. Height of armscyes 12.2 and 10.5 cm. The incomplete hem width is 50 cm.

The garment is divided in a skirt part and an upper, the latter is made up from a patchwork of six rectangular pieces of woolen cloth. It has a round neckline, straight tubular sleeves and is decorated with piping. With the exception of the left side of the skirt where the triangular gore is missing, the garment is completely preserved. It was made for a child approximately 4 to 5 years old.

The skirt of the garment is of evaded shape, narrow at the top and widening towards the hemline. At the waistline it is 37.5 cm wide, the incomplete hem width is 50 cm.

The sleeves of this garment are in a generally tubular shape but with cuffs slightly narrower, and armscyes slightly broader. Each is made of two pieces of red striped woolen cloth sewn together. None of the pieces has a selvage.

The garment is made from six different kinds of woolen cloth: brown-colored woolen tabby, white-colored woolen tabby, woolen cloth striped in blue and red, red striped woolen cloth, red woolen tabby and red gauze-like woolen cloth.

The brown-colored woolen tabby is used for the skirt part of the garment and for the added triangular gores. Both selvages are preserved, the loom width of the fabric is 44 cm. Warp and weft threads are Z-spun, and the warp thread count is 13 ends per cm, weft thread count is 16 picks per cm.

White-colored woolen tabby is used as small pieces on the upper front and back of the garment. It retains one selvage, the maximum preserved width is 14.3 cm. Warp and weft threads are both Z-spun, the warp thread count is 14 ends per cm and the weft is 14 picks per cm.

The blue- and red-striped woolen cloth is used as small pieces on the upper front and back of the garment. No selvages were found, the maximum preserved width is 13 cm. The fabric is weft-patterned, with 3/5 weft-float stripes on tabby ground. Warp and weft are arranged in stripes of blue and red threads; in the tabby areas the weft stripes are five picks high, resulting in rows of checks of red and blue-overlaid-with-red color, and of blue and red-overlaid-with-blue color. In between these rows, red and blue weft threads float in staggered 3/5 weave, four picks usually forming one stripe which is alternately red or blue. Warp and weft threads are all Z-spun, thread count of warp is 18 ends per cm, of weft it is 26 picks per cm (fig. 1).

Red-striped woolen cloth is used for the two sleeves; no selvage was found. Its preserved width is 6.2 cm. It displays a weft-oriented stripe through change in the weave, that is, composed by tabby weave and 1/3 weft-floats, which makes a striped appearance. The alternation is three picks of tabby and five picks of staggered 1/3 weft-floats weave. Warp and weft threads are both Z-spun; the warp thread count is 24 ends per cm, weft is 34 picks per cm (fig. 2).

Red-colored gauze-like woolen cloth is used as small pieces on the garment's upper. No selvages have been found, the maximum preserved width is 12 cm. Warp and weft threads are all Z-spun, with variable thread count. For about 14-15 picks (0.3 cm wide) the weft density is relatively high, and for the next 4 picks (0.4 cm wide) it is low, resulting in square-shaped holes in the sparse areas (fig. 3).

Red-colored woolen tabby is used as small pieces of woolen cloth on the garment's upper. No selvages were found, the maximum preserved width is 13 cm. Warp and weft both are Z-spun. The warp thread count is 16 ends per cm, weft is 18 picks per cm.

Ornamental edging decorates the neckline, the cuffs, and the armscyes. It is of two kinds: one is S-plied from two ends, the other is single-strand woolen yarn.

1 蓝、红条纹毛布 Blue- and red-striped woolen cloth

2 红条纹毛布 Red-striped woolen cloth

3 红色毛纱 Red-colored woolen gauze-like weave

白地棕条纹毛布背心 (96QZIM55:25)

身长 38 厘米，肩宽 29.5 厘米，下摆宽 24.5 厘米。肩袖部开口，口宽 8 厘米。

小孩服，无袖，因穿着的时间长，式样有些变形。呈斜肩，小立领，开襟，下摆略收。

两襟边各保存一根系绳，为 10 根 Z 重捻的线绳，长 12 厘米。系绳由襟边穿过。

背心用了四种毛布：白地棕条纹毛布、棕色平纹毛布、驼色地棕条纹毛布和驼色平纹毛布（图 1）。

白地棕条纹毛布（A），是背心的主要用布。保存两面幅边，幅宽 60 厘米。纬纱白色，经纱白、棕两种色，分区，显棕条纹（图 2）。经、纬纱皆 Z 捻，经密 11 根 / 厘米，纬密 7 根 / 厘米。

棕色平纹毛布（B），处于背心的右前胸部，为倒三角形的一片毛布，保存一面幅边，残幅宽 10 厘米。毛布长 35.5 厘米，宽 9.5 厘米，应该是一片补丁。羊毛相对粗一些，经、纬纱皆棕色，Z 捻，经密 11 根 / 厘米，纬密 9 根 / 厘米。

同时，在棕色平纹毛布的外侧，加了一片三角形白地棕条纹毛布（C），长 18.5 厘米，宽 2 厘米。

驼色地白、棕条纹毛布（D），处于背心的左前胸，也呈三角形，保存一面幅边，残幅宽 10.5 厘米。也应该是补丁。纬线大部分是白色纱，少部分是驼色羊毛和白色羊毛的混捻纱，显白色。经纱分白、驼、棕等三种色，分区，显驼色地白和棕色的条纹。经、纬纱皆 Z 捻，经密 11 根 / 厘米，纬密 8 根 / 厘米。

驼色平纹毛布（E），处于背心后背底部，呈三角形，也应该是补丁。长 10.5 厘米，宽 16 厘米。经纱是驼色，纬纱是白色羊毛和驼色羊毛的混捻纱，皆 Z 捻，经密 12 根 / 厘米，纬密 8 根 / 厘米。

小立领，由两层黄色平纹毛布缝制，呈长方形，宽 5.5 厘米，高 2.5 厘米。

VEST MADE OF WHITE WOOLEN CLOTH WITH BROWN STRIPES (96QZIM55:25)

The body is 38 cm long and the width at the shoulders is 29.5 cm. The lower hem is 24.5 cm wide. The armholes each are 8 cm wide.

This is a sleeveless garment that was worn by a child. Since it was worn a long time, it is somewhat out of shape. Its shoulders became slanted, it has a small upright collar, a front opening, and a hem that is slightly drawn in. Each of the two sides of the front opening retains a string, which is made of 10 threads plied and finally Z re-plied. Each is 12 cm long. The strings pass through the fabric of the front of the vest.

The vest is made of four kinds of woolen cloth: a woolen cloth with white ground and brown stripes, a brown woolen tabby, a woolen cloth with camel ground and white and brown stripes, and a camel-colored woolen tabby (fig. 1).

The main piece of the garment (A) is cut from the white-ground woolen tabby with brown stripes. It retains both selvages and shows that the fabric was woven 60 cm wide. The weft threads are white, the warp threads are white and brown, in discrete sections, creating a brown striped pattern (fig. 2). Warp and weft threads are all Z-spun, the thread count of warp is 11 ends per cm, of weft it is 7 picks per cm.

34

The brown-colored woolen tabby (B) is located on the right front part of the garment and is in an upside-down triangular form. It retains one selvage, the maximum preserved width is 10 cm. This piece is 35.5 cm long, 9.5 cm wide and was probably a patch. The wool is relatively coarse, both warp and weft yarn are Z-spun, the warp thread count is 11 ends per cm, the weft is 9 picks per cm. The outer edge of the brown-colored woolen tabby has had another triangular piece added to it (C) that is 18.5 cm long and 2 cm wide and cut from the woolen cloth with white ground and brown stripes.

Part (D), a camel-colored tabby with white and brown stripes, is stitched on the left front side of the vest. It is also triangular-shaped and retains one selvage, the maximum preserved width of the cloth is 10.5 cm. It is probably also a patch. Most of the weft threads are white yarn, with some camel-colored and white mottled yarn. The warp threads are divided in sections of white, camel-colored, and brown yarns, which produces a white ground with camel-colored and brown stripes. The warp and weft threads are both Z-spun; warp thread count is 11 ends per cm, weft is 8 picks per cm.

Part (E), a camel-colored woolen tabby, is located on the lower part of the back of the garment. Again it is triangular-shaped and probably a patch. It is 10.5 cm high and 16 cm wide. The warp yarn is camel-colored, the weft is white mottled with camel, and both are Z-spun. The warp thread count is 12 ends per cm, the weft is 8 picks per cm.

The small upright collar is sewn from two layers of yellow woolen tabby and is sewn onto the vest body. It is rectangular and measures 5.5 cm in width and 2.5 cm in height.

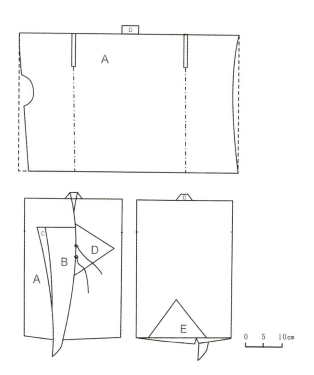

1 结构图 Cut and construction diagram   2 组织图 Woolen cloth with stripes

蓝地几何动物纹锦残片 (96QZIM54:3-2)

展开：长 13.7 厘米，宽 10.4 厘米。

长方形，没有保存幅边，锦下原衬有蓝色平纹毛布。

经锦，夹纬经二重平纹组织。经、纬线皆不加捻。纬线蓝色，有的地方退色，显蓝绿色。经线分蓝、紫红、白等三种色。排列比 1:2。经密 192 根／厘米，纬密 36 根／厘米（图 2）。

在蓝地上，以几何纹为骨架，隐隐约约显动物纹（图 1）。

1 几何纹 Geometrically-shaped framework

SILK COMPOUND WEAVE (JIN), BLUE GROUND AND STYLIZED ANIMAL PATTERNS (96QZIM54:3-2)

Height and width when laid out: 13.7 cm high, 10.4 cm wide. Rectangular, with no selvages preserved. Under the silk fabric was a lining of blue tabby woolen cloth.

The weave is a warp-faced compound tabby. Neither warp nor weft threads are noticeably twisted. The weft threads are a blue which in some areas has faded, looking more blue-green. The warp threads are divided into three colors: blue, purple-red, and white, and there are three series of warps. The warp thread count is 192 ends (64 ends per warp series) per cm, the weft is 36 picks per cm (fig. 2).

Animal patterns can be seen very indistinctly on a blue ground, inside a geometrically-shaped framework (fig. 1).

2 组织图 Warp–faced compound tabby

35

239

蓝地动物纹缂毛绦 (96QZIM34:50)

长 28 厘米，宽 13 厘米。

长方形。保存两面幅边，幅宽 13 厘米。边缘有缝缀的针眼，应是附属在某件服饰上的装饰绦。

地组织是平纹，经密 10 根 / 厘米，纬密 27 根 / 厘米。经线羊毛较粗，纬纱羊毛较细。经线 S 双捻，显棕色，是白色羊毛和棕色羊毛的混捻纱。纬纱 Z 捻，缂织花纹，有蓝、白、红、红棕、黄色等五种色（图 1）。

图案主要是动物纹，布局有序。在纵向的曲折带纹上显动物纹，带纹分红地和蓝地两种，宽 2.6~2.8 厘米。毛绦两边缘是连续的、填有动物纹的三角纹。

动物的嘴分方直和钩形两种，前者像羊或鹿的嘴，后者像鹰雕猛禽的喙。动物头上有彩带状角饰，大耳，作回首状。短尾，屈腿，作奔跳状。钩嘴和方直嘴动物在曲折带纹上呈交错状，正、反方向排列。

TAPESTRY-WOVEN BLUE WOOLEN BAND WITH ANIMAL PATTERNS (96QZIM34:50)

Height 28 cm, width 13 cm.

The textile is rectangular in shape and preserves both selvages; the width of the fabric is 13 cm. Along its border are the needle holes of previous sewing, so this was perhaps a decorative piece attached to some item of clothing.

The basic weave structure is tabby, with a warp thread count of 10 ends per cm, and a weft thread count of 27 picks per cm. The wool of the warp threads is relatively heavy, and for the weft threads it is relatively fine. The warp threads were S-plied from 2 ends, they look brown and are the result of spinning white and brown wool together. The weft threads were Z-spun. The tapestry-woven patterns includes the five colors blue, white, red, red-brown, and yellow (fig. 1).

The patterns are mainly animal motifs, distributed in an orderly manner. These patterns are displayed on wavy vertical bands, which have blue or red ground and are between 2.6 and 2.8 cm in width. At the side edges of the tapestry band, the band leave triangles with animal motifs inside.

The animals have two different kinds of mouths: one is square and straight, the other is curved. The former looks like the mouths of sheep or deer, the latter like the beaks of wild birds. The animals' heads have colored band-like horn decorations, they have large ears and are depicted in looking-back posture. They have short tails, and bent or curved legs, as though they were running. The hooked and the straight-mouthed animals alternate along the bands and are arrayed with each successive animal facing in the opposite direction.

1 组织图 Tapestry weave

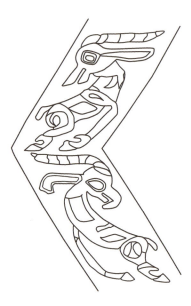

2 动物纹 Animal pattern

缂花毛罗套头上衣 (96QZIM34:15-1J)

衣身长80厘米，下摆宽77厘米，肩残宽55厘米，领径13厘米。肩袖口宽31.5厘米。

袖缺失，保存衣身部分，套头，圆领，下摆两侧加三角。加三角，底宽3、3.5厘米，长33.5厘米。衣领右侧开有小口。

衣的前、后身各用两幅毛罗，上、下拼接缝缀而成，幅宽42厘米。同时，衣身饰有红色编织绦。

毛罗除了平纹和罗组织外，上面还有红色的缂织花纹。缂织花纹处于衣身的前、后，呈绦带形式。罗组织多为白色，中间一条绿色带纹，也是罗组织。罗组织为二经纠。经纱Z捻，纬纱S捻。经纱为白色，纬纱有白和绿两种，平纹部分，经密15根／厘米，纬密36根／厘米。

绿色罗组织和红色缂织花纹构成了一条宽10.5厘米绦带纹，红色缂织花纹处于绿带纹的两侧，宽2厘米，为阶梯式山纹。

圆领由红色编织绦制作，宽2厘米，2/2斜编。在衣服的肩、肩袖和前、后身，也饰有红色编织绦，较窄，宽0.5厘米，也是2/2斜编。

红色牙线，为17根S双捻线，饰于衣身两侧。

1 组织图 Centre front with decorative band

PULLOVER JACKET IN TAPESTRY-PATTERNED WOOLEN GAUZE (96QZIM34:15-1J)

The jacket is 80 cm long, with a lower hem that is 77 cm wide. The incomplete breadth across the shoulders is 55 cm, the diameter of the neckline 13 cm. The armscye is 31.5 cm high.

The jacket's sleeves are missing, but the body part is largely preserved. It was put on over the head, has a round neckline, and triangular gores have been inserted on both sides at the bottom. These are 3 and 3.5 cm wide at their basis and are 33.5 cm long. There is a small opening on the right-hand side of the collar.

Both front and back of the body part of the garment are made from two pieces of woolen gauze, joined together with a horizontal seam at waist level. The width of the fabric was 42 cm. The garment is decorated with red-colored braided bands.

In addition to tabby weave and *luo* or gauze weave, the garment also has red tapestry-woven patterns. These are in the form of stripes on the front and back of the garment. The gauze weave is mostly white, with exception of one central stripe of green color. The weave is a patterned two-end simple gauze, with the gauze pick floating on the reverse in areas where there is no warp crossing, and with groups of tabby picks in between two gauze picks. The warp yarn is Z-spun, the weft is S-spun. The warp yarn is white, the weft is both white and green. The tabby weave part has a warp thread count of 15 ends per cm, and weft of 36 picks per cm.

The green gauze weave and the red tapestry-woven stripes form a band that is 10.5 cm wide. The red tapestry-woven patterning is on either side of the green band and is 2 cm wide. It is in a stair-stepped zigzag pattern.

The round collar is made of a red braid, it is 2 cm wide and is a 2/2 twill oblique interlacing. Red braids are also attached on the shoulders of the garment, on the armscyes and in the center front and back. It is relatively narrow, 0.5 cm wide, and it too is 2/2 twill oblique interlacing.

Red-colored cording, S-plied from 17 ends, adorn the side seams of the garment.

红色毛绣矮腰毡靴 (96QZIM34:16-21)

皮底长 27 厘米，腰高 16 厘米，腰口直径 15 厘米。

毡靴圆尖，矮腰，平底。红色毛布面，毡里，蓝绢缘边。毡靴，从后跟及腰部缝合，分不出左右。一只腰较完整，保存残皮底。腰部蓝绢保存较好。皮底呈束腰形，前、后宽，中间窄。后宽 9 厘米，前宽 5 厘米。另一只毡靴，腰部残缺严重，皮底缺失。

红色毛布面，为 2/2 Z 斜纹。经线 S 双捻，纬纱 Z 捻。经线捻得紧，纬纱捻得较松。经线白色，纬纱红色，先染后织。经密 15 根／厘米，纬密 92 根／厘米。

鞋面帮下缘边有三条绣线，为钉针绣，即将三根并线缝缀固定。绣线是毛线，S 双捻，两白一蓝，中间是蓝色线（图 1）。

毡，白色，厚 0.3 厘米。

蓝绢包在靴腰口缘，高 7.5 厘米，向里折进 1 厘米宽。丝线不加捻，经密 68 根／厘米，纬密 41 根／厘米。

38

FELT ANKLE BOOTS MADE OF EMBROIDERED RED WOOLEN CLOTH (96QZIM34:16-21)

The length of the leather sole is 27 cm, the height of the shaft is 16 cm. The diameter of the opening at the ankle is 15 cm.

The felt boots are round-pointed at the toes. They have a short shaft and flat soles. The upper is made from red woolen cloth, the lining is felt, and blue *juan* silk decorates the opening. The shoes are formed with one back seam from heel to ankle. Left and right cannot be distinguished from each other. One of the uppers is relatively complete, the leather sole remains in fragmentary form. The blue silk at the ankle is better preserved. The leather sole is pinched in at the middle, with front and back wide and middle more narrow. The back is 9 cm wide, the front 5 cm wide. The other felt shoe has suffered greater damage to the upper portion and the leather sole is completely gone.

The red woolen cloth is a 2/2 Z twill weave. The warp threads are S-plied from two ends, the weft threads are Z-spun. The warp threads are tightly twisted, the weft threads are relatively loose. The warp threads are white, the weft are red: they were first dyed and then the fabric was woven. The warp thread count is 15 ends per cm, and weft is 92 picks per cm.

The lower rim of the face part of the shoes has three lines of laid cording couched onto the fabric with stitches that run through the cord. The decorative threads are wool, S-plied from two ends, two threads white one blue, with the blue one being in the middle (fig. 1).

The felt is of white color and 0.3 cm thick.

The blue silk covers the upper edge of the shafts. It is a 7.5 cm high stripe of fabric and is folded 1 cm to the inside. The silk threads have no noticeable twist; the warp thread count is 68 ends per cm, and weft is 41 picks per cm.

1 结构图 Decorative couching

38

247

（三）1998年发掘墓葬出土纺织品珍宝

1998年在一号墓地发掘了58座墓葬，39座属第二期文化。这里介绍8座墓葬出土的35件纺织品。推测墓葬年代顺序是：98QZIM113、98QZIM136、98QZIM103、98QZIM114、98QZIM147、98QZIM139、98QZIM129和98QZIM124。

98QZIM113墓葬（第四章图39~42）

位于1998年南区第一发掘点。长方形竖穴二层台墓。墓向东西向。属第二期文化早段墓葬。

4人葬。随葬服饰有帽（98QZIM113：1，第四章图39）和白色毛布上衣。D个体，身上穿粉红色斜纹开襟长袍；B个体，身上穿长袍；A个体，身上穿白地"龙"纹缂罽长袍（98QZIM113：26-1A，第四章图41）；C个体，穿编织毛绦裙（98QZIM113：24C，第四章图40）。同时，D个体的头下枕头里有一件黄色毛布长袍。

98QZIM136墓葬（第四章图43~45）

位于1998年发掘的南区第一发掘点。长方形竖穴二层台墓。墓向东西向。墓口长3.54米，宽3.1米。墓深1.82米。属第二期文化早段墓葬。

4人葬，人成干尸，上下叠压。A、B和C三个体为成年男性，D个体为成年女性。A个体穿深红色衣服（98QZIM136：9-1A，第四章图44）。B个体保存有头发、眉毛和胡须，纹手，穿棕色长衣，着淡红色毛布裤（98QZIM136：10B，第四章图43）。C个体头发、眉毛保存尚好，穿白色毛布裤，两眼塞有毛线团。D个体保存有辫饰，两耳穿着红毛线，脸上涂抹红、黄两种颜色。

EXCAVATED IN 1998: 35 TEXTILES FROM 8 GRAVES

In 1998, we excavated 58 graves in Cemetery #1. Thirty-nine of these belonged to Second-period culture. Below, we discuss 35 textiles from 8 different graves. We hypothesize that the dating sequence of the graves is (from earliest to later): 98QZIM113, 98QZIM136, 98QZIM103, 98QXIM114, 98QZIM147, 98QZIM139, 98QZIM129, and 98QZIM124.

GRAVE 98QZIM113 (CAT. NOS 39–42)

Located in the 1998 southern region's first excavation site. This was a rectangular, vertical, two-layered platform grave. The grave orientation was east-west. It belonged to the early phase of Second-period culture.

Four people were buried here. Garments buried with them included a hat (98QZIM113:1, cat. no. 39) and a white woolen jacket. Person D was wearing a long gown, open at the front, of pink red twill; Person B was wearing a long gown; Person A was wearing a long gown with white dragon patterns painted on it (98QZIM113:26-1A , cat. no. 41); Person C was wearing a braided woolen-strip skirt (98QZIM113:24C, cat. no. 40). In addition, a yellow woolen gown was inside the pillow under the head of Person D.

GRAVE 98QZIM136 (CAT. NOS 43–45)

Located in the 1998 southern region's first excavation site. This was a rectangular vertical-pit type grave with two levels. The orientation of the grave was east-west. The grave opening was 3.54 meters long and 3.1 meters wide, the grave was 1.82 meters deep. It belongs to the early phase of Second-period culture.

Four people were buried in this grave. They had become naturally mummified and lay one on top of the other. Persons A, B, and C were adult males, D was an adult female. Person A was wearing dark-red-colored clothing (98QZIM136:9-1A, cat. no. 44). B still retained hair, eyebrows, beard and moustache, had tattooed hands, and was wearing a brown gown (98QZIM136:10B, cat. no. 43) and light-red-colored woolen pants. C also had well preserved hair and eyebrows, and was wearing white woolen pants. His eye sockets were stuffed with clumps of woolen yarn. D, female, still had braids, red woolen threads were put through her ears, and her face was daubed with red and yellow pigments.

98QZIM103（第四章图46）

位于1998年发掘的第一发掘点。长方形竖穴二层台墓，墓向东西向。属第二期文化早段墓葬。

墓口长4米，宽2.3~2.4米。

2人葬。A个体为男性，身裹棕色毛布，头发缠有红线。B个体为女性，身上缠着红色平纹毛布和白地"虫"纹缋𰐷残上衣（98QZIM103:11B，第四章图46），身旁有一顶编织帽和芦苇束捆。

98QZIM114墓葬（第四章图47）

位于1998年第一发掘点。长方形竖穴土坑墓，墓向呈西东向。墓口长3.4米，宽2.5米。墓深1.24米。

2人葬。A个体身上盖有毛单，附近有1件编织帽（98QZIM114:2A，第四章图47）。在墓室底部发现两件编织帽。

98QZIM147墓葬（第四章图48~51）

位于1998年南区第三发掘点。单墓道长方形竖穴棚架墓，墓道处于墓口北壁中部，墓向南北向。属第二期文化晚段墓葬。

墓口长10.1米，宽6.4米。墓深2.32米。

24人葬。出土的木器有单柄木罐、单耳木罐、单柄木盆、木盒、木钎、木手杖、木腰牌、木勺、箭杆、弓、木纺轮、木梳、木扣、木盘、木桶、木别子、木件；陶器有陶钵、单耳陶壶、陶罐；骨角器有骨针、骨梳、角杯。同时，随葬的还有毛布袋、皮带、皮刀鞘、皮手套、皮袋、铜镜、串珠、麦子、食物、色料等。

GRAVE 98QZIM103 (CAT. NO. 46)

Located at the 1998 excavation's first excavation site. This grave was a rectangular vertical-pit type grave with two levels. Its orientation was east-west. It belongs to the early phase of Second-period Culture.

The grave opening was 4 meters long, and between 2.3 and 2.4 meters wide.

Two people were buried in this grave. Person A was male, with his body wrapped in a brown woolen cloth. A red thread was wrapped around his hair. Person B was a female, with her body wrapped in a red tabby woolen cloth as well as a part of a jacket with white ground and red-painted worm patterns (98QZIM103:11B, cat. no. 46). Beside her body was an looped hat and a bundle of reeds tied together.

GRAVE 98QZIM114 (CAT. NO. 47)

Located in the 1998 first excavation site. This grave was a rectangular vertical-pit type grave, its orientation was west-east. The grave opening was 3.4 meters long and 2.5 meters wide. The grave was 1.24 meters deep.

Two people were buried in this grave. Person A was covered with a woolen cloth (98QZIM114:2A, cat. no. 47), and nearby was an looped hat. Two other looped hats were found on the bottom of the grave chamber.

GRAVE 98QZIM147 (CAT. NOS 48–51)

Located in the 1998 southern region's third excavation site. This grave had a single entryway and was a rectangular vertical pit-type grave with canopy. The entryway was located in the center of the northern wall of the grave. The orientation of the grave was south-north. The grave belongs to the late phase of Second-period Culture.

The grave opening was 10.1 meters long, 6.4 meters wide. The grave was 2.32 meters deep.

Twenty-four people were buried here. Wooden items that were excavated include: a single-handled wooden jar, single eared wooden jar, single-handled wooden basin, wooden box, wooden drill for making fire, wooden walking stick, wooden belt plaque, wooden spoon, arrows, bow, wooden spindle, wooden comb, wooden buttons, wooden tray, wooden bucket, wooden clip or brooch. Ceramic items included: ceramic *bo* or bowl, single-eared ceramic kettle, ceramic jar. Bone and horn items included: horn cup, bone needle, bone comb. In addition, a woolen bag, leather belt, leather knife sheath, leather gloves, and leather bag were also in the grave, as well as a bronze mirror, a string of beads, wheat, foodstuffs, and pigments.

98QZIM139 墓葬（第四章图 52~54）

位于 1998 年南区第三发掘点。单墓道长方形竖穴棚架墓，墓道处于墓室的西角。墓向东西向。属于第二期文化晚段墓葬。

墓口长 10 米，宽 5.2 米。墓深 2.5 米。

13 人葬。墓葬中发现的木器有带流木罐、小木桶、四足木盘、木盒、木碗、木纺轮、木刀、木梳、木鞭杆、木扣、木箭杆、钻木取火器；骨角器有骨梳、角杯；陶器有小陶罐、双耳陶罐、单耳陶杯。另外，还发现皮带扣、帽、布袋、箭袋、木柄铁刀、芦苇束捆等。

98QZIM129 墓葬（第四章图 55~68）

位于 1998 年北区第一发掘点。单墓道竖穴棚架墓，墓道处于墓室的西北偏东位置。墓向西北—东南向。属第二期文化晚段墓葬。

墓口长 5.6 米，宽 5 米。墓深 1.9 米。在填土中发现木梳、木鞭杆、四足木盘、木箭杆、木器足、木扣和骨套、角勺、角杯、珊瑚珠、竹条、竹排箫、残漆器等。同时，还发现不少的残丝、毛织物。

98QZIM124 墓葬（第四章图 69~72）

位于 1998 年北区第一发掘点。单墓道竖穴棚架墓，墓道处于墓室的西北角。墓向东西向。属第二期文化晚段墓葬。

墓口长 6 米，宽 5 米。墓深 2.3 米。

在填土里发现一些东西，竹木器有木梳、竹条、竹排箫、木鞭杆、四足木盘、残漆木桶、木耜、木扣、彩绘虎纹木牌和木箭杆；陶器有双耳陶罐；装饰品和骨角器有蚌壳骨套、角勺和角杯、蚌壳、绿松石和珊瑚串珠。另外，还发现一些残丝、毛织物。

GRAVE 98QZIM139 (CAT. NOS 52–54)

Located in the 1998 southern region's third excavation site. This grave had a single entryway, and was a rectangular vertical pit-type grave with canopy. The entryway was on the western corner of the grave chamber. The orientation of the grave was east-west. It belongs to the late phase of Second-period culture.

The grave opening has a length of 10 meters, and width of 5.2 meters. Depth of grave 2.5 meters.

Thirteen people were buried in this grave. Wooden articles found in the grave include: wooden jar with spout, small wooden bucket, wooden basin with four legs, wooden box, wooden bowl, wooden spindle, wooden knife, wooden comb, wooden whip stick, wooden buttons, wooden arrows, wooden board for making fire. Bone and horn articles include a bone comb and a horn cup. Ceramic articles include a small ceramic jar, a two-eared ceramic jar and a one-eared ceramic cup. There were also a leather belt buckle, a hat, a cloth bag, a quiver for arrows, a wooden-handled iron knife, bundles of reed, and so on.

GRAVE 98QZIM129 (CAT. NOS 55–68)

Located in the 1998 northern region's first excavation site. This grave had a single entryway, and was a vertical pit-type grave with canopy. The entryway was on the northwest side of the grave chamber, slightly to the east. The orientation was northwest-southeast. It belongs to the late phase of Second-period culture.

The length of the grave opening was 5.6 meters, the width was 5 meters. The grave was 1.9 meters deep. Items found in the disturbed earth of the grave included: wooden comb, wooden whip stick, wooden basin with four legs, wooden arrows, wooden feet to an object, wooden buttons, and bone covering, horn ladle, horn cup, agate bead, bamboo strips, vertical bamboo flute, fragments of lacquered items. There were also quite a few fragments of silk and woolen textiles in the disturbed earth.

GRAVE 98QZIM124 (CAT. NOS 69–72)

Situated in the 1998 northern region's first excavation site. This was a single entryway, vertical-pit type grave with canopy. The entryway was located at the northwest corner of the grave chamber. The orientation of the grave was east-west. It belonged to the late phase of Second-period culture.

The grave opening was 6 meters long and 5 meters wide. The grave was 2.3 meters deep. Various articles were found in the disturbed earth. Bamboo and wooden items included wooden comb, bamboo strips, bamboo vertical flute, wooden stick, four-legged wooden basin, fragments of a lacquered wooden bucket, wooden shovel, wooden buttons, wooden plaque with painted tiger designs, and wooden arrows. Ceramic items included: double-eared ceramic jar. Ornaments and bone and horn items included: freshwater mussel shells, horn ladles and horn cups, shells, turquoise and coral necklaces. In addition, fragments of silk and woolen textiles were found.

毛编织帽 (98QZIM113:1)

高 24.5 厘米，口径 30 厘米。

帽呈圆锥体。环编组织。[10] 顶上有个小环，通过六条主要脊线，从帽尖延伸到帽口。附近有一些短的线脊，则是由短到长变换，逐渐扩大，最后到了帽口。

羊毛较粗，纱为棕色，两根 S 双捻。

39

10 环编组织，又可称圈编组织，以单线成环为主要特征。一般认为古代环编由引针穿线绕织而成。

WOOLEN LOOPED HAT (98QZIM113:1)

Height 24.5 cm, diameter 30 cm.

The shape of the hat is conical, round at the bottom and pointed at the top. It is of an interconnected loop structure (*huanbian*).[2] There is a small thread ring at the top of the hat, with six key ridges starting from it and extending from the tip of the hat to the rim. Short rows in their vicinity gradually get longer, allowing the bottom of the hat to be wider.

The wool of the hat is quite heavy; the yarn is brown-colored and S-plied from 2 ends.

---

2 Looping, *huanbian*, can also be called *quanbian*. It is characterized by a single thread forming the loop. It is generally felt that ancient looping techniques were worked with a needle.

1 帽身组织 Interconnected loop structure

2 帽尖 Ring at the top of the hat

编织毛绦裙 (98QZIM113:24C)

裙长 44.5 厘米，宽 83 厘米。

直筒形。由 14 根编织毛绦上、下拼接缝缀而成。保存有腰带。

编织绦，除 1 根是用三根 S 捻线 1/1 斜编外，其余的皆为 2/2 斜编，用线多为 Z 捻，3 根并股，很少用两根并股的。自下而上分别是：a.棕色编织绦，宽 4.5 厘米，3 根并股线；b.蓝绿色编织绦，宽 3.5 厘米，3 根并股线；c.红色编织绦，宽 3.5 厘米，3 根并股线；d.蓝色编织绦，宽 3.5 厘米，3 根并股线（图 3）；e.酱紫色编织绦，宽 4.2 厘米，3 根并股线；f.淡黄色编织绦，宽 3 厘米，2 根并股线；g.酱紫色编织绦，宽 3.5 厘米，3 根并股线；h.大红色编织绦，宽 3.2 厘米，3 根并股线；i.紫红色编织绦，宽 3 厘米，3 根并股线；j.土黄色编织绦，宽 3.5 厘米，3 根并股线；k.菱格纹编织绦（图 2），宽 3 厘米，3 根并股线，由淡黄色和酱紫色两种色线编织；i.黄棕色编织带，宽 2.5 厘米，3 根并股线；m.紫红色编织绦，宽 2 厘米，3 根并股线；n.菱格纹编织绦，宽 2 厘米，3 根 S 捻，1/1 绞编，由黄色和酱紫色线编织菱格纹。

编织绦的经头，穿有毛绳（图 1）。经尾则是毛边，或折卷缝缀。

腰带，红色，上面有个结扣。3 根并股纱编织，Z 捻，2/2 斜编。残长 56 厘米，宽 2 厘米。

40

SKIRT MADE OF BRAIDED WOOLEN BANDS (98QZIM113:24C)

Height of the skirt is 44.5 cm; width is 83 cm.

The skirt is in straight tubular form, and is composed of fourteen bands that were sewn together one on top of the other. The garment retains a waist belt or strap.

With one exception, which is 1/1 oblique twining, the structure of all the bands is 2/2 twill oblique interlacing, with tripled Z-spun threads. Very rarely doubled threads are used. From bottom to top are: a. brown braided band, 4.5 cm wide, tripled threads; b. blue–green braided band, 3.5 cm wide, tripled threads; c. red braided band, 3.5 cm wide, tripled threads; d. blue braided band, 3.5 cm wide, tripled threads (fig. 3); e. dark purple braided band, 4.2 cm wide, tripled threads; f. light yellow braided band, 3 cm wide, doubled threads; g. dark purple braided band, 3.5 cm wide, tripled threads; h. pure red braided band, 3.2 cm wide, tripled threads; i. purple-red braided band, 3 cm wide, tripled threads; j. earth yellow braided band, 3.5 cm wide, tripled threads; k. diamond-pattern braided band, 3 cm wide, tripled threads, braided from two colors, light yellow and dark purple (fig. 2); l. yellow-

1 编织绦的经头 Starting edge of braided band (j)

brown braided band, 2.5 cm wide, tripled threads; m. purple-red braided band, 2 cm wide, tripled threads; n. diamond-pattern braided band, 2 cm wide, worked in 1/1 oblique twining with S-plied threads from 2 ends in yellow and dark purple to form the diamond pattern.

The starting edges of the bands have woolen strings onto which the threads are knotted with lark's head knots (fig. 1). The warp threads' 'tails' are unfinished, folded in and stitched.

The waist belt is red and still tied to a knot. It is worked in 2/2 twill oblique interlacing, with Z-spun tripled threads. The remaining fragment is 56 cm long and 2 cm wide.

2 菱格纹编织绦 Diamond-patterned braided band (k)

3 蓝色编织绦 Blue braided band (d)

白地 "龙" 纹缋罽长袍残片 (98QZIM113:26-1A)

经拼对：长 76 厘米，宽 108 厘米。

保存三幅缋罽，以幅边方向纵向缝合。其中有两幅保存两面幅边，一幅没有保存幅边，幅宽 40.5 厘米。

右侧一幅边上有牙线，可能是前右襟部分，其余两幅是后背的左、右部分，其中缝上也饰有牙线。这样一来，牙线饰于前襟和中缝，比较合理。

缋罽为平纹组织，羊毛中等粗，经、纬线皆 Z 捻，经密 20 根／厘米，纬密 10 根／厘米（图 1）。

牙线为棕色，里面夹杂少量的其他颜色羊毛。前襟牙线是两根并股，后背中缝牙线是单根。牙线为 4 根 Z 重捻。

缋罽，用红彩绘似 "龙" 的纹样。图案残缺严重，主体图案，是线条勾画的一正一反两个像牛股骨头的纹样，头部有须，身体上有点纹和短弧线纹等，连续斜向排列。看似像龙纹，大 小也有些差别。

FRAGMENT OF A WHITE WOOLEN LONG GOWN PAINTED WITH DRAGON-LIKE PATTERN (98QZIM113:26-1A)

Overall dimensions of the assembled fragments: height 76 cm, width 108 cm.

Three lengths of the painted fabric have been preserved, sewn together lengthwise along the selvages. Of the pieces, two have retained both selvages, one piece has no selvage; the fabric was woven 40.5 cm wide.

On one selvage on the right side is a decorative edging which may have formed the right front edge of the garment. The other two pieces are the right and left parts of the back, their join is also decorated with an edging cord. It would be appropriate for edging to adorn the front edges and the middle seam.

The painted fabric is tabby weave, woven of medium-weight wool with warp and weft threads both Z-spun, and a warp thread count of 20 ends per cm and weft of 10 picks per cm (fig. 1).

The edging thread is brown but mottled with various other colors of wool. The edging on the front opening is doubled, that on the back seam is single. The edging cord is Z re-plied from altogether four ends.

Red pigment was used to paint the 'dragon' pattern on the fabric. The damage to the pattern is severe. The main pattern is in outline form with the animals facing each other in opposition, their shapes somewhat like the curves of the thighbone of a cow. Their heads have whiskers, their bodies are decorated with both spots and curvilinear lines. They are portrayed in continuous diagonal rows. This appears to be a dragon pattern, but there are also differences in size.

1 组织图 Painted woolen tabby

编织带 （98QZIM113:30-1B）

长 171 厘米，宽 1 厘米。

用 6 根 Z 重捻的红、蓝、棕、黄等四种色线，2/2 斜编而成。带面显长方格纹，由数条齿纹组成。长方格纹长短有些变化，3、4.5、5.5 厘米不等。格纹色分红蓝和黄棕两种（图 1），两面颜色互换，如正面显红、蓝色，其反面则显棕、黄色。

穗，一端保存较好穗饰，长 20 厘米（图 2）。

BRAIDED BELT (98QZIM113:30-1B)

Length 171 cm, width 1 cm.

The belt uses four different colors of thread, all Z-re-plied from altogether 6 ends: red, blue, brown and yellow. It is worked in two-layer twill oblique interlacing with complementary passages. The larger pattern on the belt is rectangles, with each rectangle made up of many variegated zigzag lines. The rectangles are uneven in length, being 3, 4.5, 5.5 cm and so on. The patterning is done in two combinations of colors, red/blue and yellow/ brown (fig. 1). The colors on either side of the belt alternate, if the front is red and blue, then the reverse side is brown and yellow.

The fringe is well preserved on one end and is 20 cm long (fig. 2).

1 纹饰 Zigzag pattern

2 穗 Fringe

42

紫红色毛布开襟长袍 (98QZIM136:10B)

袍身长 104 厘米，肩袖通宽 167 厘米。两袖分别长 57.5 厘米、60.5 厘米，袖口宽 11.5 厘米，肩袖口宽 19.5 厘米。肩宽 51 厘米，下摆宽 82.5 厘米，臀宽 83 厘米。

袍服呈窄肩、对领、宽臀、宽下摆、窄口袖形式，并饰有牙线。

衣身为两幅毛布，前后对折拼接、后背缝合而成。两袖各为一幅毛布，上、下对折缝合而成（图1）。袍服没有剪裁，肩胸部和两袖皆以其形向内折，多少有些变化，下摆则保留两幅毛布的幅宽。

毛布皆保存两面幅边。左侧毛布：前身幅宽 40 厘米，后身则宽 44.5 厘米；右侧毛布：后身幅宽 38 厘米，前身幅宽 44.5 厘米。毛布纺织的松紧有些变化。袖毛布幅宽 42 厘米。平纹，经、纬纱皆 Z 捻，经密 11 根／厘米，纬密 8 根／厘米（图3）。羊毛中等粗，棕色为羊毛原色，上面染红色后显紫红色。

牙线，为红色纱，布于前襟、下摆底缘边、袖口、肩袖口缝、后背中缝上（图2）。

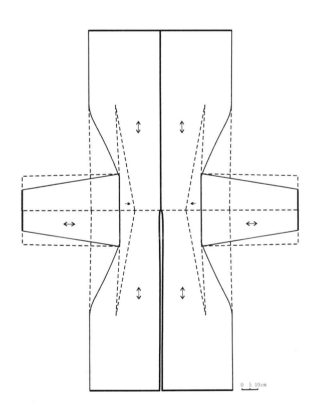

0 5 10cm

1 结构图 Cut and construction diagram

LONG GOWN WITH OPEN FRONT MADE OF PURPLE-RED WOOLEN CLOTH (98QZIM136:10B)

The length of the gown is 104 cm, the overall sleeve-and-shoulder width is 167 cm. The two sleeves are 57.5 and 60.5 cm long, the cuffs are 11.5 cm wide, the armscye is 19.5 cm high. The gown has a shoulder width of 51 cm. The lower hem is 82.5 cm, and the hip portion 83 cm wide.

The gown has narrow shoulders, edge-to-edge front, wide hips, wide lower hem, narrow sleeves and is adorned with piping.

The body is made from two pieces of woolen cloth, folded at the shoulders and sewn together along the center back and at the seams. The two sleeves are each made of one piece of fabric, with top and bottom folded and sewn together (fig. 1). There was no cutting in making this garment; to shape it, the fabric was folded to the inside at the shoulders and sleeves, with varying degrees of latitude. At the lower hem both cloth lengths retain their full loom width.

Since the woolen cloth retains both selvages, we know that the loom width of the left side of the gown is 40 cm in front and 44.5 cm in back. The loom width of the right side of the gown is 44.5 cm in front and 38 cm in back. The fabric has various degrees of looseness or tightness of the weave. The woolen cloth of the sleeves is 42 cm wide. The cloth is tabby, with both warp and weft yarn Z-spun; the thread count of the warp is 11 ends per cm, of the weft, it is 8 picks per cm (fig. 3). The wool is of medium weight and originally of a brown color which, after being dyed red, gives the appearance of purple-red.

Piping is done in red yarn, and placed on the front edges, the lower hem, the cuffs, the armscyes, and the central seam in the back (fig. 2).

2 牙线 Piping

3 组织图 Woolen cloth

红色毛布开襟长袍 <small>(98QZIM136:9-1A)</small>

袍身长 135 厘米，肩袖通宽 174 厘米。袖长 58 厘米，袖口宽 11.5 厘米，肩袖口宽 18.5 厘米。肩宽 58 厘米，下摆宽 77.5 厘米。

窄肩，宽臀、宽下摆形式，对领、开襟、窄袖口，饰有牙线。

袍身由两幅毛布纵向拼接、前后对折缝制。两袖各为一幅毛布，上、下对折缝合（图 1）。

袍服没有剪裁，肩和两袖口皆将布幅内折缝合而成，内折多少也有些变化，下摆则保留着两幅毛布的幅宽。

毛布保存两面幅边，幅宽 39 厘米。平纹，经、纬纱皆 Z 捻，经纱捻得紧，纬纱捻得松。经密 14 根／厘米，纬密 8 根／厘米（图 2）。

牙线饰于前襟边、袖口、肩袖、后身中缝、下摆底缘，为黄色四根 S 捻。

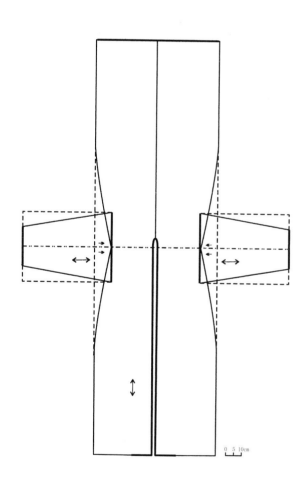

1 结构图 Cut and construction diagram

LONG GOWN WITH OPEN FRONT MADE OF RED WOOLEN CLOTH (98QZIM136:9-1A)

The body is 135 cm long; the overall sleeve-and-shoulder width is 174 centimeters. The sleeves are 58 cm long; the cuffs are 11.5 cm wide and the armscyes are 18.5 cm high. The measurement across the shoulders is 58 cm; the lower hem is 77.5 cm wide.

This garment has narrow shoulders, a broad hip area, a broad lower part, and an edge-to-edge front; it is open in the front, has narrow sleeves, and is adorned with piping.

The gown was made from two pieces of woolen cloth put together lengthwise, with front and back folded at the shoulder and sewn together along the center back. The two sleeves are each made from a piece of woolen cloth with top and bottom folded together and sewn (fig. 1).

The gown did not involve any cutting. At shoulders and cuffs, the fabric was folded to the inside, tapering off along the sleeve and towards the hip. The lower hem retains the width of the two pieces of cloth.

The woolen cloth retains both selvages: the width of the fabric is 39 cm. It is tabby, with warp and weft yarn both Z-spun, with warp yarn spun tightly and weft yarn spun loosely. The warp thread count is 14 ends per cm; weft is 8 picks per cm (fig. 2).

Piping adorns the front opening edges, cuffs, armscyes, the rear seam, and the lower edge. It is yellow S-ply from four ends.

44

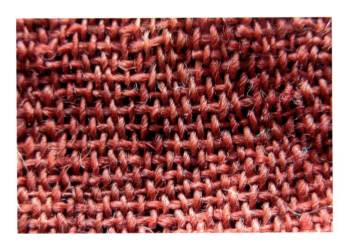

2 组织图 Woolen cloth

白色缂毛筒裙 (98QZIM136:13D)

裙长 100 厘米，腰宽 81 厘米，下摆 82 厘米。

直筒裙，三幅毛布纵向拼接缝合而成。毛布皆保存两面幅边，幅宽分别为 52、55.5、56 厘米。2/2 Z 斜纹毛布，经密 8 根／厘米，纬密 32 根／厘米。纬纱白色。经纱比较杂，多数是白色纱，少数棕色纱，分区，但没有明显的规律。皆 Z 捻，经粗、纬细。

裙腰边是经纱绞编带饰，宽 0.4 厘米。下摆边是卷边缝合。

缂织花纹为横绦式纹样，宽 1.2 厘米。图案由连续的几何小曲波纹、三角纹组成，有蓝、酱红、红、天青、军绿、黄棕色、黄和白等八种色，相间搭配。缂织花为 2/2 斜纹，纬纱两根并股（图 1）。

WHITE TUBULAR SKIRT WITH TAPESTRY-WOVEN PATTERN (98QZIM136:13D)

Length of the skirt 100 cm, width at the waist 81 cm, at lower hem 82 cm.

This straight tubular skirt is composed of three pieces of woolen cloth put together lengthwise and sewn with three seams. The three pieces of woolen cloth all retain both selvages, the loom widths are 52, 55.5, and 56 cm. The cloth is woven in 2/2 Z twill weave, with a warp thread count of 8 ends per cm and weft of 32 picks per cm. The weft yarn is white. The warp yarn is mixed, most of it white yarn, some brown yarn divided into sections but without any clear rules. All threads are Z-spun, and are heavy-weight for the warp and fine for the weft.

At the waist edge there is a 0.4-cm-band of intertwined warp ends. The lower hem is rolled and stitched.

1 组织图
Tapestry decoration in 2/2 Z twill weave

The tapestry-woven pattern is a horizontal strip, 1.2 cm wide. The pattern is a continuous row of small geometric wave patterns made up of triangles, done in eight different colors: blue, dark red, red, sky-blue, army green, yellow-brown, yellow, and white. They are in alternating groupings. The tapestry pattern is also woven in 2/2 Z twill with most of the weft yarn being doubled (fig. 1).

45

白地"虫"纹缋罽残上衣 (98QZIM103:1-1B)

衣身长 58 厘米。肩袖通宽 84 厘米，右肩宽 30 厘米，袖长 52 厘米。肩袖口宽 18 厘米，袖口宽 11 厘米。只剩了右半部分衣身和袖，右袖较完整。衣身和袖各为一幅毛布，皆保存了两面幅边，幅宽 43 厘米。

衣身为前、后折，袖为上、下对折缝制。前襟缘边和袖口饰枣红色牙线。衣没有剪裁痕迹，袖两头窄、中间宽，衣身肩窄、下摆宽，都是布幅的内折或卷边缝合效果，显现出扎滚鲁克早期服饰制作的特点。

从前身中缝的下部缝合看，似套头上衣。如是，那么衣身下部的牙线就会因对折缝合而埋没于里面，起不到牙线的装饰作用，这不太符合衣服饰牙线的目的。由此推想，最初可能是开襟上衣，人死后穿着时，将前襟缝合，所以给人以套头上衣的感觉。

缋罽为白色地，平纹组织，羊毛中等粗，经、纬纱皆 Z 捻，经密 14 根 / 厘米，纬密 10 根 / 厘米（图 2 ）。红彩绘画，纹样似"虫"纹。"虫"纹由线条勾勒，呈曲折状，两头尖、中间粗，有蠕动感。虫体上有三个螺旋纹，由弧平行线相连。衣身前襟上可以看出三排虫纹，袖上也是三排，横向排列。衣身后背，有一骆驼纹和一只羊纹，形象不很典型，骆驼的单峰则比较明显。"虫"纹的大小、形状都有些变化，一般长 23~24 厘米，宽 3.5~6 厘米，线条粗细不匀。同时，在缋罽的面上有颜料的滴珠。

衣前襟、袖口的枣红色牙线，是两根并股纱。

衣身前襟有用平针补绣的曲折花纹（图 1 ）。

1 平针绣　Repair with flat stitch embroidery

2 组织图
Front and back side of the
woolen tabby with selvage
and piping

WHITE WOOLEN JACKET, RED-PAINTED IN A WORM PATTERN (98QZIM103:1–1B)

Length of the body of the jacket is 58 cm. The overall width of the fragmentary jacket is 84 cm; the right shoulder is 30 cm wide and the sleeve is 52 cm long. The armscye is 18 cm high and the cuff is 11 cm wide.

Only the right half remains of this jacket, and the sleeve is fairly complete. Both sleeve and body-half were made from one piece of woolen cloth; both pieces of cloth retain two selvages. The fabric is 43 cm wide.

46

The body was folded front and back and then sewn, and the sleeve was folded top and bottom and then sewn. The front opening and cuff have piping that is a date-red color. The garment shows no traces of having been cut. The two ends of the sleeve are narrower than the middle and the top of the jacket is narrower than the bottom hem, but this is all the result of folding or tucking fabric to the inside and then sewing. This is characteristic for early Zaghunluq garments.

Given the central seam of the jacket in the front, this seems to have been a jacket put on over the head. But if this were so, the piping on the lower part of the body would have been hidden due to folding and sewing and would not serve the function of being edging. This does not tally with the purpose of edging on a garment. We hypothesize that, at the beginning, the garment was perhaps open in front, but after the person died and the garment was put on, the seam in the middle was sewn together so that it now appears to have been put on over the head.

The painting of the pattern is on a white ground. The fabric is tabby weave, wool is of medium weight, and both warp and weft yarn are Z-spun. The warp thread count is 14 ends per cm, the weft is 10 picks per cm (fig. 2). The red painting depicts in outline form the pattern of worms. They are shown in wavy fashion. The two ends of the worm are pointed and their middles are fatter, as if they were wriggling. Three whorl patterns are painted on the body of each worm, they are linked together with curving lines. Three rows of worms can be seen on the front of the garment and another three lines on the sleeves that are lined up horizontally. The back of the jacket has a camel and a sheep that are not totally accurate but the single hump of the camel is quite clear. The sizes and shapes of the worms are all a little different. Generally they are between 23–24 cm long, and 3.5–6 cm wide. The lines used to depict them are of varying thickness. There are also extraneous drops of paint on the fabric.

The date-red piping at the front opening and cuff is made with doubled thread. On the front part there is a repair executed in flat stitch forming a complicated zigzag pattern (fig. 1).

46

273

彩条、几何纹缂毛单 (98QZIM114:2A)

长 93 厘米，宽 144 厘米。

长方形，饰有穗。由四幅毛布纵向拼接缝缀而成，其中有一幅毛布保存两面幅边，幅宽 58 厘米。

平纹组织，羊毛粗中等，经、纬纱皆 Z 捻，经密 7 根／厘米，纬密 70 根／厘米。经纱为棕色，羊毛色有些杂，夹有少量的白色羊毛。纬纱有红、蓝、白、姜黄、酱红、棕等六种色，分区，形成横向的彩条纹。彩条纹宽 0.8~1 厘米，三条为一组。

彩条纹的地色有红色和酱红色两种，素彩条纹有蓝、白、姜黄等三色（图 2）。同时，仅在酱红地的彩条上缂织几何花纹（图 1）。缂织花纹是在斜长菱格上显水波纹、回纹、小叶纹等。彩条纹与缂织花纹成组交错分布。缂织花纹地主要是三色，即蓝、白、姜黄。三色循环变化。

毛布单下缘边是 8 厘米的红色宽带纹，边穗为 6 根 S 双捻线绳，长 5 厘米，拴系有结。单的上缘是棕宽带纹，宽 8.5 厘米。残留有卷边缝缀的痕迹。

WOOLEN CLOTH WITH TAPESTRY-WOVEN STRIPES AND GEOMETRIC PATTERNS (98QZIM114:2A)

Height 93 cm, width 144 cm.

The cloth is rectangular and adorned with fringes. It is made from four pieces of woolen cloth put together lengthwise and sewn together with vertical seams. One of the pieces retains two selvages; the fabric is 58 cm wide.

The piece is woven in weft-faced tabby weave, of medium-weight wool, both warp and weft yarn Z-spun. The warp thread count is 7 ends per cm, the weft is 70 picks per cm. The warp thread is different shades of natural brown colors, with a small amount of white wool mixed in. The weft yarn includes six colors: red, blue, white, ginger-yellow, dark red, and brown, divided into sections to form horizontal colored stripes. The width of the colored stripes varies from 0.8 to 1 cm, and every three lines constitutes a 'grouping' of stripes.

The ground color of the multicolored stripes is both red and dark red. The single-colored stripe groups are blue, white, and ginger-yellow on red ground (fig. 2). They repeat in cycles. In the dark red ground sections are stripes of tapestry-woven geometric patterns (fig. 1). These depict diagonally slanted waves made up of elongated diamonds, also small leaf patterns and so on. The tapestry-woven patterning and the colored bands alternate.

The lower edge of the woolen cloth has a red-colored 8-cm-wide band, and a fringe that is made from cords that are S plied from 6 ends, 5 cm long, and tied with knots at the end. The upper edge is a band of brown, 8.5 cm wide. It bears traces of having been rolled and sewn.

1 缂织几何纹 Tapestry-woven stylized pattern

2 素彩条纹 Color stripes

动物纹缂毛提袋 (98QZIM147:26)

全长 27 厘米，穗长 8 厘米，提绳长 19 厘米。袋体长 16.3 厘米，宽 15 厘米。

长方形，由提绳、袋体和穗组成。袋体为一幅毛布缝缀，保存两面幅边，幅宽 15 厘米。自下向上对折，两侧边缘缝合，口缘内折卷边缝缀。一侧的缝线保存较好，一侧缝线已脱开。

袋体缂毛，为蓝地，显白、红、黄、紫、绿五色纹样。纬纱 Z 捻，经纱 S 双捻，有棕、白两种色。地组织为平纹，经密 8 根 / 厘米，纬密 26 根 / 厘米。

提绳，红色，8 根纱 Z 复捻绳，绳头有结。

穗，红色毛线，饰于袋体底缘边的两侧。袋体的右侧穗上拴系蓝色羊毛。

缂织的动物似鹿或羊，头上有角。回首，作屈肢奔跑状。

WOOLEN BAG WITH ANIMAL PATTERNS WOVEN IN TAPESTRY-WEAVE (98QZIM147:26)

Overall height 27 cm, tassels 8 cm long, carrying strap 19 cm long. The body of the bag itself is 16.3 cm high and 15 cm wide.

The bag is rectangular, and made up of the bag itself, a rope handle, and tassels. The bag itself is a sewn piece of woolen fabric that retains two selvages; the loom width is 15 cm. It was folded in half at the bottom and the two sides were sewn together, with the border at the mouth being rolled to the inside and sewn. The stitching is fairly well preserved on one side, but has come loose on the other side.

The tapestry-weave of the bag is on a blue ground with the pattern shown in the five colors white, red, yellow, purple, and green. The weft yarn is Z-spun, the warp yarn S-plied and both brown and white. The basic weave is tabby with a warp thread count of 8 ends per cm and a weft thread count of 26 picks per cm.

1 组织图 Tapestry weave

The handle is red and made of 8 threads of yarn that are Z plied, with knots at either end. The tassels are from red woolen yarn, they decorate either side of the bottom of the bag. On the right-hand tassel a clump of blue-colored wool is tied to the threads.

The animal patterns that are woven into the fabric appear to be either deer or ibexes, their heads have horns. They are looking backwards, with legs curved as though running.

48

白色毛罗立领套头上衣 (98QZIM147:61-2)

衣身长 69 厘米, 肩袖通宽 86 厘米 (残宽)。肩宽 60 厘米, 下摆宽 68 厘米。袖残长 23 厘米、8 厘米, 肩袖口宽 20 厘米。

衣身为直筒形。圆立领, 套头, 饰编织绦。

衣前、后身各为上、下两幅毛罗横向缝缀。上幅毛罗保存两面幅边, 幅宽 35 厘米; 下幅保存一面幅边, 幅残宽 34.5 厘米。衣身一侧残缺, 一侧稍好, 可以看出是裁剪后缝合。两肩皆已开线, 缝合痕迹不明显。

袖, 各由一幅毛罗上、下对折、加三角缝制, 毛罗保存一面幅边 (图 1)。

毛罗, 经、纬纱皆 Z 捻, 羊毛细, 捻得比较紧。经纱为白色, 纬纱以白色为主, 还有红、蓝两种色纱。毛罗的平纹组织和罗组织呈绦式分布, 罗组织为二经纠。平纹组织部分, 宽 1.1 厘米, 经密 11 根 / 厘米, 纬密 18 根 / 厘米。罗组织部分宽 0.3~0.6 厘米 (图 2)。经密 0.6 厘米 /7 根, 纬密 0.3 厘米 /1 根。

在衣身的前、后中轴和两侧肩袖, 都有一宽带纹。带纹的中间是红色, 两侧边是绿色。带纹宽窄有些变化, 后身宽 4~5 厘米, 前身和袖一样宽, 为 4 厘米。

立领, 由编织绦和平纹毛布缝合。编织绦为红色, 较宽。残长 10 厘米, 宽 2.8 厘米。两根并纱, 2/2 斜编。经边系折卷收边缝缀, 一侧开口, 并饰有毛系绳。平纹毛布也为红色, 分成了三段, 长 5.5、6、10.5 厘米。两侧缘折边缝缀, 没有发现幅边。羊毛较细, 经、纬纱皆 Z 捻, 经密 9 根 / 厘米, 纬密 28 根 / 厘米。

编织绦, 处于前、后身的中轴部分, 为三根并股纱的 1/1 斜编绦。后身编织绦保存较好, 前身残缺严重。绦稍窄, 宽 0.6 厘米。另外, 在肩部残留一条编织饰绦, 绦宽 0.5 厘米, 残长 7.8 厘米, 也是三根并股纱的 1/1 斜编绦。

2 组织图 Woolen gauze

WHITE WOOLEN GAUZE PULLOVER JACKET WITH STANDING COLLAR (98QZIM147:61-2)

The body of the jacket is 69 cm long, the maximum width of the remaining fragment is 86 cm. The shoulder width is 60 cm, the lower hem is 68 cm wide. The length of the incomplete sleeve is 23.8 cm, the armscyes are 20 cm high.

The jacket is in straight tubular form. It has a round neck with standing collar, was put on over the head and is decorated with braids.

Front and back were made by sewing two pieces of woolen gauze together horizontally. The upper piece of woolen gauze retains both selvages; the fabric is 35 cm wide. The lower retains one selvage, the maximum preserved width is 34.5 cm. One side of the garment is fragmentary, the other slightly more complete. One can see that the garment was sewn together after being cut. The stitching at the shoulders has come apart, and the traces of the seam are hard to see. Each of the sleeves was made from one piece of woolen gauze, top and bottom folded together and stitched, with triangular gussets added at the underarm seam. This piece retains one selvage (fig. 1).

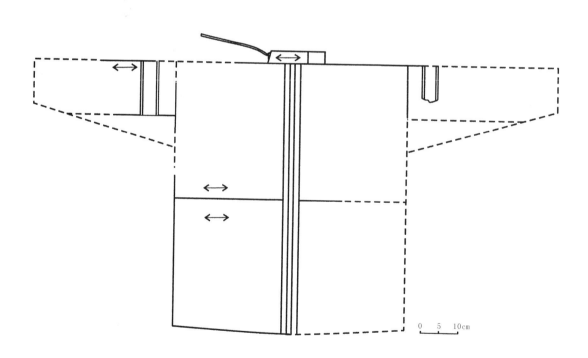

1 结构图 Cut and construction diagram (front of garment.)

The warp and weft yarn of the woolen gauze were both Z-spun, the wool is fine and the spinning was fairly tight. The warp yarn is white; the weft is mainly white, with some red and blue. The alternation tabby and gauze weave structures creates a striped pattern; the weave is a patterned two-end simple gauze, with the gauze pick floating on the reverse in areas where there is no warp crossing. The tabby weave parts are 1.1 cm wide, with warp count of 11 ends per cm, weft of 18 picks per cm. The gauze parts are between 0.3 and 0.6 cm wide; their warp density is 7 ends per 0.6 cm, and there is 1 weft pick per 0.3 cm (fig. 2).

There is a decorative gauze-woven band on the center front and back of the jacket and on the sleeve near the shoulder. The middle of this band is red, with green on both sides. Its width varies: on the back it is 4-5 cm, on the front is the same width as on the sleeves, 4 cm.

The standing collar is sewn together from an braided band and tabby woolen cloth. The braided band is red and fairly wide. The length of the fragment is 10 cm, width is 2.8 cm. It is worked with doubled yarn, 2/2 twill oblique interlacing. The narrow ends are folded in and stitched. There is an opening on one side that has a woolen tie-string. The tabby woolen cloth is also red and is in three sections, 5.5, 6, and 10.5 cm long. The edges are folded in and stitched, no selvage has been discovered. The wool is fairly fine, warp and weft threads both Z-spun, with a warp thread count of 9 ends per cm, and weft of 28 picks per cm.

The red braided band stitched on front and back along the central vertical axis is made from tripled threads and worked in twill oblique interlacing. On the back, it is preserved in considerable length while on the front much more is missing. It is quite narrow, 0.6 cm wide. In addition, another red braided band decorates the armscyes, it is 0.5 cm wide and its maximum preserved length is 7.8 cm. Again it is made from tripled threads and worked in twill oblique interlacing.

阶梯十字形白色毛布裤裆 (98QZIM147:68)

长 38 厘米，幅宽 40 厘米。

呈阶梯"十"字形。专为裤纺织的毛布裆，经纱头反穿插在了纬纱上（图 1）。

羊毛较粗。经纱 Z 捻，有两种色毛，一为纯白色羊毛；一为棕、白两种色的羊毛混捻纱，棕色毛多一些，白色毛少，显棕色。纬纱白色，S 捻。1/2 Z 斜纹组织。经密 5 根／厘米，纬密 39 根／厘米。

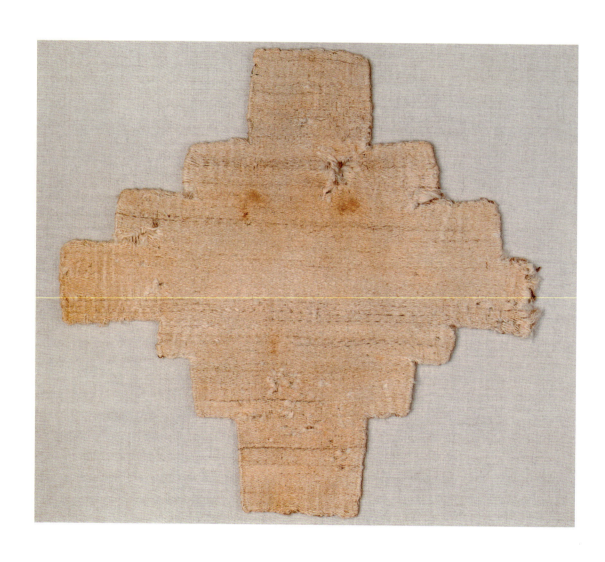

WHITE WOOLEN-CLOTH CROTCH OF PANTS, IN STAIR-STEPPED CROSS FORM (98QZIM147:68)

Height 38 cm, width of the fabric (with selvage) 40 cm.

The shape of this piece was specifically woven for use as a crotch in a pair of pants. It is in a stair-stepped cross shape. The warp yarn ends are turned around and pulled back into the fabric again (fig. 1).

The wool is fairly thick. The warp yarn was Z-spun and of two colors, one pure white, the other brown and white mixed together. The brown predominates with less white so the appearance is of brown. The weft yarn is white and S-spun. The weave is 1/2 Z twill. The thread count of the warp is 5 ends per cm, of the weft, 39 picks per cm.

1 组织图 Warp edge (reverse)

白地红、灰网格纹缋罽上衣残片 (98QZIM147:70)

长 56.5 厘米，宽 28.5 厘米。

长方形，为衣身部分，残留了前身和后身的肩背部分。同时下摆底缘、肩袖口、肩部都有折卷边缘缝缀的痕迹。前身保存了右襟，是保存两面幅边的一幅毛布，幅宽 41 厘米。同时，可以看出右襟缘边和外侧部分，襟缘边上保存了 3 根均匀分布的系绳，皆 S 捻。其中的一根较长。

在衣身右外侧，保存了肩袖口，宽 19.5 厘米。肩袖口为剪裁口，不是剪刀裁剪效果，略显毛边。右袖残迹保存很少的幅边，袖以幅宽为袖的长，上、下对折而成。

后背的残毛布紧连着前身右襟，肩结合部有拼接缝缀残迹。与前身右襟相拼接的后背是两幅毛布，以幅边纵向拼接，皆保存一面幅边。残幅宽 12 厘米，残长分别为 11、6 厘米。由此可以看出，后背有可能是三幅毛布，至少两幅是经过剪裁。

在前身的襟缘边和肩袖部分都残留了牙线。牙线为棕色，S 捻。

毛布为平纹组织，羊毛较细，经、纬纱皆 Z 捻。经、纬纱都是白色，纬纱每织六行就会出现一行两根并股纱。经密 14 根 / 厘米，纬密 12 根 / 厘米。

毛布地色是白色，由红、灰两种色的宽带斜向交叉，形成了宽带网格纹。带纹是绘上去的，有一些色滴珠。带纹，红带纹宽 5.5 厘米，灰带纹稍窄，宽 4.5 厘米。红、灰两种色相交、重叠处，显灰红色。所以，称它是"白地红、灰网格纹缋罽上衣残片"。

FRAGMENT OF WOOLEN JACKET WITH PAINTED RED-AND-GREY NETTING PATTERN (98QZIM147:70)

Height 56.5 cm, width 28.5 cm.

Rectangular in shape, this textile was part of a garment with the extant part being the front and the shoulder part of the back. The lower hem, the armscye, and the shoulder line all were folded in and show the traces of rolling and sewing. The right front of the body is preserved as one piece of fabric, with both selvages. The loom width is 41 cm. Three regularly spaced tie-strings are preserved on the front edge, which are all S-spun. Among them, one is slightly longer.

An armscye is preserved on the right side of the jacket front, it is 19.5 cm high. The armscye is a cut opening; because it was not cut with scissors, it shows some rough ends of the wool. A very small portion of selvage is left on the vestige of the right-sleeve fragment. The length of the sleeve corresponded to the width of the fabric, whose top and bottom were folded together.

The fragmentary back is still attached to the right front part; the remains of a stitched seam appear at the shoulder where they join together. The back consisted of two pieces of woolen cloth, joined selvage to selvage with a vertical seam. The fragments are 12 cm wide, and 11 and 6 cm long. From this it can be seen that the back part was perhaps made of three pieces of woolen cloth, and that at least two of them had been cut.

Traces of piping remain on the front edge and the armscye seam. The piping is brown and S-spun.

The woolen cloth is tabby weave, the wool is relatively fine, with both warp and weft yarn Z-spun. Warp and weft yarn are both white; the weft has one pick of double yarn woven in every six picks. The warp thread count is 14 ends per cm, the weft is 12 picks per cm.

The basic color of the cloth is white, with bands of two colors, red and grey that run diagonally across the fabric forming a banded netting pattern. The bands are painted on and there are occasional drops of the pigment on the fabric. The red strips are 5.5 cm wide; the grey ones are slightly narrower, 4.5 cm wide. Red and grey intersect and where they overlap the resulting color is grey-red. Therefore, the description of this textile is 'fragment of a jacket with white ground and painted red-and-grey netting pattern.'

51

蛇纹缂毛绦 (A.98QZIM139:9，B.98QZIM139:53-6C)

A. 长 44 厘米，宽 4.5 厘米。

B. 三片：长 37.5、21.5、18 厘米，宽 5 厘米。

蓝地，显纹样。羊毛中等粗，经线 S 双捻，为棕、白两种羊毛的混捻纱，其中棕色羊毛多一些，显棕色。纬纱 Z 捻，有紫红、蓝、白和酱紫等四种色。地组织为平纹，经密 9 根／厘米，纬密 40 根／厘米（图 1）。

白纱和紫红色纱显 "X" 形纹，相间分布，以分隔纹样。间隔宽 5.7 厘米左右。主纹样是蛇纹，蛇头作六边形，方眼，曲状嘴，小耳。头作白色，嘴和眼眶为紫红色，酱紫色为眼仁和小耳。蛇身呈折线的弯曲状，以紫红、白两种色的小方格纹形式附着在紫红的（当地大红的）曲条纹上（图 2）。

WOOLEN STRIPS IN TAPESTRY WEAVE WITH SNAKE PATTERN

(A: 98QZIM139:9, B: 98QZIM139:53-6C)

A Height 44 cm, width 4.5 cm.
B Three pieces of 37.5, 21.5, and 18 cm length, width is 5 cm.

The textile has a blue ground which sets off the pattern. The wool is of medium weight, warp threads are S-ply from two ends, and from brown and white natural wool mixed and spun together. The brown slightly predominates, making the color look brown. Weft yarn is Z-spun, and comes in four colors, purple-red, blue, white, and dark purple. The basic weave structure is tabby, thread count of warp is 9 ends per cm, of weft it is 40 picks per cm (fig. 1).

The white yarn and purple-red yarn alternatively display a diagonal cross that divides the motif of the pattern. The crosses are spaced at roughly 5.7 cm intervals. The main motif is a snake pattern with the snakes' heads woven in hexagonal shape, their eyes are square, their mouths curved, and

52

287

they have small ears. The heads are white, the mouths and eye sockets purple-red. The pupils of the eyes and the small ears are woven in dark purple. The snakes' bodies are curved and made up of a band of alternating purple-red and white shapes adjoining a band of purple-red, locally of pure red color (fig. 2).

52

1 组织图 Tapestry weave (A)

2 蛇纹 Snake pattern (A)

曲折纹残缂毛 (98QZIM139:53-5C)

长 27.5 厘米，宽 13.5 厘米。

裤形。腿长 18.5 厘米，裤腿宽 5、4.5 厘米。沿着毛布的缘边有内折缝缀的痕迹，可能是一件小裤服。为一幅缂花毛布，没有发现幅边。基础组织为 2/2 Z 斜纹，经纱 Z 捻，纬纱 S 捻，经密 7 根 / 厘米，纬密 26 根 / 厘米（图 1）。

经纱深棕色，纬纱为蓝、红两色。用纬纱缂织出蓝、红两色的带状曲折纹，给人感觉是蓝地红纹或红地蓝纹。

FRAGMENT OF WOOLEN TAPESTRY CLOTH WITH STAIR-STEP PATTERNING (98QZIM139:53-5C)

Length 27.5 cm, width 13.5 cm.

This fragment is in the shape of a pair of pants. The legs are 18.5 cm long, the width of legs is 5 and 4.5 cm. Traces of a former rolled seam are along the edge of the cloth so this may once have been a small pair of pants. It is a tapestry-woven woolen cloth, no selvages are preserved. The basic weave structure is 2/2 S twill with warp threads Z-spun and weft S-spun. The warp thread count is 7 ends per cm, the weft is 26 picks per cm (fig. 1).

1 组织图 Twill tapestry weave

The warp thread is dark brown; the weft is divided between blue and red and is used in the tapestry weave to display ribbon-like stair-stepped patterning which gives the sense of being either red on blue or blue on red.

53

棕色菱格纹残缂毛毯 (98QZIM139:53-16-2C)

长 208 厘米，宽 53 厘米。

一幅毛布制作，仅保存一面幅边，残幅宽 53 厘米。羊毛中等粗，纱也比较粗。经纱 Z 捻，纬纱 S 捻。经纱为棕色和白色羊毛的混捻，多为白毛色，显白色。纬纱分白色和棕色两种色。地组织为 2/2 Z 斜纹，经密 4 根 / 厘米，纬密 10 根 / 厘米（图 1 ）。

白地，缂织棕色菱格网纹和宽带纹。图案以分区的形式表现，饰棕边的宽白带纹为隔带，在隔带中间缂织棕色的菱网格纹。隔带间宽 51 厘米，棕条纹宽 2 厘米。保存了四个隔带，其中两个隔带间的纹样比较完整。棕色羊毛是原色，里面含有少量的白羊毛。

FRAGMENT OF A TAPESTRY-WOVEN WOOLEN BLANKET WITH LATTICE PATTERNS (98QZIM139:53-16-2C)

Height 208 cm, width 53 cm.

This textile is made of a piece of woolen cloth with only one remaining selvage; the fragment's incomplete loom width is 53 cm. It is of medium-weight wool, woven with fairly thick yarn. Warp threads are Z-spun; weft threads are S-spun. The warp yarn is spun of brown and white fibers with white predominating, giving a whitish color. Weft yarn is divided into white and two kinds of brown color. The basic weave is 2/2 S twill, with a warp thread count of 4 ends per cm and a weft thread count of 10 picks per cm (fig. 1).

The tapestry weave displays a brown diagonal lattice pattern with white and greyish fillings, alternating with white horizontal bands that separate the pattern sections. The pattern bands are

1 组织图 Twill tapestry weave

51 cm wide, and the brown lines are 2 cm wide. Four pattern bands are preserved; the pattern is complete on two of them. The brown-colored yarn is the natural color of the woolen fibers, spun with a slight amount of white fibers.

54

酱紫色毛罗残片 (98QZIM129:3-1)

长 38 厘米，宽 31.5 厘米。

不规则长方形，是衣服下摆部分。有两幅毛罗拼对缝合在一起，皆保存一面幅边，残幅宽 38 厘米。

毛罗上面有平纹和二经绞组织，呈宽带状纵向排列，罗组织宽 1.6 厘米，平纹组织宽 3.8 厘米。

先织后染，羊毛较细，经、纬纱皆Z捻，捻得比较紧。平纹组织，经密16根／厘米，纬密12根／厘米（图1）。

FRAGMENT OF DARK PURPLE WOOLEN GAUZE (98QZIM129:3-1)

Height 38 cm, width 31.5 cm (warp running horizontally).

This fragment is an irregular rectangle in shape and was part of the lower hem of a garment. Two pieces of woolen gauze cloth were sewn together. Both retain one selvage; the incomplete loom width is 38 cm.

Both tabby sections and patterned two-end simple gauze sections alternate, creating longitudinal stripes: the width of the patterned gauze weave stripes is 1.6 cm, that of the tabby is 3.8 cm.

The piece was first woven and then dyed. The wool is quite fine, with warp and weft both fairly strongly Z-spun. In the tabby weave areas, warp thread count is 16 ends per cm, weft is 12 picks per cm (fig. 1).

1 组织图 Woolen two–end simple gauze

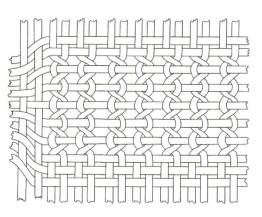

2 组织图 Weave diagram

动物纹缂毛残片 (98QZIM129:3-3)

残长 17 厘米，残宽 27 厘米。

长方形，没有保存幅边。羊毛中等粗，经、纬纱皆 Z 捻，地组织为平纹，经密 10 根／厘米，纬密 12 根／厘米。缂织花纹的地方纬线较密，纬密多的可达 42 根／厘米。经纱白色，纬纱有红、橘红、蓝、白、绿、酱紫、姜黄和黄等八种色。

缂织纹样保存不全，两条长带纹之间有一残动物纹，头缺失，可以看出有立状的两腿、翼和翘起的尾巴，给人的感觉是酱紫地上显动物纹。有三根竖立的条带，似翼，由蓝、白、红、黄等色组成。两条长带纹，其中一条保存较好，由白、蓝、红、黄色条构成，宽 2 厘米，晕繝效果不明显，颜色的变化与两种色的羊毛比例有关系。其旁是小长方格组成的带纹，小长方格内填对三角和四菱叶纹等。在小长方格的旁边有酱紫色条纹和白色边缘，白色缘边宽 9 厘米，长 1.5 厘米。经密 10 根／厘米，纬密 12 根／厘米。

另外，在动物的腹下有弧形和曲折的条带纹，红、黄色条纹。

FRAGMENT OF TAPESTRY-WOVEN CLOTH WITH ANIMAL PATTERNS (98QZIM129:3-3)

Height 17 cm, width 27 cm.

This textile is rectangular in shape, without any selvages. Its medium-weight yarn has both warp and weft Z-spun. The basic weave is tabby, with a warp thread count of 10 ends per cm and a weft thread count of 12 picks per cm for the plain areas. The tapestry is woven in tabby as well, its weft thread count is 42 picks per cm. The warp yarn is white; the weft yarn is in eight colors, red, tangerine-red, blue, white, green, dark purple, ginger-yellow, and yellow.

The tapestry-woven area is incompletely preserved. Between two long bands is fragmentary animal patterning. The head of the animal is missing but the strongly planted legs are visible, also wings and an uplifted tail. The pattern is set off against a dark purple background. Three multi-colored strips rise from the back of the animal, wing-like, woven in blue, white, red, and yellow. One of the two long horizontal bands on either side is better preserved and is woven in white, blue, red, and yellow, altogether 2 cm wide. The band presents a slight shading effect, due to the gradation of colors and the relative amount of the two colors in the wool. Next to this multi-colored strip is an area of rectangles filled with opposing triangles and flowers with four diamond-shaped petals. Next to that follow a narrow dark-purple band and an area of white tabby, 9 cm wide and 1.5 cm

1 反面 Reverse side

high. It has a warp thread count of 10 ends per cm, and weft of 12 picks per cm.

Beneath the stomach of the animal are four curved lines woven in red and yellow that are sprouting from the front legs.

2 组织图，反面 Tapestry weave, reverse

3 组织图 Tapestry weave with sewn slits

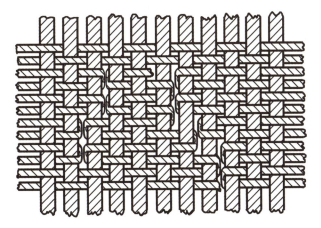

4 组织图 Weave diagram

花草纹缂毛带 (98QZIM129:3-4)

长 20.5 厘米，宽 13 厘米。

长方形。两侧经缘边折卷缝缀。保存一面幅边，残幅宽 20.5 厘米。

羊毛较细，经、纬纱皆 Z 捻，地组织为平纹。经密 9 根／厘米，纬密 50 根／厘米。经纱白色，纬纱有蓝、白、红、酱紫、橘黄、黄和绿等七种色。

毛带的中间有两条蓝、白色带纹，毛布的上、下缘边各有一排小长方格组成的带纹。两条蓝、白带纹宽 1.7 厘米，其间有宽 5.3 厘米，为酱紫色地、"十"字形的花纹。其中相对的花瓣纹较长，花瓣间是花蕊。与花瓣呈十字相对的是两个小"十"字纹，表现的可能是叶片。花瓣分白边蓝体和白边橘黄体，小"十"字纹分白地蓝"十"字和白地红"十"字纹。

毛布上、下缘边的小长方格纹宽 2.3 厘米，为红地，长方格内填对三角和四菱叶纹等，用色有些变化。

另外，两条蓝、白色带纹的蓝色带纹有晕繝效果，由白色羊毛和蓝色羊毛的混捻纱织成，颜色变化与两种色的羊毛比例有关。

TAPESTRY-WOVEN BAND WITH FLORAL PATTERNS (98QZIM129:3-4)

Height 20.5 cm, width 13 cm.

Rectangular in shape; the two warp-end sides have been rolled in and sewn. One selvage remains; incomplete loom width of the fabric is 20.5 cm.

The piece is made of relatively fine wool, with both warp and weft Z-spun. The basic weave structure is tabby. The thread count of warp is 9 ends per cm, of weft it is 50 picks per cm. The warp yarn is white; weft yarn is seven colors: blue, white, red, dark purple, tangerine-yellow, yellow, and green.

Two stripes of blue and white traverse the middle of the belt; the borders above and below them each have a row of rectangular segments. The blue and white stripes are 1.7 cm wide, with a distance of 5.3 cm between them. This area has a dark purple ground with a roughly cross-shaped pattern on it, composed of elongated symmetrical petals with stamens or pistils. The other crossbar is formed by two white shapes, perhaps depicting leaves, each containing a small cross. The petals are in white-edged blue and white-edged tangerine-yellow. Small cross motifs are blue on white and red on white.

The upper and lower bands of the belt, with the rectangular segments, are 2.3 cm wide. The segments are filled with opposing triangles and four diamond-shaped petals on a red background, with some variation in coloring.

The strips of blue and white employ a shading technique which is the result of weaving the strips from mottled blue and white yarn, with varying proportion of the two colors mixed before spinning and thus resulting in shades of yarn.

动物纹缂毛绦 (98QZIM129:3-5)

拼对：全长 106 厘米，宽 12.5 厘米。

羊毛较粗，经线 S 双捻，纬纱 Z 捻。地组织为平纹，经密 8 根／厘米，纬密 38~48 根／厘米。

经线是棕色羊毛和白色羊毛的混捻，棕色羊毛多一些，显棕色。纬纱有红、黄、白、粉红、酱紫、蓝、天青等七种色。天青色是白色羊毛和蓝色羊毛的混捻，蓝色羊毛为染色羊毛。

纹样残缺不全，大体可以看出是龙纹，残留了鸟首及喙状嘴；有的残留了鹿头，头上有角，颔下有垂饰，肩部有翼翅，腿呈站立状，有爪。

TAPESTRY-WOVEN WOOLEN BAND WITH ANIMAL PATTERNS (98QZIM129:3-5)

Reconstructed from several fragments, the band is 106 cm long and 12.5 cm wide.

The wool used in this weaving is relatively coarse. The warp threads are S-plied from two ends, the weft threads are Z-spun. The basic weave structure is tabby, with a warp thread count of 8 ends per cm and weft of 38 to 48 picks per cm. Warp threads are spun from brown and white wool mixed together with brown predominating. Weft yarn includes seven colors: red, yellow, white, pink red, dark purple, dark blue, and sky-blue. The sky-blue is the result of spinning white and dark-blue fibers together, the dark-blue being a dyed color.

The pattern is incomplete but one can mostly make out a pattern of dragon-like animals that have a bird's head with beak-like mouth. There is also the fragmentary part of a deer-like head with antlers and some decoration hanging from its chin. This animal has wings on its shoulder and sturdily upright legs with claws.

红色菱格三角纹提花毛绦 (98QZIM129:3-6)

片拼对：长 53.5、34 厘米，宽 16.8、20 厘米。

长方形。残，保存两面幅边，幅宽 16.8 厘米。在红色菱格三角纹提花毛绦上缝缀着蓝色提花毛织物残片，还残留有牙线，应该是服饰上的装饰绦残片。

毛绦为平纹组织，羊毛中等粗，经、纬纱皆 Z 捻，经密 14 根／厘米，纬密 34 根／厘米。经、纬纱相交的地方保存有缺少染色的白点，应该是先织后染的效果。

毛绦面的中部以提花的形式织有一排菱格纹，在绦边缘的菱格纹之间织有三角纹，构成了两边排列三角纹，中间是菱格纹的效果。

在正面，由浮出的一个个纬纱小方块构成大的菱格和三角纹。小方格由四根纬纱并成，给人一种提花的感觉。在反面，则是经纱浮于面上，隔一行织一道（图 1、2）。

蓝色提花毛织物残片，与毛绦以幅边拼对缝缀，保存一面幅边。它的局部残留有与红色菱格三角纹提花毛绦相同的组织，经、纬皆 Z 捻，经纱是白色羊毛和棕色羊毛的混捻纱，显棕白色。纬纱显蓝色，属先染后织。经密 10 根／厘米，纬密 26 根／厘米。

牙线，橘黄色，处于毛绦和毛布的结合部。

SELF-PATTERNED RED WOOLEN STRIP WITH TRIANGLES AND
DIAMONDS (98QZIM129:3-6)

Two fragments: 53.5 cm and 34 cm long, 16.8 and 20 cm wide.

The textile is rectangular in shape and fragmentary, but it retains both selvages; the loom width of the fabric is 16.8 cm. A blue-colored self-patterned fabric was sewn on above the red strip with diamond and triangular self-patterning; the blue strip is now fragmentary. The seam retains piping, however, which was likely part of the decoration of an item of clothing.

The red woolen strip is woven with tabby ground of medium-weight wool with both warp and weft Z-spun. Thread count of warp is 14 ends per cm, of weft it is 34 picks per cm. Since the underlying white of the yarn shows through where warp and weft intersect at certain places, we know the fabric was first woven and then dyed. In the central part of the woolen strip, a row of diamond patterns is woven in self-patterning and between this row and the edge of the strip are two rows of self-pattern triangles. If put the other way round, the diamond shapes in the middle are the result of an edging pattern of triangles.

On the right side of the fabric, one can see floating weft threads that create the appearance of small squares (each composed of four weft picks floating over five warp ends, and alternating with unaltered tabby picks), which constitute the overall larger pattern of triangles and diamonds. On the reverse side, this technique results in warp threads floating on the surface, again alternating with 'common' tabby warp ends (figs 1, 2).

The fragments of blue fabric include a selvage edge that is sewn onto the red fabric. The blue fabric is the same self-patterned structure as the red, with warp and weft both Z-spun and the warp threads spun from mottled white and brown yarn with a brownish-white result. Weft yarn is blue and was dyed first and then woven. The thread count of the warp is 10 ends per cm; of the weft it is 26 picks per cm.

The piping thread is tangerine-yellow and is located at the juncture between woolen strip (red) and woolen cloth (blue).

1 正面 Self-patterning, obverse   2 反面 Self-patterning, reverse

三角条纹缂毛残片 (98QZIM129:3-8)

长 16.5 厘米，宽 30.5 厘米。

三角形，没有保存幅边。纹样呈横向排列，两边是宽窄不同的条带纹，中间是连续重叠的三角纹。一侧的条带纹保存较好，可以看出有红、蓝、白、驼等色的条带。红色带纹较宽，残宽 6.5 厘米。白带纹上还有橘黄色的三角纹，蓝色带纹、驼色带纹都显晕繝效果。

角纹，由白、棕、橘黄三种色构成一组，连续排列。

经线为橘黄色，S 双捻；纬纱 Z 捻，有红、蓝、白、橘黄、酱紫、驼、棕等七色。除红色带纹外，余皆为缂织纹样。地组织为平纹，经密 8 根 / 厘米，纬密 42 根 / 厘米。

FRAGMENT OF TAPESTRY-WEAVE WOOLEN CLOTH WITH TRIANGULAR

PATTERNS (98QZIM129:3-8)

60

Height 16.5 cm, width 30.5 cm

This fragment is triangular in shape, and retains no selvages. The pattern is horizontal with bands of differing width on either side. In the middle band are overlapping aligned triangular patterns. One side of the fragment is better preserved and the zones of red, blue, white, and camel-colored stripes are clearly visible. The red band is wider, 6.5 cm remains of it in the fragment. In the upper part of the white band are tangerine-colored triangular patterns, the blue and camel-colored strips both display the effect of shading.

The triangles in the middle band are arrayed in groups of lines of three colors, each forming a unit composed of white, brown, and tangerine-yellow.

The warp threads are tangerine-yellow and S-plied from two ends. Weft yarn is Z-spun and includes seven colors: red, blue, white, tangerine-yellow, dark purple, camel-colored, brown. Except for the band of red, all are patterned in tapestry weave. The basic weave structure is tabby, with a warp thread count of 8 ends per cm, and a weft thread count of 42 picks per cm.

1 组织图 Tapestry weave

白地蓝菱格纹丝编织带 (98QZIM129:3-10)

残长 20 厘米，宽 4.2~4.5 厘米，厚 0.22 厘米。

长方形。由白、蓝、绿等三种色线编织而成。地色为白色，菱格纹是蓝色，蓝色菱格纹内有一个绿色和三个棕黄色的小方菱格组成的大方菱格纹。

丝线为 Z 双捻，捻度强。3/3 斜编组织，比较厚，编织细密（图 1）。

61

BRAIDED SILK BAND WITH BLUE DIAMONDS ON WHITE GROUND (98QZIM129:3-10)

Length 20 cm, width 4.2-4.5 cm. Thickness 0.22 cm.

The fragment is rectangular in shape, and braided from three colors of yarn: white, blue, and green. The ground is white and the diamonds are blue, with four smaller lozenges inside each larger lozenge field. One of the four-lozenge groups is green and three are brownish-yellow, probably as a result of color deterioration. The pattern is identical on both sides of the band.

The silk threads are Z-ply from two ends and spun relatively tightly. The piece is worked in multiple-layer 3/3 twill oblique interlacing, relatively thick, and is finely braided (fig. 1).

61

1 组织图
Multiple–layer 3/3 twill oblique interlacing

白地蓝网格纹丝编织带 (98QZIM129:3-11)

残长9厘米，宽3~3.5厘米，厚0.19厘米。

长方形。由白、蓝两种色线编织而成，显白地蓝色网格纹，两面图案完全相同。
丝线为Z双捻，捻度较强。3/3斜编组织，比较厚，编织得比较密（图1）。

62

BRAIDED SILK BAND WITH BLUE NETTING PATTERN ON WHITE GROUND (98QZIM129:3-11)

Length 9 cm, width 3-3.5 cm. Thickness 0.19 cm.

This fragment is rectangular and worked of two different colors, white and blue, with the white ground setting off a blue netting pattern that is identical on both sides of the band.

The silk yarn is fairly tightly Z-plied from two ends. Multiple-layer 3/3 twill oblique interlacing, fairly thick and worked quite finely (fig. 1).

1 组织图 Multiple-layer 3/3 twill oblique interlacing

晕繝彩条纹毛布服饰残片 (98QZIM129:3-15)

两片：长 22、17.5 厘米，宽 27.5、9.5 厘米。

一大一小，保存一面幅边，残幅宽 15.3 厘米。

大片，由两幅毛布纵向拼接缝合，一幅是蓝色平纹毛布，一幅是晕繝彩条纹毛布。缝痕呈弧线状，应该是服饰残片。

小片，上面有彩条纹。

经线为浅蓝色。纬纱有浅蓝色、红色、绿色、蓝色和黄色，分区。其中浅蓝是地色，红色和蓝色之间分界明显，蓝色和黄色之间出现宝石蓝、藏蓝、浅绿的过渡色。同时在黄色上又可分出黄色和浅黄色。红和黄之间、蓝和黄之间分界不明显，呈一种过渡色地形式。红和蓝之间，红色有大红和紫红的区别。这就是人们常说的晕繝效果。

羊毛中等细，经线 S 双捻，纬纱 Z 捻。经密 11 根 / 厘米，纬密 40 根 / 厘米。

FRAGMENT OF A WOOLEN GARMENT WITH SHADED COLOR STRIPES (98QZIM129:3-15)

The fragment is in two pieces. Heights are 22 and 17.5 cm; widths are 27.5 and 9.5 cm.

The fragments both retain one selvage, the fragmentary loom width is 15.3 cm.

The larger of the two fragments consists of two pieces of woolen cloth sewn together lengthwise. One piece is tabby weave and blue; the other is graduated colors woven in a pattern of stripes. The seam is curved, so most likely this was part of a garment. The smaller of the two fragments still has the colored stripes at one end.

The warp is light blue. The weft is divided into stripes of light blue, red, green, blue, and yellow. Among these, light blue is the ground color. From top to bottom, the distinction between red and blue is very clear while the transitional colors between blue and yellow produce such colors as lapis lazuli-blue, greenish-blue, and light green. In the yellow portions, one can make the further distinction between yellow and light yellow. In between red and yellow, and in between blue and yellow, the line is indistinct, forming a transitional hue. Between red and blue, the pure red gradually shades into purple-red. This is the result of the technique so often heard about called *yunjian* (shading).

The wool is of medium weight, warp threads are S-plied from two ends, weft threads are Z-spun. The warp thread count is 11 ends per cm, the weft thread count is 40 picks per cm.

1 组织图 Color–shading

白地葡萄纹毛绣带 (98QZIM129:4)

全长 54 厘米, 宽 33.5 厘米。穗长 26 厘米。

由带体和穗组成, 带身呈长方形。由一幅白色平纹毛布制作, 保存两面幅边, 幅宽 33.5 厘米。两侧缘边都有缝缀的针眼痕迹, 可能是双层的毛布绣带。带体底缘饰以刺绣, 刺绣部分宽 11.5 厘米。

毛布为平纹, 羊毛很细, 经、纬纱皆 Z 捻。经密 26 根／厘米, 纬密 15 根／厘米。穗是六根经纱的捻线绳, 头端打结。

锁针绣, 刺绣花纹是葡萄纹, 绣线有白、红、粉红、蓝、天青、黄、绿等七种色。图案花纹分主纹饰和上、下边缘纹饰。上、下边缘纹饰相同, 由内、外框线和连续的椭圆纹构成, 外边框线上垂饰椭圆纹, 形成一种垂帐效果。内边框线则与垂纹间有一定的距离。内、外框线皆为蓝色, 椭圆纹分外缘和圆心部分。椭圆纹的外缘皆为蓝色, 分别在里面填以红、粉红、天青、黄、绿等五色, 以相同色的两个椭圆纹为一组, 红、天青、黄、粉红、绿连续排列。椭圆纹的刺绣基本上是随纹样的形状呈螺旋形式的走向（图 1）。

主纹饰是一条较粗的曲线葡萄枝, 枝的弯曲度比较大, 一端是叶花, 一端是渐细的枝尾。藤枝有四道弯曲, 在每一个弯曲的中部, 垂着一串葡萄和叶花。粗葡萄枝是蓝色的缘边, 里面填红、天青、黄、粉红、绿等五色的线段, 连续变化, 成为一条蓝边的五彩藤枝。葡萄果实为带茎的小圆形, 呈互生的串状, 吊在枝上的葡萄果实有白、粉红、绿、红、天青等五色。葡萄叶花呈五瓣形, 分花瓣和叶瓣两个部分。叶瓣与藤茎相接, 呈相对的螺旋三角形。花瓣附着在叶瓣相拼的三角纹底平面上, 显出三瓣花纹, 两侧是螺旋形花瓣, 中间是较长的花蕊。叶花也都是蓝边, 内填红、粉红、天青、黄、白等五色。叶花色的组合有些变化, 一般一枝叶花只用四种色线。

1 组织图 Chain stitch embroidery

EMBROIDERED WOOLEN SASH WITH GRAPE PATTERN ON WHITE GROUND (98QZIM129:4)

Entire height 54 cm, width 33.5 cm, length of fringe is 26 cm.

This textile is composed of the main part of the sash and the fringe, the sash forming a rectangular shape. It is made of a piece of white tabby woolen cloth which retains both selvages; the loom width is 33.5 cm. Both sides of the piece have the remains of needle holes and the sash may once have been double-layered or lined. The lower end of the piece of fabric constituting the sash is embroidered, and the embroidered part is 11.5 cm in height.

The cloth is tabby weave, the wool is extremely fine, with warp and weft threads both Z-spun. The warp has a thread count of 26 ends per cm; the weft of 15 picks per cm. The fringe is made of six warp ends plied into strings and knotted at the ends.

The pattern embroidered on the piece is of grapes, with embroidery threads being white, red, pink red, blue, sky-blue, yellow and green, all worked in chain stitch. The pattern is composed of a central motif edged with upper and lower bands. The upper and lower bands are identical and made up of aligned embroidered oblong shapes with a straight line on either side. The shapes hang down from the outer line like a hanging curtain. There is a gap between the oblongs and the inner line. Both inner and outer framing lines are blue, the oblong dots are variegated in five colors, red, pink red, sky-blue, yellow, and green, all outlined in blue. Always two subsequent oblongs have the same color, and the sequence of red, sky-blue, yellow, pink red, and green is constantly repeated. The embroidery stitches of the oblong dots follow the direction of the curve (fig. 1).

The main pattern in the central portion of the fragment is a curvilinear stem with bundles of grapes on it, with the curvature of the stem being quite considerable. At one end of the vine is a leaf pattern, at the other end the stem gets progressively thinner. The grape-vine has four curves in it and in the center of each curve a bunch of grapes and leaves hangs down at an oblique angle. The thicker grape-vines are blue on the outside and filled in with five colors in succession, red, sky-blue, yellow, pink red, and green, so the vine is five-colored with a blue outline. The grapes themselves are small circles with short stems, emerging from both sides of a twig, and done in six different colors, white, pink red, green, red, sky-blue, and yellow. The floral pattern is five-lobed and divided into two parts, petals and the fairly leaves. These are linked to the stem and form a triangular whorl pattern. Where leaves and petals meet, the leaves broaden into a triangular shape from which the petals are displayed forming two spirals and a fairly long stamen enclosed between them. The leaves also have blue outlines, they are filled in with the five colors red, pink red, sky-blue, yellow, and white. The arrangement of the colors is somewhat varying, but each of the flowers combines no more than four filling colors.

蓝地对龙纹锦 (98QZIM129:4-3)

两片拼对：上片较大，长 38 厘米，宽 28.5 厘米；下片小，长 28.5 厘米，宽 16.5 厘米。

长方形，下片保存一面幅边，残幅宽 16.5 厘米，幅边宽 0.8 厘米。

经锦。经、纬线都不加捻，经线蓝、黄两种，纬线蓝色。夹纬经二重平纹组织，排列比 1:1。经密 108 根 / 厘米，纬密 36 根 / 厘米。

蓝地，纹样是纬向排列，两只对龙呈立状，在颈和腰部呈交会状。四条腿，三爪。胸间和尾间饰花纹。

65

SILK COMPOUND WEAVE (JIN), BLUE GROUND, WITH OPPOSING DRAGONS (98QZIM129:4-3)

Reconstructed from two pieces: the upper is larger and is, in warp direction, 38 cm long and 28.5 cm wide. The lower is smaller and is 28.5 cm long and 16.5 cm wide.

This textile is of roughly rectangular shape. The smaller fragment preserves one selvage, the maximum preserved loom width is 16.5 cm, the width of the selvage is 0.8 cm. Neither the warp nor the weft threads have been noticeably twisted; the warp threads are blue and yellow; the weft threads are blue. The weave is a warp-faced compound tabby with two series of warps. Warp thread count is 108 ends (54 ends per warp series) per cm, weft is 36 picks per cm.

Blue ground, the patterning is aligned in weft direction and shows opposing dragons in sinuous standing position that cross over each other at neck and waist. They have four legs with three claws. The chests and shoulders are patterned.

1 组织图 Warp-faced compound tabby with selvage

绿地对鸟纹残锦带 (A.98QZIM129:4-2，B.98QZIM139:53-14C)

A. 二片：残长 30、38 厘米，残宽 6.9、7.5 厘米。

B. 残长 46.5 厘米，宽 7.2 厘米。保存一面幅边，残幅宽 0.5 厘米。

长方形。经锦。经、纬丝线皆不加捻，经线红、绿和白等三种色，纬线白色。夹纬经二重平纹组织，排列比 1:2，经密 162 根 / 厘米，纬密 36 根 / 厘米。

绿地，纹样边显红色，中间显白色。图案不是很清楚，可能是对鸟纹。

66

SILK COMPOUND WEAVE (JIN) BAND, GREEN GROUND AND BIRD

PATTERNS A (98QZIM129:4-2), B (98QZIM139:53-14C)

A is in two fragments that are 30 and 38 cm long, and 6.9 and 7.5 cm in width.
B is a fragment 46.5 cm long, 7.2 cm wide. It retains one selvage which is 0.5 cm wide.

The fragments are rectangular and woven from silk in a warp-faced compound tabby. Neither warp nor weft has been given a noticeable twist, the warp threads are red, green and white, the weft threads are white. The weave is warp-faced compound tabby, with three series of warps. The warp thread count is 162 ends (54 ends per warp series) per cm, weft is 36 picks per cm.

The ground is green, with patterning displayed, at the sides, in red and, in between, in white. The pattern is indistinct and may be opposing birds.

动物头像缂毛绦残片 (98QZIM129:32-3)

长 14 厘米，宽 9 厘米。

长方形。保存两面幅边，幅宽 9 厘米。

地组织为平纹，羊毛稍粗，经线 S 双捻，纬纱 Z 捻。经线显棕白色，为棕色羊毛和白色羊毛的混捻，棕色毛多一些。纬纱有紫红、白、黄、棕、砖红、浅驼等六种色。经密 9 根 / 厘米，纬密 36 根 / 厘米（图 1）。

毛绦经边保存一条白缘，纬纱为两根并股，蓝色地，紫红、白、黄、棕、砖红、浅驼色显纹样，可以看出来有一个动物的头像。表现出了动物的长耳（或角），梯形头，方眼，嘴有点像兔嘴。动物头的上面又有许多几何形线条。

用色方面，红和白色比较明显，棕色表现眼仁。另外，在动物头上部的几何条纹中可以看到黄色。

FRAGMENT OF A TAPESTRY-WEAVE WOOLEN BAND WITH ANIMAL-HEAD PATTERNS (98QZIM129:32-3)

Height 14 cm, width 9 cm. The fragment is rectangular and retains both selvages, its loom width is 9 cm.

The basic weave structure of this textile is tabby, from slightly heavier yarn; warp threads are S-plied from two ends, weft threads are Z-spun. The warp threads are brownish-white and are spun from brown and white wool mixed together, with brown somewhat predominating. The weft yarn includes purple-red, white, yellow, brown, brick-red, and light-camel colors. The warp thread count is 9 ends per cm, the weft is 36 picks per cm (fig. 1).

The warp end of the band retains a border of white that uses doubled weft yarn. The main field of the band has blue ground and purple-red, white, yellow, brown, brick-red and light camel colored yarn to display the pattern. A kind of animal's head is visible. Most noticeable is the animal's long ear (or it may be a horn), his trapezoid head, square eye, and a mouth that resembles the mouth of a rabbit. Stylized patterning adorns the band above the animal's head.

Coloration: the red and white are fairly bright, the pupil is shown in brown. Moreover, one can see some yellow in the stylized patterns above the animal's head.

1 组织图 Tapestry weave

红地龙纹锦衣残片 (98QZIM129:5-1)

两片：大片，长 65.5 厘米，宽 59.5 厘米；小片，长 42 厘米，宽 44 厘米。

大片，长方形，没有幅边。小片，圆形，由两片呈半圆形锦拼对，皆保存一面幅边，残幅宽 22.5 厘米。

纬锦，绵经绵纬。经、纬纱皆 Z 捻，夹经纬二重平纹组织，夹经并股，排列比 1:2。经密 15 根 / 厘米，纬密 48~54 根 / 厘米。经纱棕黄色，纬纱为白、棕黄和红三种色。其中白纱松、粗，棕黄、红纱较细（图 1）。

红地，曲折的枝干骨骼贯通全幅，其间填以动物纹。动物有些变形，为龙纹，作回头状，头呈虎头状，额面有短线状饰。前腿平伸，后腿屈，为三趾爪。龙纹为白体，棕黄色饰边。

新疆考古中发现了许多这样的龙纹，早在西汉时期的铜、金饰件上就有类似的动物纹样。同时随着时间的推移存在一些演化。曲折的枝干骨骼，显然具有汉风云气纹骨骼演化的特点。

1 组织图 Weft–faced compound tabby (taquete)

SILK COMPOUND WEAVE (JIN), RED GROUND AND DRAGON-LIKE PATTERN (98QZIM129:5-1)

In two pieces. The large piece is 65.5 cm high and 59.5 cm wide. The small piece is 42 cm high and 44 cm wide.

The large piece is rectangular in shape and does not retain selvages. The small piece is round in shape and is made up of two semicircular pieces of fabric put together, each of which retains one selvage. The maximum preserved width is 22.5 cm. These seem to be fragments of clothing.

This is a piece of weft-faced compound weave with both warp and weft of spun silk. Warp and weft yarn are both Z-spun, the weave is a weft-faced compound tabby or taqueté, the main warp is doubled, the proportion of binding warp ends to main warp ends is 1:2. The thread count of the warp is 15 ends (10 main warp ends and 5 binding warp ends) per cm, of the weft it is between 48 and 54 picks (16-18 passes) per cm. Warp yarn is brownish-yellow, weft yarn is white, brownish-yellow, and red. Among these three colors, the white yarn is looser and thicker, while the brownish-yellow and red yarns are finer (fig. 1).

The textile has a red ground and curving branches that serve as a skeletal framework for the entire piece, within which are set animal patterns. The animals are somewhat distorted and appear to be dragons in reverse-head posture with heads like tigers and, on their foreheads, short linear ornamentation. Their front legs are straight, the rear legs are curved and have three claws. The dragons are white and set off in brownish-yellow.

Similar animal motifs have been found already on Western Han bronze and gold objects discovered by various archaeological excavations in Xinjiang. With the passage of time, the motifs are modified somewhat. For example, the curvilinear branch framework begins to evolve into characteristic Han (Chinese) style cloud patterns.

蓝地菱格曲线纹锦残片 (98QZIM124:8-1)

两片：一片长 56.5 厘米，宽 16.8 厘米；一片长 28.5 厘米，宽 16.8 厘米。

长方形。没有保存幅边。经、纬丝线皆没有加捻，经锦。排列比 1:2，夹纬经二重平纹组织。经密 168 根／厘米，纬密 46 根／厘米（图 1）。

经线蓝、绿和白三种色，纬线绿色。蓝地，显菱格曲线纹。菱格是主体纹样，菱格饰白边，内填绿色。曲线纹处于菱格纹内，为绿色，上面有两个白色圆点。

以菱格为框架填充自然花纹的图案形式，具有汉风特点。

1 组织图 Warp-faced compound tabby

69

SILK COMPOUND WEAVE (JIN), BLUE GROUND WITH DIAMONDS AND CURVED LINES (98QZIM124:8-1)

In two pieces. One piece is 56.5 cm high and 16.8 cm wide; the other piece is 28.5 cm high and 16.8 cm wide.

The assembled textile is rectangular in shape. No selvages are preserved. Neither warp and weft threads have been given a noticeable twist; the weave is a warp-faced compound tabby with three series of warps. The warp thread count is 168 ends (56 ends per warp series) per cm, and weft is 46 picks per cm (fig. 1).

Warp threads are in three colors: blue, green, and white. Weft threads are green. The piece has a blue ground, setting off a diamond-and-curved-line pattern. The diamonds are the primary motif. They are rimmed with white and filled with green. Wavy lines are located within the diamond patterns, they are green, and above each one, inside the diamonds, are two small white dots.

Using a diamond-framework and filling each diamond with a natural pattern is a form that is characteristic of Han-Chinese styles.

蓝地植物纹锦残片 (98QZIM124:8-3)

两片：长 16、11.5 厘米，残宽 6、3.3 厘米。

没有发现幅边。经、纬丝线皆不加捻，经锦。排列比 1：2，夹纬经二重平纹组织。经密 186 根 / 厘米，纬密 32 根 / 厘米（图 1）。

经线蓝、红和白三种色，纬线白色。蓝地，红、白两色显花纹。主体花纹似四方连续的叶纹。这一纹样的织锦在新疆尚属首次发现，感觉上有汉锦遗风，或有着承上启下的纹样特点。

SILK COMPOUND WEAVE (JIN) WITH BLUE GROUND AND VEGETAL PATTERNS (98QZIM124:8-3)

In two pieces. Heights are 16 and 11.5 cm, and widths are 6 and 3.3 cm.

No selvages remain on this textile. Neither warp nor weft silk threads have been given a noticeable twist; the weave is warp-faced compound tabby with three series of warps. The warp thread count is 186 ends (62 ends per warp series) per cm, weft is 32 picks per cm (fig. 1).

Warp threads in this textile are blue, red, and white; weft threads are white. A blue ground sets off the pattern which is shown in red and white. The main motif is a continuous square pattern with a leaf motif.

This is the first of this kind of brocade to be found in Xinjiang. It looks somewhat like Chinese patterned silks, but may be a kind of connecting link with its own characteristics.

1 组织图 Warp-faced compound tabby

红地回菱纹毛绣残片 (98QZIM124:8-6)

长 23 厘米，宽 26 厘米。

不规则形，没有保存幅边。在红色平纹毛布上，以钉线绣绣出回菱纹。经、纬纱皆 Z 捻，经密 10 根／厘米，纬密 24 根／厘米。

将深棕、白两色线摆放成菱格纹样，而后用菱纹本色线缝缀在织物上面，也叫钉线绣或缠绕针。图案残缺严重，为双重菱格纹，里面的菱纹中饰斜"十"字纹。

纹样分深棕色和白色两种，呈间隔状排列，即上下、左右的排列，比较整齐，都是一棕色、一白色变换分布。毛绣线较粗，是 4 根 S 双捻。钉线则是两根纱的并线，缝缀时上下穿绕，间隔较宽，绣线表面可以看出钉线，钉线用色与绣线相同，即棕色绣线使用的是棕色钉线，白色绣线使用的是白色钉线（图1、2）。

FRAGMENT OF RED WOOLEN CLOTH EMBROIDERED WITH DIAMONDS (98QZIM124:8-6)

Height 23 cm, width 26 cm.

The textile is irregular in shape, with no selvages retained. The diamonds are embroidered on red woolen tabby. Both warp and weft have been Z-spun, the thread count of warp threads is 10 ends per cm, of weft it is 24 picks per cm.

The diamond patterns were made by first laying out the pattern in white and dark brown threads, and then stitching that onto the fabric using the same color of thread, using a couching stitch which is also called overcast stitch. Little of the pattern remains due to damage, but it was a double-outlined diamond pattern with slanted crosses inside the diamonds.

The pattern is in two different colors, dark brown, and white, alternating in rows that are vertically oriented, one diamond on top of the other, as well as lined up right and left, so in quite regular order. In both directions, dark brown and white diamonds alternate regularly. The woolen embroidery thread is rather coarse, it is a S-plied thread from four ends. The couching thread (to tie the diamonds down) is doubled and uses the same color as the embroidery, so brown was used to tie down the brown diamonds and white for the white (figs 1, 2).

1 正面 Couching, obverse

2 反面 Couching, reverse

橘黄地栽绒毛毯 (98QZIM124:8-9)

长 10 厘米，宽 18.5 厘米。

椭圆形。地组织为平纹，经线是 3 根 S 双捻，纬线是 Z 捻，两根、三根、四根纱的并股，交错排列，规律不明显。

地色为橘黄色，由红、蓝、棕、黄等四种色线栽绒起花。栽绒毛线头磨损严重，看不出花纹式样。起绒线是两根并股纱，起绒较密。一般隔两行纬线，在经线上栽一行绒。应该是以色线的变化显图案纹样，结扣为波斯扣，也叫生纳扣（图 2）。

WOOLEN RUG WITH ORANGE GROUND (98QZIM124:8-9)

Height 10 cm, width 18.5 cm.

This fragment of a rug is oval in shape. Its ground weave is tabby, warp threads are S-plied from three ends, weft threads are Z-spun, doubled, tripled, or fourfold, alternating but without any clear order.

The ground color is orange-yellow, with four colors of thread to create the patterning, namely red, blue, brown, and yellow. The pile has suffered severe damage and it is not possible to see the original pattern. The pile threads used doubled yarn and were tied quite densely. Generally a row of pile was tied in on the warp threads after every two weft picks. The changing pile yarn colors are what created the pattern. The knot used was the Persian knot, also called the Senna knot (fig. 2).

1 组织图 Tabby with pile

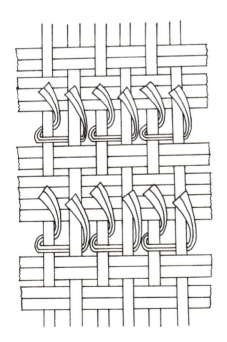

2 组织图 Persian or Senna knot

二 第三期文化墓葬出土纺织品珍宝

在 1996 年和 1998 年扎滚鲁克墓地考古发掘中，发现了第三期文化墓葬，共 30 座。其中 1996 年发掘 11 座，1998 年发掘了 19 座。

选取了 8 座墓葬（96QZIM60、96QZIM49、98QZIM141、98QZIM149、98QZIM122、98QZIM105、98QZIM156 和 98QZIM131）的 13 件纺织品残片、服饰和制品等，多数是丝织品，少数是毛织品。

（一） 1996 年发掘墓葬出土纺织品珍宝

选取了 96QZIM49 和 96QZIM60 两座墓葬的 2 件丝织品。

96QZIM60 墓葬（第四章图 73）

位于 1996 年发掘的南西区的第三发掘点。长方形竖穴墓，墓向南北向。墓室的东南壁上有一方形小龛，有木棺葬具。墓葬出土的"延年益寿大宜子孙"锦（96QZIM60:2，第四章图 73），与民丰县尼雅东汉墓和古楼兰地区发现的东汉织锦相似，年代推测为东汉（公元 25~220 年）。96QZIM60 墓葬属第三期文化墓葬。

96QZIM49 墓葬（第四章图 74）

位于 1996 年发掘的南东区发掘点。方形竖穴土坑棚架墓，墓向呈南北向。属第三期文化墓葬。

墓口长 3.82 米，宽 3.8 米。墓深 1.6 米。葬具为箱式木棺，处于墓室的西南角，呈南北方向放置。

墓室和填土中出土了一些东西，有木耜、木盘、玻璃杯、漆案、漆耳杯、漆匕、陶罐等。

墓葬出土的玻璃杯与斯坦因 20 世纪初在楼兰 LK 遗址墓葬中出土的 2 件相似，年代推测为公元 5~6 世纪。出土的木案和耳杯与南京象山东晋早期墓 7 号墓（公元 4 世纪）的相似。出土的刺绣与吐鲁番阿斯塔那古墓 177 号葡萄禽兽纹刺绣和 382 号墓神鸟纹绣红绢的图案相似，年代推测为南北朝时期（公元 420~589 年）。

TEXTILES EXCAVATED FROM THIRD-PERIOD CULTURE GRAVES

Thirty graves were discovered in the course of excavations in 1996 and 1998 that belonged to Third-period culture graves at Zaghunluq. Eleven of these were excavated in 1996, and nineteen in 1998.

Thirteen textile fragments or garments, from eight graves, were selected for discussion below. Most of these are silk textiles, a small number are woolen textiles. The graves from which they were excavated are: 96QZIM60, 96QZIM49, 98QZIM141, 98QZIM149, 98QZIM122, 98QZIM105, 98QZIM156, and 98QZIM131.

EXCAVATED IN 1996: 2 TEXTILES

Two silk textiles were selected from the two graves 96QZIM49 and 96QZIM60.

GRAVE 96QZIM60 (CAT. NO. 73)

Located in the 1996 southwest region's third excavation site. Rectangular vertical-pit type grave, orientation north-south. There was a square niche in the southeast wall of the grave chamber and grave equipment such as a wooden box-like coffin. The compound-weave *jin* with inscription (96QZIM60:2, cat. no. 73) excavated from this grave, is similar to the textiles excavated from Eastern-Han graves in Niya, in Minfeng County, as well as to the Eastern-Han textiles from the ancient Loulan area. We propose that the dating is Eastern Han (25–220 CE). Grave 96QZIM60 belongs to Third-period culture graves.

GRAVE 96QZIM49 (CAT. NO. 74)

Located in the 1996 southeast region's excavation site. This was a rectangular vertical-pit type earthen grave with canopy, orientation north-south. It belongs to Third-period culture graves.

The grave opening was 3.82 meters long, and 3.8 meters wide. The grave was 1.6 meters deep. Equipment in the grave included a box-type coffin, located in the southwestern corner of the grave chamber, placed in a north-south orientation.

Items excavated from the chamber as well as from the disturbed earth include: a wooden shovel (*si*), a wooden basin, a glass cup, a lacquered table (*an*), a lacquered ear-cup, a lacquered ladle, a ceramic jar and so on.

The glass cup is similar to two examples found in the LK gravesite at Loulan in the beginning of the last century by Aurel Stein, which has been dated to the 5th – 6th centuries CE. The wooden *an* or small table and the ear-cup are similar to those from grave M7 at the early Eastern-Jin site at Xiangshan in Nanjing, dating to the 4th century CE. The embroidery from this grave is similar to the grape-and-bird embroidery from Grave 177 at Astana in Turfan, and to the animal-and-sacred-bird embroidery on red *juan* silk from Grave 382 there, both of which are believed to date from the beginning of North-South Dynasties period (420–589 CE).

"（亟）年益寿大宜子孙" 锦残片 (96QZIM60:2)

长 51 厘米，宽 40 厘米。

长方形，是服饰残片，较大的 5 片，还有一些碎片。这是最大的片，保存一面幅边，残幅宽 40 厘米。经锦，经、纬丝线皆不加捻，经线单根，纬线两根并股。夹纬经二重平纹组织，排列比 1∶2。经密 138 根／厘米，纬密 28 根／厘米（图 2）。

纬线为白色，经线有三色，即蓝、白和红。原是红地上显蓝、白和红花纹，因蓝和红退色严重，锦面显棕色，花纹不是很明显。

图案分区隐约能看出曲折的藤杆、动物纹等，里面分布着文字，为隶书"亟年益寿大宜子孙"，比较清楚，红色。

另外，在幅缘边上有墨书的五个汉字，其中"王大吉"三字比较清楚（图 1）。

73

1 墨书文字 Ink-written characters

2 组织图 Warp-faced compound tabby

SILK COMPOUND WEAVE (JIN) WITH EIGHT-CHARACTER INSCRIPTION (96QZIM60:2)

Height 51 cm, width 40 cm.

Rectangular in shape, these are fragments from an article of clothing, and include five larger pieces and many smaller ones. The largest piece is shown here. It retains one selvage, and the fragmentary loom width is 40 cm. Warp-faced compound tabby, with neither warp nor weft silk threads given a noticeable twist. The warp threads are single, the weft threads are doubled. There are three series of warps. Thread count of warp threads is 138 ends (46 ends per warp series) per cm, of weft it is 28 picks per cm (fig. 2).

The weft threads are white, the warp threads are in three colors: blue, white, and red. The patterning, in blue, white and red was originally set off against a red ground. Since the blue and red have suffered serious fading, the entire fabric looks somewhat brownish, with indistinct patterning.

The pattern is divided into sections and one can vaguely make out the curvilinear lines of scrolls, and of animal patterns, and amongst them some characters of Chinese script. The script is written in *lishu* Chancellery Script calligraphy. The eight characters (延) 年益寿大宜子孙 (*yannian yishou dayi zisun*) say "longevity and long life is most desirable to the descendants." These characters are quite distinct and are written in red. The one character *yan* is missing.

In addition, five more Chinese characters are written in black ink along the side of the selvage. Among the five, three are quite clear, and they read 王大吉 (*wang da ji*) (fig. 1).

绿绢双头鸟纹刺绣 (96QZIM49:9)

长 32 厘米，宽 38.5 厘米。

原为三角形的残制品，推测是鸡鸣枕的一个角。现展开呈长方形，保存两面幅边，幅宽 38.5 厘米。平纹，经密 50 根／厘米，纬密 40 根／厘米。

绿绢的两侧缘饰有带纹，带纹宽 1 厘米。带纹上饰有小圆环纹。主体图案居中，以经向自上而下分布，上中部是花盖，由横的带纹和弧边垂帐纹构成；其下是双头鸟。双头鸟为一体，呈半椭圆形的两翅，长尾。鸟头相对，头上饰冠（图 1）。这一组图案宽 10.3 厘米，高 8 厘米。双头鸟两侧和下部纹饰，皆为草叶、藤枝纹等，以圆点为主，绣出藤枝、叶纹等。

锁针绣，绣线有白、红、酱紫、蓝、宝蓝等五种色。双头鸟纹样汉代十分流行，在汉代神话中又称共命鸟，表示夫妻相依为命的意思。

1 双头鸟纹 Two-headed bird pattern
2 组织图 Chain stitch embroidery

DOUBLE-HEADED BIRD PATTERN EMBROIDERED ON GREEN SILK JUAN TABBY (96QZIM49:9)

Height 32 cm, width 38.5 cm.

This was originally a triangular-shaped piece that we surmise was a corner of a 'crowing-cock' pillow. Spreading out, it is now rectangular in shape, with both selvages that show the fabric width to be 38.5 cm. Tabby weave, warp thread count 50 ends per cm, weft thread count 40 picks per cm.

The two sides of the green *juan* silk have embroidered ornamental bands, each 1 cm wide. Small circular patterns adorn the bands. The main pattern is in the center of the piece and is distributed top to bottom in warp direction. In the top center there is a flower canopy, made of a horizontal band and lobed hanging-curtain shapes. Below this is the two-headed bird, which has half-oval-shaped wings and a long tail. The two heads face each other, and are adorned with crowns (fig. 1).

The width of this group of patterns is 10.3 cm, its height is 8 cm. On either side of the bird and below it are grasses and leaves, tendrils and so on, mostly with round circles interlaced with the embroidered tendrils and leaves. The embroidery is done in chain stitch, using five colors: white, red, dark purple, blue, and sapphire blue.

A two-headed bird pattern was very popular in the Han dynasty, and was called a 'shared-life' bird in Han-dynasty mythology, signifying the lifelong bonding of husband and wife.

74

（二） 1998 年发掘墓葬出土纺织品珍宝

选取了 98QZIM105、98QZIM122、98QZIM131、98QZIM141、98QZIM149 和 98QZIM156 等 6 座墓葬的 11 件丝织品。

98QZIM141 墓葬（第四章图 75~76）

位于 1998 年南区第二发掘点。洞室墓。墓向东南 — 西北向。属第三期文化墓葬。

洞室在墓道的南侧，呈长椭圆形，长 2.42 米，宽 0.6~1.3 米。墓道深 2.6 米。葬具木梯架式，用粗、细原木棒制作，皆为榫卯结构，长 2.36 米，宽 0.7 米。盗掘严重，出土遗物有残木弓和木扣，纺织品有绮裙残片和毛布裤。

98QZIM149 墓葬（第四章图 77~78）

位于 1998 年南区第二发掘点。洞室墓。属第三期文化墓葬。梯架式葬具。随葬品在尸架的西南头，有马鞍和毛布食品袋、毡帽等。

98QZIM122 墓葬（第四章图 79）

位于 1998 年南区第二发掘点。长方形竖穴土坑，壁上设龛。墓向东北 — 西南向。属第三期文化墓葬。

墓口长 3.6 米，宽 1.8 米。墓深 2.2 米。保存了木棺四根方木立柱、两块底板和一侧的挡板。单人葬，主人是成年男性。

墓葬出土器物有木马鞍、木马镳、木扣、木箭和残弓、铜带扣等。另外，还出土了纺织品残片。

EXCAVATED IN 1998: 11 TEXTILES

Eleven silk textiles have been chosen from articles excavated from the following six graves: 98QZIM105, 98QZIM122, 98QZIM131, 98QZIM141, 98QZIM149, and 98QZIM156.

GRAVE 98QZIM141 (CAT. NOS 75–76)

Located in the southern region's second excavation site, this was a grave with side-chamber. The grave orientation was southeast-northwest, and the grave belonged to Zaghunluq Third-period culture.

The chamber was on the southern side of the grave shaft, and was oblong, 2.42 meters long and between 0.6 and 1.3 meters wide. The grave was 2.6 meters deep. Grave equipment included a wooden bier made of logs of differing size, all of mortise and tenon construction, 2.36 meters long and 0.7 meters wide. The grave had been severely robbed. Remaining objects included fragments of a wooden bow and a wooden buckle. Among textiles, the fragments of a skirt woven of *qi* damask and woolen pants were found.

GRAVE 98QZIM149 (CAT. NOS 77–78)

Located in the 1998 southern region's second excavation site. This was a side chamber grave that included a bier. It belongs to Third-period culture graves. Accompanying grave goods were on the southwestern side of the bier, and included a saddle, a woolen cloth bag for holding foodstuffs, and a felt hat.

GRAVE 98QZIM122 (CAT. NO. 79)

Located in the 1998 southern region's second excavation site. This was a rectangular vertical-pit type earthen grave, with a niche placed on the eastern wall. The orientation of the grave was northeast-southwest, and it belongs to Third-period culture graves.

The grave opening was 3.6 meters long, and 1.8 meters wide. The grave was 2.2 meters deep. Four square vertical posts of a wooden coffin were preserved, also two of the bottom boards and one of the side boards. This was a single-occupancy grave holding one adult male.

Items excavated from this grave included a wooden saddle, a wooden bit cheek, a wooden toggle, wooden arrows and fragments of a bow, a bronze belt buckle and so on, as well as fragments of textiles.

98QZIM105 墓葬（第四章图 80~81）

位于 1998 年南区第二发掘点。洞室墓。墓向大体呈东西向。属第三期文化墓葬。

墓口长 2.5 米，宽 1.72 米。墓深 1.9 米。

墓主人为青年男性，在胸部发现弓的残片，身体右侧发现残箭杆。同时，还出土了木马鞍桥、锦绦、长衣和毛布袋等。

98QZIM156（第四章图 82）

位于 1998 年南区第二发掘点。长方形竖穴土坑墓，墓向东西向。属第三期文化墓葬。

墓口长 3.2 米，宽 1.9 米。墓深 2.4 米。

盗掘严重，墓底残留有木棺腿和陶罐。填土中出土男性骨架及残织物。

98QZIM131（第四章图 83~85）

位于 1998 年南区第二发掘点。长方形竖穴土坑墓，墓向东西向。墓内残留箱式木棺的足腿。

墓口长 3 米，宽 2.1 米。墓深 2.2 米。在填土中发现墓主人的零星下肢骨、肋骨和丝织品残片。

GRAVE 98QZIM105 (CAT. NOS 80–81)

Located in the 1998 southern region's second excavation site. This was a side chamber type grave, generally east-west oriented. It belongs to Third-period culture graves.

Length of grave opening 2.5 meters, width 1.72 meters. Depth of grave 1.9 meters.

Occupant was a young male. Fragments of a bow were discovered near his chest. Arrows were discovered to the right of his body. Also excavated from this grave are a horse saddle arch, fragments of compound weave, a gown and a woolen bag.

GRAVE 98QZIM156 (CAT. NO. 82)

Located in the 1998 southern region's second excavation site. This was a rectangular vertical-pit type earthen grave, with east-west orientation. It belongs to Third-period culture graves.

The grave opening was 3.2 meters long, 1.9 meters wide. The depth of the grave was 2.4 meters. The grave had suffered severe damage from robbery. The legs to a casket and a ceramic jar remained on the grave floor. The skeleton of a male corpse was found in the disturbed earth, as well as fragments of textiles.

GRAVE 98QZIM131 (CAT. NOS 83–85)

Located in the 1998 southern region's second excavation site. Rectangular vertical-pit earthen grave, orientation east-west. The legs of a box-type coffin were found.

The grave opening was 3 meters long and 2.1 meters wide. The grave was 2.2 meters deep. In the disturbed earth were the scattered lower limbs of the occupant's skeleton, his ribs, and fragments of silk textiles.

棕地挖花毛布裤 (98QZIM141:1)

裤长 119 厘米，腰宽 75 厘米。裤腿口宽 23 厘米。

由裤身、裤腿口缘边、裆和附加三角组成，腰口不整齐，有补丁，为窄腿裤。

两条裤腿各为一幅毛布，皆保存两面幅边，幅宽 44 厘米。裤裆展开为菱形，对折呈三角形，前长、后短，长 29.5、33.5 厘米，底边宽 15.5 厘米。裤裆两边又附加一片倒三角形毛布，上宽、下窄，前短、后长，前长 66.5、后长 79 厘米。裤腿口缘边，左长 8 厘米，右长 7 厘米。

毛布非常的细、软，2/2 S 斜纹，纬纱 Z 捻，两根并股；经线 S 双捻。经密 28 根 / 厘米，纬密 28 根 / 厘米。正侧斜纹毛布。

挖花处于裤的大腿部分，长 40 厘米，前后都有。由红、白、绿、黄和蓝等五色 S 双捻线织出。图案以平行曲线纹为主，还有平行短线构成横带纹。曲线纹三条为一组，宽 1.4、1.5 厘米不等；带纹宽 3.5 厘米。

另外，在带纹下缘残留锦绦饰。锦绦宽 0.3 厘米，为经锦。纬线蓝色，经线为黄、蓝和白三种色。

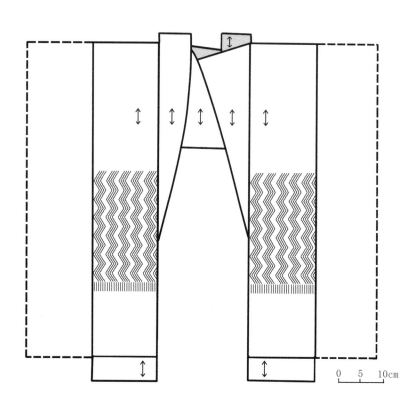

1 结构图 Cut and construction diagram

75

WOOLEN-CLOTH PANTS, BROWN GROUND WITH BROCADING (98QZIM141:1)

Length of pants 119 cm, width at the waist 75 cm. Cuffs 23 cm wide.

The pants are composed of the main part plus a border or band at the cuffs, and a crotch as well as triangular insets that have been added. The waistline is irregular and was patched in antiquity. The pants are narrow in the leg.

Each of the legs is made from one piece of fabric. Both legs retain two selvages showing the loom width of the fabric to have been 44 cm. The crotch, when opened out, is a diamond shape, folded into a triangular shape with a longer front and a shorter rear, measuring 29.5 and 33.5 cm in length and 15.5 cm in width. Two triangular pieces of woolen cloth have been sewn between crotch and trouser legs, with narrow lower part and wide upper part, front short, rear longer. They measure 66.5 cm in length in front, and 79 cm in length at the rear. The band along the trouser cuffs is 8 cm in width on the left leg and 7 cm on the right leg.

The woolen cloth is extremely fine and soft, woven in 2/2 S twill weave, with weft yarn Z-spun and doubled. The warp threads were S-plied from two ends. Warp thread count 28 ends per cm, weft 28 picks per cm, the twill slant is approximately 45°.

The brocaded patterning with supplementary weft (*wa hua*) is located on the thigh part of the legs and is 40 cm long. Both front and back carry this patterning, which is woven from five colors, red, white, green, yellow and blue, and with S-plied yarn from two ends. The pattern is mainly parallel zigzag-lines, but also parallel short lines forming cross-bands. Three parallel lines are forming groups of zigzag patterning, each group being between 1.4 or 1.5 cm wide, i.e., not of equal width. The width of the cross-bands is 3.5 cm.

Below the cross-band is a fragment of compound weave (*jin*) which measures 0.3 cm in width and is warp-faced compound weave. Its weft threads are blue, its warp threads are yellow, blue and white.

2 毛布组织 Woolen 2/2 S twill   3 挖花组织 Brocaded supplementary wefts (wa hua)

白色缣地葡萄纹刺绣残片 （98QZIM141:2-2C）

长 12.5 厘米，宽 9 厘米。

没有保存幅边。丝线皆不加捻，白色缣地，经密 68 根 / 厘米，纬密 44 根 / 厘米。绣线为 S 双捻，有三种色，即蓝色、酱色和黄棕色。

锁针绣，纹样有藤枝、萄萄串和叶、花等，用色上有些变化。萄萄圆形果，两粒并列成串状，用色有变化，或果显酱色，果芯是黄棕色和白色；或果显蓝色，果芯是黄棕色。葡萄叶的形状及用色也有变化，或黄棕色叶，或酱色叶饰以黄棕色边。花是一种，两瓣圆芯花（图 1）。

FRAGMENT OF GRAPE-PATTERN EMBROIDERY ON WHITE JIAN SILK GROUND (98QZIM141:2-2C)

Height 12.5 cm, width 9 cm.

No selvages remain on this textile. Neither warp nor weft threads of the white *jian* ground are noticeably twisted. It has a warp thread count of 68 ends per cm, and a weft thread count of 44 picks per cm. The embroidery thread is S-plied from two ends and in three colors, blue, dark brown, and yellowish brown.

Embroidery is done in chain stitch, with patterning of branches, bunches of grapes and leaves, and flowers. The coloration of these varies. The grapes are shown in round form with bunches represented by parallel lines of grapes in a row, the centers of each grape being yellowish-brown and white, with outlining done either in dark brown or blue. In the case of blue grapes the centers are yellowish-brown. The shape and coloring of the grape leaves also varies, either yellowish-brown leaves or dark brown leaves with yellowish-brown edging. The flowers are of one kind, two-petalled flowers with pistil or stamen (fig. 1).

1 组织图 Chain stitch embroidery

彩条纹毛布袋 (98QZIM149:2)

长 62 厘米, 宽 16.5 厘米。

长方形。一幅毛布缝制, 横向对折缝合 (图 2)。毛布保存两面幅边, 幅宽 33.6 厘米。羊毛较粗。经纱 Z 捻, 捻得较紧, 白色。纬纱 S 捻, 有棕、白、蓝、红、浅红、黄和绿等七种色。毛布为平纹, 经密 6 根 / 厘米, 纬密 20 根 / 厘米 (图 1)。

袋口为白色宽边, 以下是彩条纹。蓝、红、黄、绿、浅红彩条和白棕彩条纹相间分布, 彩条宽窄有些变化, 在 1.3~2 厘米之间。白棕条纹上显小方格纹, 为一行白一行棕, 错位布局形成 (图 1)。

毛布袋出土时, 在一小马鞍上。袋里保存有面食碎渣。

1 组织图
Plain stripes and brown-and-white color-and-weave pattern

77

350

WOOLEN BAG WITH STRIPED PATTERN IN VARIOUS COLORS (98QZIM149:2)

Height 62 cm, width 16.5 cm.

This textile is rectangular and was made of one piece of cloth, folded crosswise and sewn (fig. 2). The woolen cloth retains both selvages. The loom width of the fabric is 33.6 cm. Woolen yarn is fairly coarse; warp yarn is white and relatively strongly Z-spun, weft yarn is S-spun and comes in seven colors: brown, white, blue, red, and light red, yellow, and green. The woolen cloth is tabby weave with warp thread count of 6 ends per cm and weft thread count of 20 picks per cm (fig. 1).

The top or opening to the bag is bordered in a band of white, below which is the striped patterning. The stripes in plain blue, red, yellow, green, and light red alternate with white-and-brown stripes and there is slight variation in their width, which is between 1.3 and 2 cm wide. The white-and-brown stripes are woven in a small square color-and-weave pattern made by alternating one pick of white and one pick of brown and reversing the shuttling order after every four picks (fig. 1).

When this bag was excavated, it was found on a small saddle. Preserved traces of wheaten food were inside the bag.

2 毛布的拼对缝缀 Seam joining two selvages

红色毛罗残片 (98QZIM149:2-3)

长 114 厘米，宽 47 厘米。

形状比较规则，为长方形，保存一面幅边（经拼对有了两面幅边），宽 47 厘米。面为红色毛罗，里面衬垫白色平纹毛布，可能是被子一类的东西。

毛罗为二经纠罗，经、纬纱皆 Z 捻，红色，捻得比较紧。经密 12 根／厘米，纬密 18 根／厘米（图 1）。

白色平纹毛布衬里，残缺严重，保存一面幅边。残长 105 厘米，残幅宽 45 厘米。中间絮有浅黄色羊（驼）绒，残留得很少。经、纬纱皆 Z 捻，经密 14 根／厘米，纬密 9 根／厘米。

FRAGMENT OF A PIECE OF RED WOOLEN GAUZE (LUO) (98QZIM149:2-3)

Height 114 cm, width 47 cm.

The original shape was a quite regular rectangle. Reconstructed, the warp length has two selvages that show the loom width of the fabric to be 47 cm. The surface of the piece is red woolen gauze or *luo*; the lining is a white tabby-woven woolen cloth. This may have been a kind of quilt or blanket.

The woolen gauze is two-end simple gauze, with groups of three tabby picks in between two gauze twistings. Warp and weft are both Z-spun and of red color. The threads are twisted fairly tightly. Warp thread count is 12 ends per cm, weft is 18 picks per cm (fig. 1).

The white tabby lining is severely damaged, but retains one selvage. The length of the fragment is 105 cm, the maximum preserved loom width 45 cm. The warp and weft yarn are both Z-spun. Warp thread count is 14 ends per cm, weft is 9 picks per cm. Between lining and gauze are remnants of light-yellowish sheep or camel's-hair fleece, of which very little remains.

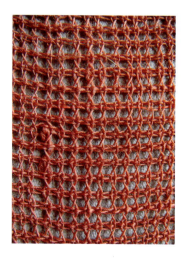 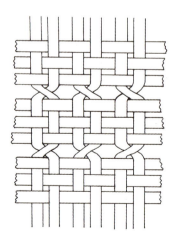

1 组织图 Two-end simple woolen gauze 2 组织图 Weave diagram

353

烟色地动物纹锦衣饰绦 (98QZIM122:4-2)

两条：长 28、27 厘米，宽 3 厘米。

剪裁制成。没有保存幅边，残幅宽 28 厘米。纬锦。经、纬纱皆 Z 捻，绵经绵纬。经纱捻得紧，纬纱捻得松。经纱橘黄色，纬纱有红、白、黄、烟等四种色，烟色纱为两根并股。用色分区，排列比 1:2。夹经纬二重平纹组织，夹经 2 根并股，经密 24 根／厘米，纬密 96 根／厘米（图 1）。

图案残缺严重，似为几何形动物纹，有羊的头和角等。

SPUN-SILK COMPOUND WEAVE (JIN), PALE BROWN WITH ANIMAL PATTERNS (98QZIM122:4-2)

In two parts: lengths 28 and 27 cm, width 3 cm.

The textile was formed by cutting a larger piece of fabric. No selvages remain. The maximum preserved loom width is 28 cm, and the weave is weft-faced. These are decorative strips from an item of clothing.

The warp and weft yarn are both Z-spun silk, the warp yarn is spun tightly, the weft yarn loosely. Warp yarn is tangerine-yellow, weft yarn includes four colors, red, white, yellow and very light brown. The latter yarn is doubled. The coloring is divided into sections and there are never more than three lats altogether. The weave is a weft-faced compound tabby (taqueté). The main warp ends are doubled, with a warp thread count of 24 ends (16 main warp ends and 8 binding warp ends) per cm, and a weft thread count of 96 picks (32 passes) per cm (fig. 1).

The pattern has been badly damaged but appears to be stylized animal motifs, with sheep's heads and horns.

1 组织图 Weft–faced compound tabby (taquete)

红地植物纹锦绦 (98QZIM105:3)

长 100 厘米，宽 5.5 厘米。

剪裁制成，为衣服的缘边。中间折叠缝缀，呈折角的圆弧形。两端是幅边，幅宽 100 厘米（图 1）。纬锦。经、纬纱皆 Z 捻，绵经绵纬。经纱捻得松，纬纱捻得紧。经纱白色，纬纱有红、白和黄等三种色。组织排列比 1：2，夹经纬二重平纹组织，夹经两根并股，经密 19 根／厘米，纬密 72 根／厘米。红地，显白和黄色的植物纹。图案不完整，可以看出来有曲折枝干骨骼及小朵的花。

80

SPUN-SILK COMPOUND WEAVE (JIN), PALE BROWN WITH ANIMAL

PATTERNS (98QZIM105:3)

Length 100 cm, width 5.5 cm.

This textile was made by cutting a piece of fabric; it was originally the border to a garment. The center part was tucked in and sewn, to give the fabric the shape of a slightly pointed arch. The two ends are the selvages of the fabric, which had a loom width of 100 cm (fig. 1).

The piece is weft-faced. Both warp and weft yarn are Z-spun silk; the white warp yarn was spun loosely, the weft yarn was spun tightly and includes three colors: red, white, and yellow. It is a weft-faced compound tabby (taqueté) with three lats, with doubled main warp ends. The warp thread count is 19 ends (12–14 main warp ends and 6-7 binding warp ends) per cm, and the weft thread count is 72 picks (24 passes) per cm.

The textile has a red ground, exhibiting floral patterning in white and yellow. The pattern is incomplete, but one can see a framework of curved branches with small-petalled flowers.

1 组织图 Selvage

2 组织图 Selvage

黄色毛布开襟长衣 (98QZIM105:4)

衣身长 107 厘米，肩袖通宽 178 厘米。袖长 55 厘米，袖口宽 14 厘米。下摆宽 70 厘米，胸宽 61 厘米。

有领，窄袖、开襟、束腰、宽下摆，衣身两侧开叉。

衣领呈梯形，背部饰锦，宽 15 厘米，长 54 厘米，高 8 厘米（为上、下两片）。

袖由缘边、接袖组成，袖口有锦缘边，宽 3.3 厘米（图 1，B）。接袖部分，左宽 14 厘米，长 39 厘米；右宽 13.5 厘米，长 12 厘米（图 1，A）。

衣服用布，主要是黄色斜纹毛布，剪裁而成。衣身和衣袖为一幅毛布，保存两面幅边，幅宽 126 厘米。经、纬纱皆 S 捻，经纱捻得紧，纬纱捻得比较松，1/2 Z 斜纹，经密 13 根／厘米，纬密 39 根／厘米。

衣领、袖缘和下摆开叉处饰白地"十"字纹锦绦。锦绦属纬锦，经、纬纱皆 Z 捻，绵经绵纬。经纱白色，纬纱有红、白和黄等三种色。组织排列比 1:2，夹经纬二重平纹组织，夹经两根并股。图案分区，有的区域，纬纱中缺少红纱，排列比 1:1；有的区域纬纱有红、白和黄三种色纱，排列比 1:2。纹样有"十"字、菱纹、圆点纹等。同时，白纱有粗细之分，一般在排列比 1:1 的地方，白纱为粗纱，而在排列比 1:2 的地方白纱为细纱。

81

LONG GOWN WITH OPEN FRONT MADE OF YELLOW WOOLEN CLOTH (98QZIM105:4)

The length of the body of the garment is 107 cm, its overall sleeve-and-shoulder-width is 178 cm. The length of sleeves is 55 cm, width of cuffs is 14 cm. The lower hem width is 70 cm, width across the chest is 61 cm.

This garment has a collar, narrow sleeves, is open in the front, tied at the waist, and has a wide lower hem, with slits at either side of the body.

The collar has a trapezoid shape, with the rear ornamented with figured silk. It is 15 cm wide, and 54 cm long, 8 cm high, and is composed of an upper and lower piece.

The sleeves are composed of the sleeves themselves and an adjoining piece, with figured silk bordering on the cuffs that is 3.3 cm wide (fig. 1, B). The adjoining piece[3] is different for right and left. On the left, it is 14 cm wide, 39 cm long. On the right, it is 13.5 cm wide and 12 cm long (fig. 1, A).

The fabric used for the garment is a woolen twill cloth of primarily yellow color that has been cut and sewn. The body and sleeves are one piece of cloth, preserving both selvages that show the loom width of the fabric to be 126 cm. Warp and weft are both S-spun, with warp yarn spun tightly, weft yarn spun relatively loosely. 1/2 Z twill, warp thread count 13 ends per cm, weft thread count 39 picks per cm.

---

3 I.e., the portion in between the border of the cuff and the part of the sleeve that is cut in one with the body.

2 组织图 Weft–faced compound tabby (taquete)

The collar, border of sleeves and slits at the lower hem are adorned with a spun-silk compound weave (*jin*) with cross-pattern on white ground. The weave is weft-faced, with both warp and weft yarn from Z-spun silk. The warp yarn is white; the weft yarn includes red, white, and yellow. The weave is a weft-faced compound tabby (taqueté) with altogether three lats and doubled main warp ends. The patterning is in sections, with some areas lacking red yarn in the weft and thus only two lats present. Other areas have red, white and yellow weft yarn, and all three lats are present. Patterning includes 'crosses,' diamonds and circles or dots. In addition, the white yarn is divided into areas where it is heavier and areas where it is lighter. Generally, in two-lats areas the white yarn is heavy, whereas in three-lats areas it is fine.

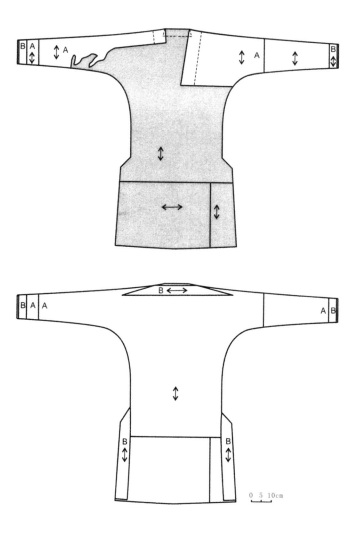

1 结构图 Cut and construction diagram

白地几何纹锦扎头带 (98QZIM156:5-1)

长 61 厘米，宽 7 厘米。

头带由织锦和毛纱组成，拼接缝缀，并保存有系结。织锦保存两面幅边，幅宽 47 厘米。丝、棉纬锦。经、纬纱皆 Z 捻，绵经绵纬。经纱白色，为丝。纬纱有红、黄棕和白等三种色，红和黄棕色纱是丝，白色纱是棉。图案分区，组织排列比 1:1，夹经纬二重平纹组织。夹经为两根并股纱，经密 22 根 / 厘米，纬密 48 根 / 厘米。

几何纹样呈绦式排列，有方菱格纹、三角纹、短线纹等。

毛纱为红色，平纹组织，有方纱孔。

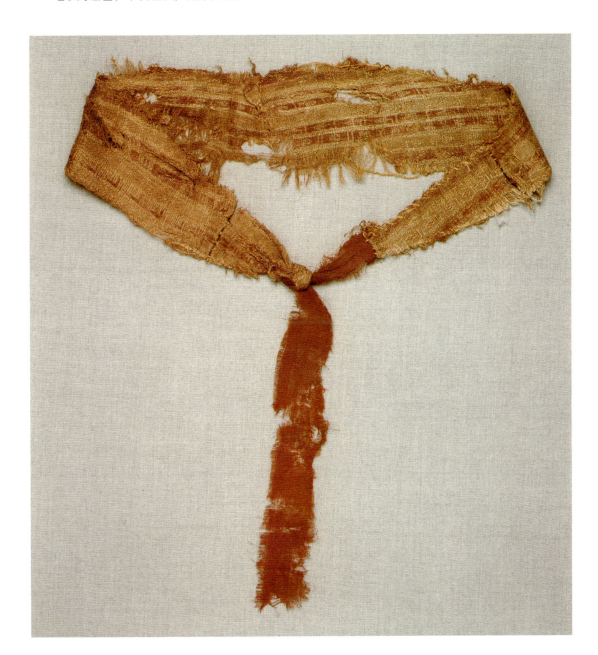

KNOTTED HEADBAND OF SPUN-SILK COMPOUND WEAVE (JIN) (98QZIM156:5-1)

Length 61 cm, width 7 cm.

The headband is made from figured silk and woolen gauze-like cloth sewn together. The knot tying the band together is still preserved. Two selvages remain on the figured silk, showing the fabric's loom width to be 47 cm. The fabric is weft-faced compound weave (*jin*) with spun silk and cotton wefts. Warp and weft yarn are both Z-spun. The warp yarn is white silk. The weft yarn includes three colors: red, yellowish-brown, and white. Red and yellowish-brown are silk threads, white is a cotton thread. The weave is weft-faced compound tabby (taqueté) with two lats, the patterning is in sections. The main warp is doubled, with a warp thread count of 22 ends (14-16 main warp ends and 7-8 binding warp ends) per cm, and a weft thread count of 48 picks (24 passes) per cm.

The patterning is geometric and set in rows, including square and diamond patterns, triangles, and short lines.

The red gauze-like wool is woven in loose tabby showing square holes.

1 组织图 Weft–faced compound tabby (taquete) with cotton weft

红地龙纹锦绦 (98QZIM131:1-2)

两片拼对：全长 24 厘米，宽 4.3 厘米。

长方形。没有保存幅边。纬锦。经、纬纱皆 Z 捻，绵经绵纬。经纱白色，细；纬纱红、白和黄棕三种色，粗。排列比 1:2。夹经纬二重平纹组织，经密 25 根 / 厘米，纬密 84 根 / 厘米。组织比较松，变形。

红地，保存了黄棕和白色的条纹骨骼，可以看出有龙头、颈和前腿部分。上面还有圆点纹、椭圆点纹，带须的叶纹和似 "汉" 字的符号。叶纹体为黄棕色，叶须和龙纹是白色。

SPUN-SILK COMPOUND WEAVE (JIN) WITH RED GROUND AND DRAGON PATTERN (98QZIM131:1-2)

This piece is in two fragments. Reconstructed, the total length is 24 cm, width 4.3 cm.

It is rectangular in shape, with no retained selvages and woven in weft-faced compound weave (*jin*). Both warp and weft are Z-spun silk. The warp yarn is white and fine; the weft yarn is red, white and yellow, and thick. Weft-faced compound tabby (taqueté) with three lats, the warp thread count is 25 ends (12-13 main warp ends and 12-13 binding warp ends) per cm, the weft thread count is 84 picks (28 passes) per cm. The weave is fairly loose and deformed.

The ground of this textile retains the linear framework of the pattern which is woven in yellowish-brown and white. The dragon's head, neck, and front legs are visible. Above are also circles, ovals, hairy leaf patterns, and what appears to be a symbol for the character 汉 *Han*. The body of the leaf pattern is yellowish-brown, the leaf hairs and the dragon are white.

1 组织图　Weft-faced compound tabby (taquete)

红地龙纹锦绦 (98QZIM131:1-4-1)

长 10.9 厘米，宽 6.5 厘米。

长方形。没有保存幅边。纬锦。经、纬纱皆 Z 捻，绵经绵纬。经纱白色，纬纱红、白和黄棕三种色。组织排列比 1:2。夹经纬二重平纹组织，经密 28 根 / 厘米，纬密 84 根 / 厘米。

红地，保存有曲折纹骨骼，填以动物纹、香炉和汉字的符号。保存完整的动物纹为龙纹，头呈虎头状，龇牙咧嘴。头上饰有曲折线的角，四腿直立。肩部饰三翼，尾作卷曲状。纹样皆为黄棕色，饰白边。

SPUN-SILK COMPOUND WEAVE (JIN) WITH RED GROUND AND DRAGON PATTERN (98QZIM131:1-4-1)

84

Length 10.9 cm, width 6.5 cm.[4]

The textile is rectangular, with no retained selvages, and is a weft-faced compound weave (*jin*). Both warp and weft are from Z–spun silk. The warp yarn is white, the weft yarn red, white, and yellowish-brown. The weave is weft-faced compound tabby (taqueté), with three lats. The warp thread count is 28 ends (14 main warp ends and 14 binding warp ends) per cm, the weft thread count is 84 picks (28 passes) per cm.

The textile has a red ground, and retains a curvilinear framework inside which are animal patterns, incense burners, and a symbol for the character 汉 *Han*. The only pattern preserved in entirety on this fragment is a dragon, with tiger-like head, and open mouth displaying teeth. The head has a curved linear horn. The four legs are straight. There are three wings on the shoulder, the tail is curved. The entire pattern is yellowish-brown and outlined in white.

---

4 This is one out of a total of five fragments of the same fabric (98QZIM131:1-4). Since this fragment does not include the hunting motif present on the other fragments, it is given the name dragon-patterned.

红地狩猎纹锦绦 (98QZIM131:1-3)

三片：经向长 17.5、16、12.9 厘米，纬向宽 6.2、5.5、5.1 厘米。

原各为衣服饰绦，皆有宽 0.5 厘米的折边。现按纹样拼对，略呈长方形，长 17.5 厘米、宽 16.4 厘米。

没有保存幅边。纬锦。经、纬纱皆 Z 捻，绵经绵纬。经纱白色，纬纱红、白和黄棕三种色，组织排列比 1:2。夹经纬二重平纹组织，经密 22~25 根 / 厘米，纬密 84 根 / 厘米（图 1）。

红地。图案不完整，保存有曲折的植物纹骨骼，填以狩猎纹、龙纹、椭圆点、"卍"字和汉字符号。汉字中，"目"、"木"字比较明显。骑马射箭者，人回首，搭箭作射击状；马身体很长，四腿直立，鬃呈直立状。纹样皆为黄棕色，饰白边。

SPUN-SILK COMPOUND WEAVE (JIN) WITH RED GROUND AND HUNTING PATTERN (98QZIM131:1-3)

This textile is in three fragments whose warp lengths are 17.5, 16, and 12.9 cm. In the weft direction, the widths are 6.2, 5.5, and 5.1 cm.

85

Originally these were strips of a garment. They all have an edge that was folded in for about 0.5 cm. Reconstructing the pattern, the piece is roughly rectangular, 17.5 cm long and 16.4 cm wide.

No selvages remain of this weft-faced compound weave (*jin*). Both warp and weft yarn are Z-spun silk. The warp yarn is white, the weft yarn is red, white, and yellowish-brown. The weave is weft-faced compound tabby (taqueté), with three lats; the warp thread count is 22-25 ends (11-13 main warp ends and 11-13 binding warp ends) per cm, the weft thread count is 84 picks (28 passes) per cm (fig. 1).

The textile has a red ground, on which the pattern is incomplete but retains a curvilinear vegetal-patterned framework inside which hunting scenes, dragons, oval dots, the character 卍 *wan*, and the symbol for the character 汉 *Han* appear. Two components contained within the character *Han*, 目 and 木, are fairly clear. The hunting scene displays a hunter mounted on a horse, with head in reverse, i.e., in backward-facing position, holding a bow and getting ready to shoot. The body of the horse is very long, its legs are straight, and its mane is standing upright. The pattern is done in yellowish-brown, outlined in white.

1 组织图 Weft–faced compound tabby (taquete), reverse

后 记

经过多年的努力，新疆维吾尔自治区博物馆与瑞士阿贝格基金会（Abegg-Stiftung）合作出版《扎滚鲁克纺织品珍宝》（中英文对照）一书，终于即将问世。这本由新疆维吾尔自治区博物馆编著、文物出版社编辑出版的图录，旨在向世界各国专业和非专业的读者介绍中国古代纺织精品和相关文化。整个合作出版项目是由瑞士阿贝格基金会（Abegg-Stiftung）提供资金赞助。

瑞士阿贝格基金会（Abegg-Stiftung）是一家私立研究收藏纺织品的公益性的基金会，由玛格丽特和维尔纳·阿贝格夫妇（Mrs. Margaret and Werner Abegg）于20世纪60年代创立。多年来收集、研究、保护了各国众多的纺织文物，并采取了博物馆特展、出版研究图书等多种形式与世人共享，目的是希望通过他们的努力让这些文物珍品走出家门，发挥其应有的文化魅力。自本世纪初，中亚广阔地区丝绸之路上文化交融的悠久历史已成为阿贝格基金会研究的重点之一。现任基金会董事长多米尼克·凯勒先生（Mr. Dominik Keller）非常重视一般西方学者很少接触的、在新疆出土的色泽鲜艳、纹饰独特、织物织法新颖的毛、丝、棉纺织品的研究。2009年他与阿贝格基金会纺织品保护研究中心主任瑞谷拉·肖特博士（Dr. Regula Schorta）一起亲赴新疆维吾尔自治区博物馆考古部考察，选择了扎滚鲁克墓地出土的纺织品、研究了织物的结构和纹饰织法等细节，并与当时在任的博物馆田馆长进行了商谈，希望合作出版一本双语的专业研究图录。在得到博物馆领导的支持后，阿贝格基金会还特别资助了德国纺织品保护维修专家安洁莉卡女士（Ms. Angelika Sliwka）专门到新疆维吾尔自治区博物馆考古部对出土的纺织品的修护进行了指导。

从2007年我开始参与到这本书的合作、策划、协商、编撰与出版等诸多事宜，深深体会到出版这样一本高质量的双语研究专辑图录所经历的艰难。新疆维吾尔自治区博物馆的王博先生不仅是著名的考古学者，也是当年新疆维吾尔自治区博物馆考古部的负责人，还是扎滚鲁克墓地发掘者和领队。在此次合作出书之前我与他曾有过多次交往，深知他的学识与人品，我认为他是与阿贝格基金会(Abegg-Stiftung)合作出版《扎滚鲁克纺织品珍宝》的最佳人选。因此，我也愿意关注这个合作项目的进展，并做些力所能及的事推进项目的成功，包括组织合作协议的商谈交流、选择联系合作出版单位、在各合作单位人员之间保持协调、联络、沟通等。王博先生告诉我新疆且末县扎滚鲁克墓地前后共经过了四次发掘。1985年考古调查时发现墓地已经有许多盗坑，考古队为了了解墓地基本情况而进行试发掘，第一次共发掘了5座墓。1989年第二次发掘是为了巴音郭楞蒙古自治州博物馆展陈的需要，考古队因此对当时已经遭盗掘破坏较严重的2座墓又进行了发掘。由于这两次发掘墓葬的数目较少，因此对其所属年代和文化内涵不是很清楚。为了解决这些问题，1996年考古所提出再进行发掘的申请，并于1996年和1998年由王博领队进行了两次发掘。这两次对扎滚鲁克墓地发掘的墓葬共计167座，经研究分为三期考古文化。其中出土纺织品较多的第二期文化年代为公元前8世纪~公元3世纪中期，第三期文化墓葬年代为公元3世纪中期~6世纪，三期文化共延续了大约16个世纪。这两次发掘整理出土的组织结构特殊和图案花纹保存较好的织品和残片共计约有200件。新疆维吾尔自治区博物馆木娜瓦尔·哈帕尔女士和郭金龙先生对纺织品进行了清洗、平整和保护工作，张素珍和马金娥也参加了具体的清洗、平整工作，万芳帮助进行了服装的绘图工作。王博和王明芳夫妇对扎滚鲁克墓地出土的这批织品进行了深入研究，他们的研究结果就整理收入在这本图录中。在博物馆领导的关心与督促下，2008年王博领导的研究团队交出了中文书稿和拍摄的数百张彩版照片。这批纺织品的研究结果清楚地表明了这一地区在早期的丝绸之路上纺织业多元文化交流与融合的发展水平。经过阿贝格基金会合作专家双方的精心挑选，特别选择了最具有代表性的86件纺织珍品和它们的研究细节，列于本册图录中，以馈国内外的广大读者。

2010年开始了中文书稿的英文翻译工作。能够对中国新疆维吾尔自治区考古工作有所了解，并且能够进行中英文翻译的专家学者本来就寥寥无几，而本书的翻译特别需要译者了解自第二章开始写入的花样众多的扎滚鲁克墓地出土的纺织品的技术细节和纺织术语，包括纺织品的组织结构、织法、色彩、颜料、染色、剪裁、缝制、编织方法、图版说明等专业术语。将中文的研究结果翻译成为国际通用的标准英语，对于我和当时一起工作的姜曦（北京科技大学博士生）是不能完成的工作。这本图录的翻译工作最终是以阿贝格基金会的纺织研究专家瑞谷拉·肖特博士（Dr. Regula Schorta）和美国学者艾美霞女士（Ms. Martha Avery）为主，美国理海大学（Lehigh University）的王东宁博士（Dr. DongNing Wang）进行了校对审译，几方共同合作一起完成的。中英文双语书稿及图版于2013年5月交给文物出版社，开始了一系列的出版准备工作。文物出版社是第一次与国外机构合作编辑出版这样的大型双语研究图录，参与编辑的李缙云先生、王戈女士等付出了极大的努力，将这本高质量的双语《扎滚鲁克纺织品珍宝》一书顺利编排完毕。 在这期间，几方合作团队之间的交流与沟通、辛勤而又认真严谨的工作态度，都是我亲身经历的。自始至终我都是这个合作项目的参与和见证者。

在此，我要衷心的感谢瑞士阿贝格基金会(Abegg-Stiftung)对这个项目的资助，感谢多米尼克和瑞谷拉对此项目所花费的心血和时间。他们几次来华专门与文物出版社的编辑以及本书的作者见面，一次次商谈如何把这本高质量的图书尽早在国内外同期出版发行。我虽然已是耄耋之年，但身体尚好，愿意为出版此书奉献微薄之力，让国内外研究古代纺织品的学者和爱好者，重新认识新疆维吾尔自治区且末县扎滚鲁克墓地出土的纺织品珍宝及其凸显的灿烂文化，是我最大的心愿和衷心的期盼。

韩汝玢教授

北京科技大学冶金与材料史研究所原所长

2015 年 7 月

POSTSCRIPT

After many years of hard work and collaboration between the Xinjiang Ugyur Autonomous Region Museum and the Abegg-Stiftung, the bilingual catalogue "Textile Treasures of Zaghunluq" is finally published and ready for all interested scholars and readers around the world. This collaborative project has been funded by the Abegg-Stiftung foundation of Switzerland, and aims to promote the little known cultural ingredients and interactions of the Qiemo region along the Silk Road by introducing the unique beauty of unearthed textiles from the Zaghunluq tombs.

The Abegg-Stiftung is a nonprofit research institute that collects and studies historical textiles from all around the world; it was founded in the 1960s by Mrs. Margaret Abegg and Mr. Werner Abegg. For many years, the foundation has shared its conservation studies and collections by publishing books, hosting exhibitions in its museum, and teaching courses through its educational program. The foundation's efforts in the research of historical textiles have resulted in the better understanding and appreciation of different cultural heritages and interactions between different regions. Since the beginning of this century, the long history of cultural interactions along the Silk Road in Central Asia has become one of the research focuses of the Abegg-Stiftung. Mr. Dominik Keller, Chairman of the Foundation, holds a strong interest in the little known and rarely studied textiles unearthed from the Xinjiang area. One of the excavation sites, Zaghunluq in the Qiemo region, has revealed many well preserved textiles and fragments made from brightly colored wool, silk, and cotton that exhibit unique decoration patterns and woven details. In 2006 Mr. Keller visited the Xinjiang Ugyur Autonomous Region Museum in Urumqi with Dr. Regula Schorta, the director of the Abegg-Stiftung. After touring the museum and holding discussions with archaeologists at the museum, the Abegg team selected the group of textiles excavated from Zaghunluq tomb site as the subject of a further study of technical details regarding weaving and dyeing as a collaborative project with the archaeology department of the museum. The aim of this collaborative study was to publish a bilingual research catalogue to benefit scholars both in China and in the West. With the support of Mr. Tian Xianrong, the director of the museum, the Abegg-Stiftung sent Angelika Sliwka, a very experienced textile conservator, to help and guide the archaeologists in Urumqi to clean and protect the fragile unearthed textiles stored in the museum.

I began my participation in this project in 2007, and learned from experience how difficult it is to coordinate the many levels of consultation, communication, planning details for meetings, and discussions required between the various collaborative teams. Mr. Wang Bo of the Xinjiang Ugyur Autonomous Museum is not only a famous archaeologist who is responsible for the archaeology department at the museum, but was also the team leader and the field archaeologist who excavated the Zaghunluq tomb sites. I had worked with Mr. Wang before this project, and was well aware of his abilities and talents. I had no doubt that he was the best candidate to coordinate this project with the Abegg-Stiftung. As a result, I was made responsible for organizing meetings, arranging visits, contacting the publishing house, and communicating with various teams to keep everyone on the same page.

According to Mr. Wang Bo, there have been a total of four field excavations at the Zaghunluq site. The first was a trial excavation in 1985 after reports of many robberies at the tomb site. Among many disturbed burial pits the archaeology team systematically excavated five pits to obtain a primary understanding of the burial conditions. The second excavation was held in 1989 in two badly damaged tombs in association with a special exhibition at the Bayingolin Mongol Autonomous Museum. The information gathered from the first two excavations in 1985 and 1989 was very limited; as a result, it was hard to fully understand Zaghunluq's cultural context and the exact date of the tombs. In 1996, the archaeology team successfully proposed more excavations at Zaghunluq. Mr. Wang Bo led the team in two more excavations in 1996 and 1998. The fieldwork in 1996 and 1998 excavated a total of 167 tombs. The results have been divided into three archaeological periods of culture graves that span the eighth century BCE until the middle of the sixth century CE, a period of well over a millennium. The second-period culture graves, which are dated from the eighth century BCE to the middle of the third century CE, have revealed more textiles than the others. About 200 pieces of well-preserved textiles and fragments from the excavation display special weaving structures and unique pattern designs. The textiles and fragments were carefully washed and cleaned with special procedures carried out by Ms. Minawar Happar and Mr. Guo Jinlong at the Xinjiang Uygur Autonomous Museum, with help from Ms. Zhang Suzhen and Ms. Ma Jin'e. Ms. Wan Fang did the drawings of the clothes' construction. Mr. Wang Bo and Mrs. Wang Mingfang conducted a thorough study of these textiles and fragments. Their working results form the core contents published in this special catalogue. In 2008, Mr. Wang Bo and his team composed the first draft of the manuscript including hundreds of color photographs of their textile studies, which clearly displayed multicultural integration and interactions from the early times of this region. After careful selection from their study by both Abegg-Stiftung and the archaeology team in Xinjiang, a total of 85 pieces of clothes and fragments from all the unearthed textiles are included in this very special publication. These pieces best represent the beauty and details of Zaghunluq's culture and its technology, and this is the first time for most of them to be seen outside the Zaghunluq region.

The translation of the Chinese manuscript into English was another challenging task, begun in 2010 by a group of international scholars from different countries. The task requires not only substantial archaeological knowledge of the Xinjiang Ugyur area but also technical details and terminologies in the textile field, including weaving and loom structures, fabric colors and dyeing agents, tailoring, sewing, and braiding. Translation work was therefore beyond the powers of my colleague Ms. Jiang Xi, a PhD student at USTB, and me. The final English manuscript of this publication was completed by Martha Avery (Boulder, Colorado, USA), Dr. Regula Schorta (Abegg-Stiftung, Switzerland), and Dr. Dong-Ning Wang (Lehigh University, USA). In May 2013, the bilingual manuscript with color photographs was delivered to Cultural Relics Press house. It turns out that this was the first time Wenwu Press ever worked with an international institute to publish such a large and detailed research catalogue. The chief editors Mr. Li Jinyun and Ms. Wang Ge have made every effort to ensure high quality and a successful publication during the whole process. I am not only one of many participants in this project, but also a witness of the hard work, the enthusiasm, the rigorous working attitude, and the effort of each team member exhibited at every step of the process.

I am especially grateful to the Abegg-Stiftung for funding this project, and I am very thankful to Dominik Keller and Regula Schorta who have spent tremendous energy and time to maintain the very high standards of this project. They have traveled many times to meet with the author and editors, discussing every detail regarding how to successfully publish such a bilingual research collection both in China and abroad. It has been my greatest honor and pleasure to work on such a wonderful international collaborative project at my age of eighty. I sincerely hope that this research publication will highlight cultural development in the Qiemo region and benefit all the scholars and readers around the world who are interested in the splendid cultural interactions and exchanges of the Xinjiang Ugyur area along the ancient Silk Road.

Prof. Han Rubin

Former Director of the Institute of Historical Metallurgy and Materials

University of Science and Technology, Beijing

July 2015

图书在版编目（CIP）数据

扎滚鲁克纺织品珍宝 : 汉英对照 / 王博等著；
新疆维吾尔自治区博物馆编著 .
—— 北京 ：文物出版社，2016.4
ISBN 978-7-5010-4516-7

Ⅰ．①扎… Ⅱ．①王… ①新… Ⅲ．①墓葬 (考古) –
毛织物 – 研究 – 新疆 – 汉语、英语
Ⅳ．① K876.94

中国版本图书馆 CIP 数据核字 (2016) 第 014030 号

扎滚鲁克纺织品珍宝

编　　著	新疆维吾尔自治区博物馆	
著　　者	王　博　　王明芳　　木娜瓦尔·哈帕尔　　鲁礼鹏	
装帧设计	雅昌设计中心	
出版发行	文物出版社	
地　　址	北京东直门内北小街 2 号楼	
邮　　编	100007	
网　　址	http://www.wenwu.com	
邮　　箱	web@wenwu.com	
经　　销	新华书店	
制版印刷	北京雅昌艺术印刷有限公司	
开　　本	965×635 毫米　　1/8	
印　　张	48	
版　　次	2016 年 4 月第 1 版	
印　　次	2016 年 4 月第 1 次印刷	
书　　号	ISBN 978-7-5010-4516-7	
定　　价	580.00 元	